Seven Grains of Paradise

a culinary journey in Africa

Joan Baxter

Pottersfield Press, Lawrencetown Beach, Nova Scotia, Canada

Library and Archives Canada Cataloguing in Publication

Baxter, Joan, author
     Seven grains of paradise : a culinary journey in Africa / Joan Baxter.
ISBN 978-1-988286-02-0 (paperback)
1. Baxter, Joan--Travel--Africa, Sub-Saharan. 2. Food--Africa, Sub-Saharan.
3. Local foods--Africa, Sub-Saharan. 4. Food habits--Africa, Sub-Saharan.
5. Cooking--Africa, Sub-Saharan. 6. Farms, Small--Africa, Sub-Saharan.
7. Africa, Sub-Saharan--
Description and travel. I. Title.
GT2853.A47B39 2017   394.1'20967   C2016-906957-5

Cover image: Roadside sellers of tamarind in Burkina Faso. Photo by Joan Baxter:

Back cover photo by Saskia Marijnissen

Cover design: Gail LeBlanc

Pottersfield Press acknowledges the financial support of the Government of Canada through the Canada Book Fund for our publishing activities. We acknowledge the support of the Canada Council for the Arts. We are pleased to work in partnership with the Province of Nova Scotia to develop and promote our creative industries for the benefit of all Nova Scotians.

Pottersfield Press
83 Leslie Road
East Lawrencetown, Nova Scotia, Canada, B2Z 1P8
Website: www.PottersfieldPress.com
To order, phone 1-800-NIMBUS9 (1-800-646-2879) www.nimbus.ns.ca

Printed in Canada   FOREST STEWARDSHIP FSC COUNCIL

Pottersfield Press is committed to preserving the environment and the appropriate harvesting of trees and has printed this book on Forest Stewardship Council ® certified paper.

I invite you on a formidable gourmand's journey, between desert and tropical forest, between continent and oceans ... I want you to discover countless unusual and delicious flavours.

– Alexandre Bella Ola
La Cuisine de Moussa

Contents

Acknowledgements

I owe every story and experience in this book to the countless people – friends, colleagues, acquaintances, guides, and mentors – who schooled me on food, farms, cooking and culinary culture, and sometimes on life itself for over three decades in many countries in Africa. Some appear in person on these pages, as they share with me their knowledge and love of their own wonderful crops, dishes, and food cultures. All I can say to them, and to all the others who shared their time and thoughts (and often their food) with me to increase my appreciation of the culinary wealth on the continent, is *asante sana, barka, i ni ce, merci beaucoup, tenki tenki* – a Very Big Thank You – for everything. I would also like to express my immense gratitude to the people who kindly read the manuscript and offered invaluable guidance, among them Dali Mwagore, Isabel Huggan, Katie Plestid, Roger Leakey, and Wayne Roberts. Thanks also to Lesley Choyce at Pottersfield Press for giving the book a home in Canada, and to Julia Swan and Peggy Amirault for their tireless and marvellous editing work. *Bon voyage and bon appetit!*

Introduction

One of the happiest, most celebratory pieces of music I know is a song called "Africa" by Malian superstar Salif Keita, known as "the golden voice of Africa." In the song, his rousing band dishes up a smorgasbord of rhythms and melodies, cheerled by a female chorus calling out their love for "Africa-oh" and "Africa-eh." Keita runs through a list of African nations, exclaiming how beautiful they are, how in Africa you eat a lot and dance a lot. He then rhymes off the names of some favourite African dishes – *attièke, futu, fufu, yassa, mafé,* exclaiming "oh, what good food." Africa, he sings, makes you "dream, vibrate, come alive and dance."

After the privilege of living for more than three decades on the continent, and sampling those wonderful dishes, I couldn't agree with him more. Precious little from Africa has been given its due, let alone celebrated in song. Not least the amazing array of foods and food crops. The rest of the world has pretty much ignored the culinary cultures of Africa, or else swallowed simplistic stereotypes about a constant continental food crisis and negative portrayals of African diets and eating habits.[1]

These stereotypes, in turn, are being used to justify the takeover of Africa's food and farms by global corporations through multi-billion-dollar initiatives, heavily backed by and benefitting multinational corporations, such as the G7/G8's New Alliance for Food Security and Nutrition, the Alliance for a Green Revolution in Africa (AGRA), and Grow Africa.[2] Ironically, just as Africa's cuisines and foods are threatened by the increasing push for industrial corporate agriculture on the continent, African chefs and cooks are making an effort to promote its diverse and rich cuisines. There has also been a proliferation of African restaurants around the world, thanks to the growing diaspora and a budding interest in new and interesting cuisines. More and more people are devoting their lives to documenting and promoting cuisines from Africa, so more and more books are being dedicated to the rich heritage and cultures of African foods and the crops grown to make them.

These champions of African cuisine are now spreading the word around the world about its fine foods and enormous potential.

Fran Osseo-Asare is the author of several books, including *Food Culture in Sub-Saharan Africa*. She founded Betumi: The African Cuisine Network (www.betumi.com) and blogs about African foods. She says the website grew out of her experiences over three decades in Africa, starting in the 1970s, that she was "galvanized to action by intense frustration over a general failure to take sub-Saharan culinary history and contributions seriously, by the distorted popular media coverage and assumptions in North America, and the biased 'scholarly' information available on Africa's food-related history, whether that information was pro or con."

And there's Marcus Samuelsson (*The Soul of a New Cuisine: A Discovery of the Foods and Flavors of Africa*); Alexandre Bella Ola (*La Cuisine Moussa: 80 Recettes Africanes Irrésitibles*); Rachel C.J. Massaquoi (*Foods of Sierra Leone and Other West African Countries: A Cookbook and Food-Related Stories*); Judith Carney and

Richard Rosomoff (*In the Shadow of Slavery: Africa's Botanical Legacy in the Atlantic World*); and Jessica B. Harris (*High on the Hog: A Culinary Journey from Africa to America*). In 2012, for the first time, African foods were showcased by the Slow Food Movement's annual food fair and extravaganza, the *Salon Internazionale del Gusto et Terre Madre* in Italy.[3]

A landmark study published in 2015 went further to dispel myths about African food, diets, and malnutrition. It examined diets in 187 countries in 1990 and again in 2010, and found that nine of the healthiest were in West African nations. The three countries with the healthiest diets of all – Chad, Sierra Leone, and Mali – are also three of the world's poorest countries.[4]

African novelists often insert the names of their favourite foods lovingly into their books. Cameroon's Calixthe Beyala crafted an entire mischievous and bitingly satirical novel around Cameroonian recipes, fantastic flavours, longing and seduction, and African identity and called it *Comment Cuisiner son Mari à l'Africaine* (*How to Cook Your Husband in the African Way*). But even satire cannot undo stereotypes. Non-African readers may have a problem translating words on a page into real desires for unfamiliar delicacies and grasping the richness of Africa's culinary cultures.

I am speaking from experience; when I first went to Niger to join my finacé there in 1982, I was oblivious to the world of culinary wonders around me. But as time passed, and helped along by African friends and mentors, I began to realize how much I was missing by not sticking my nose into cooking pots and kitchens, farm fields and markets. It was a long and steep learning curve that involved more than three decades and living in seven countries – Niger, Cameroon, Burkina Faso, Ghana, Kenya, Mali, and Sierra Leone – with working trips to many others. It involved stints with an international agricultural research organization that focused on agroforestry and smallholder farming and gave me opportunities to visit farms and forests throughout sub-

Saharan Africa with farmers as my guides. And all of this, combined with shopping and cooking lessons from many African friends over the years, is how I eventually began to grasp that there is an enormous wealth of traditional knowledge and wisdom that goes into Africa's cooking and the complexity and sophistication of its countless culinary cultures.

It was a lovely journey, one that began with three majestic trees that graced our lives in northern Ghana.

1

Three magic trees

A tree that refuses to dance will be made to do so by the wind.

— Ghanaian proverb
The Wisdom of Africa
Pete Lewenstein, editor

At first, they just looked like big no-name trees out there in the heat and the dust, standing improbably in a bleak, bare compound of red gravel. One of them was at the entrance to our compound, just inside the wooden gate. Another stood on the north side of the house, visible through a bedroom window. The other was on the south side, visible through another bedroom window.

When I was lying on our bed, nursing another headache or fever or bout of homesickness, I had a choice. I could lie on my right side staring morosely out the south window at one thick tree trunk and its yawning canopy, or roll over and stare for a while at its twin on the north side. Just staring, not really seeing them. Not even remotely curious about them.

My diaries from the first year spent in Tamale, northern

Ghana, with two small kids and a frequently absent husband confirm that I was a rather unhappy excuse for a mother and spouse during that time. My own neuroses blinded me to much that was good and beautiful around me, including the three mighty trees that stood like guardians around the house, their branches reaching over the roof like protective arms, shading it from the worst of the sun and shielding it from the brunt of the seasonal winds that blasted across the savannah.

I fretted about all the things we were missing in Tamale. Electricity. Running water. Telephone. Medical facilities. Grandparents, uncles, aunts, cousins. Cold, fresh, frothy milk. Cheddar cheese. The brisk, cool breeze coming off the Atlantic Ocean on a glorious summer day in eastern North America. Meadows full of daisies and brown-eyed susans and honeybees. The surprise reprieve of a snow day.

At the same time, I panicked about all the things we were not short of in Tamale. Stifling and oppressive heat. Frequent bouts of malaria. Raging infections of staphylococcus and streptococcus.

There was, fortunately, an excellent doctor around when my son split open his forehead on the eve of his first birthday. Dr. Tinorgah is a wonderful physician and medical researcher with profound knowledge of tropical diseases and their treatment, who would go on to join the World Health Organization. But at that time he was working as a medical advisor on a development pro-ject in the area and not officially practising medicine. So he didn't have on hand any emergency medical materials to deal with the wound. He very kindly spent several hours frantically combing the town of Tamale to come up with some strands of sterile catgut to stitch up my son's head. He did that without anaesthetic. By candlelight. In the sweltering stifling heat. While I pinioned my son to the floor on his back, Dr. Tinorgah sewed up the gash in his forehead, my dripping sweat mingled with my own and my son's tears. The doctor was calm, cool, compassionate, and competent beyond imagining.

The children were still tiny little beings, largely and happily oblivious to all their near-death experiences. They were open to everything and everyone who offered fun, excitement, and friendship in their new Ghanaian home. They had many Ghanaian friends who took them under their wings, and who carted my son around like a beloved ragdoll. Adults rapidly became their "aunties" and "uncles" and tossed them in the air, played with them, danced with them, dressed them up in colourful Ghanaian clothing – tunics or "smocks" of locally grown and woven cotton. They invited them for meals, local dishes made of yams, rice, cassava, maize, or millet topped with rich sauces made of local oils, spices, fish, and vegetables. Our dining table, set with individual plates and knives and forks, tended to feature more familiar-to-me fare involving chicken or beef, rice or potatoes and sometimes fried yams and salads. The kids far preferred to eat local fare at their friends' homes, gathered around large communal bowls on mats where everyone sat and scooped up the food with their right hands. It was the children, so unset in their ways, so open to learning, who made me slowly start to wake up to the wonders of the trees in our compound.

The period of gradual discovery began in January, when the trees sprouted fuzzy balls, richly orange as the setting sun. The balls – the trees' flowers – dangled from long stems like Christmas tree ornaments. They swayed and danced in the last of the Harmattan winds, which sweep south across West Africa from the Sahara Desert each year and blanket the whole region with a fine layer of yellow-brown dust. Sometimes, the wind knocked a few of the spheres to the ground. The kids and their friends gleefully harvested them and stockpiled them as furry orange weapons for whacking each other, while they squealed and giggled. They called the balls "bommy-knockers," a term they culled from Joy Cowley's *The Hungry Giant's Soup*, one of their favourite books.

Then they told me the balls on the trees were changing.

They dragged me outside to gaze up at the spreading canopy of the tree, where the orange orbs had begun to moult. Their furry coats were dropping off in clumps, revealing green-skinned balls underneath. Next, each small green sphere sprouted a crop of green shoots. The shoots grew into long curved pods. My daughter suggested this miraculous transformation in the bommy-knockers was "magic."

The dry season was now beginning to wane. The humidity and heat had begun their crescendo in preparation for the rains that would start to pummel us in June. Heavy storm clouds, moving up from the coast hundreds of kilometres to the south, gathered over the scrubby savannah horizon. They crouched there like muscle-bound monsters waiting to unleash their fury on the parched surface of the earth. The pods turned from green to brown. The trees developed a voice; the dry pods rattled each time a breeze tickled their branches.

I was only dimly aware of all of this, and paid no more attention to the brown pods than I would to any plants that I assumed were "just weeds," because I knew nothing about them and never paused to give them a kind or considerate thought.

Then one day our compound was invaded. Men, women, and children from the neighbouring village arrived on foot, pouring in through the open gate. No questions (permission) asked of us, the tenants in the house. They went straight to the trees, clambering over them, gathering all the brown pods and tossing them down to children below, who stacked them in neat(ish) piles.

I was watching from inside the house, pondering the twists and turns that had landed us in Tamale, where my husband was working on a Canadian- and German-funded rural development project. We'd moved south to Ghana from Ouagadougou in Burkina Faso, where I'd been reporting for the BBC and Reuters. But it wasn't obvious to me then that I would be able to do much of that from a small town in northern Ghana. We had no telephone line and if I wanted to file a report, I had to drive seven kilometres into the centre of Tamale to the post office. It boasted a telex machine that functioned only when there was a confluence of small miracles; someone had to manage to get the generator working and find money to buy fuel to keep it running for an hour or two. Email and mobile phones were still a decade away in that part of the world.

As I watched the trespassers out the window, I worked myself into a sour mood that translated into an urge to go outside and demand of them what the hell they thought they were doing on what I considered *our* compound, climbing about in what I considered *our* trees. Instead, I stood at the window watching in silence and some wonder as my two small children frolicked about with the kids. Under the tutelage of their friends and newfound "aunties" and "uncles," they were discovering the delicacies hidden inside the brown pods. With their pudgy little fingers, they pulled out chunks of the bright yellow powder that was compressed inside. They gleefully crammed the powder into their mouths, until their hands and faces were coated with it. Stuff harvested from trees on our compound that these trespassers – friendly as they were – seemed to think were theirs.

It turns out the trees were indeed theirs. The land, I later learned from friends, had been signed over by the chief of the adjacent village to the development project as a housing compound for the Ghanaian and expatriate staff. But the trees that grew on the land would always belong, in an informal traditional way, to the chief and his people. They, and a few dozen other kinds of trees indigenous to the region, were considered "economic species" that local people cherished and needed for their survival. The unwritten rights to the use of the trees and the land in the region were as complex and intricate as the traditional governance structures involving chiefs, linguists, elders, spiritual leaders, and other guardians of the resources that sustained the people.

This was just the first of many bits of enlightenment that began with those three trees that blessed our compound. In northern Ghana, they were called *dawa dawa*, from the Hausa word *dawa* that could refer to food or to medicine, a difference that is often blurred in Africa and sometimes only in the amount or dose consumed. Many parts of the *dawa dawa* tree were used as medicine.

I learned to accept it as normal that travelling medicine men and traditional healers would wander through our gate and into the compound to scrape off small patches of the trees' bark, which they would use to treat jaundice, toothache, worms, bacterial dysentery, and snakebite, or as a mouthwash and a vapour inhalant for toothache or ear problems. The bark was also mashed up and used in baths for leprosy and to treat bronchitis, pneumonia, skin infections, sores, ulcers, malaria, diarrhea, and sterility. Its roots could be used to treat sore eyes. The leaves could be used to treat fever and bronchitis.

The food, however, was what fascinated me most. It came from the pods. First, there was the yellow powder, an "instant" food, a natural culinary wonder. Neighbours showed me that all I needed to do was mix it with water and boil it for a few minutes to produce porridge, as smooth and delicious as a self-sweetening bowl of Cream of Wheat. The yellow flour also made a wonderful snack that could be eaten straight from the pod, as my children liked it. And if you didn't take the time to pick out the seeds, just stuffed powder and seeds into your mouth all at once and swallowed, the little brown seeds would go right through your digestive tract as roughage and come out the other end – evidence-based research undertaken by my son while I monitored the data in his diaper.

But generally the brown seeds cushioned in the yellow powder are collected before going through any digestive systems, and are dried, cooked, fermented, and pounded to produce a pungent brown paste that is pressed into balls or rolled into little log shapes. Cooked up in a sauce or a soup, the fermented paste from the *dawa dawa* seeds makes for a wonderful condiment and complement to cuisines in the region. It is extremely nutritious, full of proteins, lipids, carbohydrates, essential amino and fatty acids, and vitamins.

The trees in our compound were architectural delights, wider than they were tall, shaped like squat, top-heavy giant green mushrooms. Their roots, formed over decades, reached deep into the earth to anchor their crowns and pump up water and nutrients from far below the dry surface. But to appreciate any of their qualities and uses, a non-local needs to have both eyes and mind wide open.

To the foreign eye, large parts of sub-Saharan Africa can appear as infertile wasteland, degraded and deforested scrubland sprinkled sparsely with remnant trees. In the dry season, with the trees dotting brown fields, it can be difficult to believe that anything, let alone something edible or useful, could ever be coaxed out of the fields of dehydrated earth. It would be easy to believe that the trees are still there only because people have been careless in clearing land for farms and just haven't got around yet to chopping or burning them down. In other words, it is awfully easy to get it all dead wrong. Were it not for the trees, if the land were denuded and unprotected from torrential downpours and punishing windstorms, it might long since have become true wasteland.

After we left Ghana, I would come across *dawa dawa,* the tree of many names (*néré* in French, locust bean in some anglophone countries, *Parkia biglobosa* to scientists, and dozens more appellations in local languages), all over West Africa – in Benin, Burkina Faso, Côte d'Ivoire, Guinea, Mali, Niger, Nigeria, Senegal, The Gambia, and Togo. I would recognize the powerful pungency of the condiment made from its seeds (*soumbala* in Mali, *iru* in parts of Nigeria) in markets throughout the region. When, once, I thought I might take some of the *soumbala* back to North America to add some hefty flavour to my soups and stews there, the airline check-in agent in Frankfurt detected the powerful odour emanating from my suitcase and asked me if I was carrying something rotten. I earnestly and enthusiastically explained it was a delicious and nutritious spice. He listened politely then insisted I remove and dispose of the offensive stuff before he would check the bag onto the plane. I argued it didn't smell any worse or stronger than some German cheeses. He wasn't swayed; it was either my suitcase or the spice. The spice went into a rubbish bin.

There is no denying that *soumbala* has a distinctive smell that can fill a home with a powerful aroma when it first goes into the pot. My kids unkindly described this as a "stink" and complained loudly while the *soumbala* heated up. But once cooked and blended into any sauce, it packs a knockout flavour punch.

When, in 2007, our uncharted life path led my husband and me to Sierra Leone, there was the same species of tree again, growing right behind the building in which he had rented a room in the capital, Freetown. So once again I could lie in my bed and watch in awe as this wondrous tree put on a seasonal fashion show in January – adorning its greenery with those splendid dangling orange balls, then the green pods that matured to brown, full of nutritious food.

In Sierra Leone, the tree has grown rarer in the landscape, partly because the decade-long civil war took a horrific toll not just on human beings and rural communities but also on the country's vegetation and forests. The use of its seeds to produce a nutritious condiment, which Sierra Leoneans call *kenda,* was also on the decline. Not just because the trees were becoming increasingly scarce, but also because "flavour enhancers" such as Nestlé's Maggi cubes had taken over as the condiment of choice in the country, and right across Africa.

Some thought this a good thing. Take, for instance, the thoroughly modern young Sierra Leonean woman who was working as a communications officer for Addax Bioenergy, a Swiss corporation that had leased a great swath of arable land in Sierra

Leone for sugarcane plantations.

We met up one hot afternoon in the shade of a small thatched hut, beside a tin shack that served as a makeshift office for the company while it constructed the enormous modern complex that would become its permanent headquarters. Even as we spoke, in the distance I could hear bulldozers at work, clearing the land. More than 10,000 hectares of farmland were being converted from food-producing farms and fallow forests to sugarcane, which in turn would be transformed into ethanol for export to Europe, where it would feed vehicles and not people. The Addax Bioenergy plantation would be irrigated with precious river water and boom-sprayed with a cocktail of herbicides and pesticides, financed by a half-dozen European development banks.

What I wanted to know from the communications officer was whether – as a daughter of the land – she had any concerns about the loss of all the indigenous foods and fruits that might no longer be available when the landscape was reduced to a single industrial biofuel crop. She told me there was no point in my worrying about the trees that would be bulldozed to make way for the massive plantations because there would be "ecological corridors" and anyway, there was little of value on the land.

"But the land has lots of oil palm and other trees," I persisted. "There is so much biodiversity, so many locust bean trees that will have to come down. There will be no more *kenda.*"

"Why are you thinking about *kenda*?" she scoffed. "I mean, we call *kenda* the poorest man's food!" She told me the only reason people used the local condiment and not Maggi cubes was because "they have no choice." To prove her point, she sang me a couple of lines from a popular song about *kenda* being "poor man's food." I had earned her scorn with my feeble defence of a traditional (and nutritious) local food. She viewed me as backward, said I was against "development."

But many Sierra Leoneans remembered with some pride that their mothers and grandmothers had always used *kenda* and other local condiments and ingredients and cooked wonderful food, without the benefit of Maggi. They said *kenda* was always given to pregnant women because it was so nutritious. *Kenda* could turn a rather bland bowl of plain rice into a nutritious and tasty breakfast.

The National Academy of Sciences in the United States lists locust bean or *dawa dawa* as one of a marvellous array of important "lost" African crops (or at least sorely neglected and overlooked by governments, development agencies, and science).[5] Alas, today the knowledge of the food and medicines from the locust bean tree, like the tree itself, is fading and even disappearing in the chaotic storm of rapid change as Sierra Leone – indeed the entire continent – is swept up in the frenzy to modernize, industrialize, globalize, and change its eating habits. Just like the rich industrialized West, and the increasingly rich and industrialized East. Amid the media reports of famine and hunger and the images of starving children, new studies now highlight the latest big health problems in Africa – heart disease, obesity, and Type 2 diabetes, new scourges brought on by industrial diets that have no room for traditional condiments produced by family farmers.

I often think fondly about the *dawa dawa* trees that stood guard over our house in northern Ghana because they marked the first real step in my own journey of culinary learning. So close to the house, but invisible to me until my kids and their Ghanaian tutors began to school me, open my mind to the treasures and complexities of their landscapes, their farms, their foods, their lives.

2

Seven grains of paradise

Scores of little huts with grand names competed for the travellers'
custom with colourful signboards backed up with verbal appeals:
Goat meat here! Egusi soup here! Bushmeat here! Come here for Rice!
Fine Fine Pounded Yams!

– Chinua Achebe
Anthills of the Savannah

My initial inability to notice the gastronomic and medicinal
marvels of the *dawa dawa* tree was not an aberration. Nor
was it the first time I'd failed to notice what was right in front
of me, sometimes even when it was written in black and white.
When I first read the late Chinua Achebe's classic 1958 novel,
Things Fall Apart, I completely missed his many references to
food. Set at the end of the nineteenth century among the Ibo in
the fictitious village of Umuofia in what is today Nigeria, Achebe's
brilliant book illustrates how the arrival of Christian missionaries
ruptured families and societies as surely and irrevocably as a
magnitude-eight earthquake taking down a concrete bridge.

Caught up in the story, I guess I skimmed right over the many passages that Achebe devoted to celebratory foods and feasts. It didn't register that the wealth and well-being he described had nothing to do with money; both were measured instead by the size of the stacks of yams stored in family barns and by the numbers of goats and chickens in a household. He also hinted at the complexities of the farms of the time, the yam mounds that men hoed and planted, amid which women sowed maize, melons, and beans.

It took a reread many years later for my culinary curiosity to be roused by the tantalizing foods featured in *Things Fall Apart*. While I again devoured the richness of Achebe's prose and storytelling, I noticed something else happening too. I found myself salivating at every mention of yam *foo-foo*, palm oil, palm wine, alligator pepper, vegetable soup, and yam pottage. The food references wafted off the page, each one a delectable desire. I'd now had occasion to sample most of the foods and dishes that appeared on the pages so they were no longer abstract ideas and I hankered after them. There was, however, one that I didn't know – alligator pepper. Not only had I never tasted it, but I'd never seen or even heard of it beyond the pages of Achebe's novel.

I went to work to learn all I could about alligator pepper. The small red peppers (*Aframomum* species) are native to West Africa and have always had great ceremonial and even religious significance in the region, just like the much-treasured kola nut.

Back in the fifteenth century, alligator pepper was one of several local resources the Portuguese appropriated from Africans without so much as a please or thank you, and certainly no recognition for the indigenous knowledge on this and other marvellous crops. In 1469, Portugal's King Afonso V granted the exclusive right to trade the pepper to a Lisbon merchant as part of a trade monopoly for the entire Gulf of Guinea, provided he spend five years exploring about 160 kilometres of coastline.

After that, the spicy little gem made its way north from sub-Saharan Africa along trade routes and in caravans. It became popular in North African cuisine and for a time also in Europe, where it was used as a substitute for black pepper. It was exported to the Americas as part of the Columbian Exchange, the vast movement and migration of plant and animal species unleashed after Christopher Columbus landed in the New World in 1492.

The versatile pepper goes by countless names in local languages, and even in English it has many that attest to its gallivanting past and its moments of glory over the centuries. Various of its species have been known as melegueta pepper, African pepper, British pepper (trust the little island kingdom to claim possession of an African resource), Jamaican pepper (transported as it was in slave ships from Africa to the Caribbean), guinea grains, guinea pepper, mbongo spice, hepper pepper, and my favourite name of all, the exquisite "grains of paradise." Even if the outside world seems to have forgotten about this fiery African gem, at home in West Africa it still has its devotees.[6]

Alligator pepper is used to impart tongue-tingling life to goat soup, a classic favourite right across West Africa. But its importance as a spice is just a small part of the pepper's remarkable repertoire. It has long been prized as a medicine, used to prevent some infections and heal many others. Ancient knowledge about the pepper stands up very well to modern scientific scrutiny.[7] Extracts of the plant have powerful antiseptic and anti-microbial properties and can be used against some of the bacteria associated with food poisoning. It has antioxidant and anti-tumor effects and shows promise in treating diabetes.[8] The pepper can also be used to treat dysentery and diarrhea, inflammatory conditions of the throat, fever, and skin rashes caused by a host of illnesses. It's said to be an antidote to snakebite. And it's a great favourite of gorillas living in the wild in Central Africa; because it contains a powerful anti-inflammatory compound, alligator pepper is being proposed as an antidote that could be introduced to the diets of captive gorillas to reduce their incidence of heart disease.[9]

That is one powerful, peppy little pepper. But even this is not the whole story, not a full inventory of the pepper's powers, as I was to learn from Dorcas, my soft-spoken and kindly neighbour in Freetown.

When I began taking this overdue interest in alligator pepper, our children had long gone off to live their own lives and my husband and I were living in the Sierra Leonean capital, Freetown. We had moved from the apartment with the view of the locust bean tree into the ground-floor apartment of a modest house squeezed onto a miniscule "town" lot. It was snuggled uncomfortably close to a very tall concrete wall that was evidently meant to protect us from any interlopers and also spare us any view of the sky. This meant I had to go outside, open the metal door in the wall, and step out onto the narrow mud track that fronted our house before I was able to determine whether the day was going to bring sun and heat, or if dark clouds were massing on the horizon, in which case we could expect rain and heat. Making things even more secure and claustrophobic inside was the razor wire drooped along the top of the wall, a relic from the days of the civil war when those who could afford to turned their homes into veritable bunkers.

Our rented quarters included two small bedrooms and two bathrooms with lovely modern fixtures that worked only when city water was running, which was a rare happenstance in Free-town. We had a tiny but cozy living room and a miniature kitch-en that we'd equipped with a gas stove and a bucket of water, as the faucets had never been hooked up to the city water supply, which, as I've said, only supplied water once in a blue moon.

On the upper floor of the house lived Dorcas, her two-year-old daughter, her husband, and her brother-in-law. After I'd been there a few weeks, Dorcas took to coming downstairs with her daughter to visit. She suffered from homesickness; she missed her parents terribly and was desperate to move back home to Nigeria.

Her husband had come to Sierra Leone after its civil war ended, in search of work, a young architect from Nigeria where the school of architecture was pumping out graduates faster than they could possibly be employed. He went to work for a construction company, and was not finding it easy. Despite the long hours he put in, from early morning until well after dark each evening, his pay was what Dorcas called "small" and he was fed up with the job. Many people refused to pay for drawings and some wealthy businessmen owed him a lot of money and simply wouldn't pay. He'd been applying online for jobs, but he didn't have the contacts or friends in high places needed to secure a lucrative post with an international company or organization. So for now, he stuck with it and she tried to accept her life far from her home and her people, praying always for a stroke of luck, a good job for her husband, and an opportunity for her to continue her studies so she could obtain a teaching job.

One day I remarked to Dorcas I was interested in African cooking, and in learning how to make some of the Nigerian specialities mentioned in *Things Fall Apart*. She beamed at me. "We have so much, so much, we have so many foods in Nigeria! You know we have so many different ethnic groups. We have so many good foods!" Without any prompting, she immediately offered to show me how to make some Nigerian dishes.

We agreed to begin with yam pottage and set a day and a time. As she backed away from my porch, she couldn't stop saying, "Thank you, thank you ma, thank you, thank you ma," as if *I* were doing *her* a favour.

On the appointed day, Dorcas arrives with a metal platter piled high with everything we need for yam pottage. This hadn't been the plan. I had told her if she were going to give me cooking lessons, I would at least take her to the market (I had a vehicle and she didn't) and pay for all the ingredients. But there she is, standing at my door with her shy smile and a platter full of as-yet-to-be-constructed yam pottage. She moves into my kitchen, and very politely but firmly tells me I am not to help, that she will do the work. She says she hopes she isn't disturbing me.

I say if anyone is doing any disturbing, it is I. But she explains to me that she is just so happy I asked her about Nigerian food, because, she says, "We have so many good foods and no one ever talks about them."

I want to press her like a flower between the pages of my little black notebook to preserve those words and thoughts about unsung African foods, which have been going round in my own brain for years.

She's brought along a white yam, a slim cylinder of a tuber about a foot long, to show me what kind of yam can be used for pottage, if I so wish it. She carves through the brown skin to show me its tender white interior, and explains there are many types of yams for all kinds of different dishes. Perhaps the best known is *fufu,* which varies from place to place and from one cook to another, and generally seems to refer to a category of foods that I might label as porridge.

Nigerian cooks are flexible and adaptable, she tells me, and are constantly adjusting traditional recipes to accommodate new foodstuffs and, when they can afford them, kitchen gadgets and machines. These days Dorcas makes *fufu* from a variety of basic ingredients. She purchases whole wheat in the market, which comes from Guinea but originates in France, and grinds it into powder for *fufu*. Or she buys imported bags of semolina, the coarse purified wheat middlings from durum wheat, and prepares that with water. She says she can also prepare *fufu* from cassava or corn flour.

Then, much to my dismay, Dorcas sets the yam aside and announces that we aren't going to make the yam pottage with yam today. Rather, she says, we'll try a recipe that she uses a lot in Sierra Leone, where there are plenty of sweet potatoes and there isn't a great abundance of cheap and varied yams on the market as there is in Nigeria. She has brought along a couple of sweet potatoes and three "Irish" potatoes, as the potatoes I know from my childhood are called in parts of West Africa, which seems odd for a tuber that originated and was domesticated in Latin America. These she peels and cuts into large chunks, placing them in a pot on the stove to boil. Then she cuts up a bunch of spring onions, one carrot and a handful of green beans so ripe their fat seeds are already bursting out through the seams.

Next she tackles the onion, telling me the imported onions in Sierra Leone remind her of something that has been "preserved" for a long time, missing both flavour and juice. She speaks longingly of the purple onions grown in northern Nigeria, which are so succulent and strong they make you cry. But, she says, it is becoming harder to find local onions in West Africa. The one she is using comes, she thinks, from Europe.

As she chops, she talks about how difficult it was for her when she first landed in Sierra Leone. She says she finds Freetown a strange place, with very different habits from those of her native Kogi State. Even the Christians in her church here have differ-ent beliefs from the ones in her church back home. Many people in Kogi State are Muslim, as was her father's family. But her fa-ther, the eldest son in the family, converted to Christianity as a young man. He was heavily influenced by the American mission-ary who brought Christianity to their part of Nigeria; her father ran errands for him and they grew very close. She says her father still cherishes the photograph he has of himself standing with the white man who made such a mark on him. But her father's con-version was not without repercussions. When he announced he was abandoning Islam, his father – her grandfather – disowned him and sent him away from the family home.

As I stand there watching Dorcas prepare yam pottage (well, *potato* pottage), I realize I'm hearing echoes of things fall-ing apart, just as they had in Achebe's novel. In *Things Fall Apart,* missionaries intent on converting local people to Christianity in the village of Umuofia had divided families, caused hostilities between fathers and sons, and rent asunder the ties that bound the community.

By now she has finished the vegetable chopping and moved on to the chicken leg, and having washed it, is cutting it into pieces.

"The chicken here is all imported," she says. "So the meat is not hard. But I prefer the country chicken. Most people do." By "country chicken" she means lean, local breeds that are free-ranging and not fattened up with feeding.

We agree it is strange that Sierra Leone, a nation of farmers, produces so little chicken and imports so much from the United States. Then again, it's easy to forget that just over a decade earlier, as recently as 2001, war was raging in this country. While it did, farmers were on the run and rebels were eating their way through just about every cow, goat, sheep, and chicken they could lay their hands on, decimating the nation's livestock supply.

Dorcas tells me her mother still maintains a small business raising a few country chickens, goats, and sheep. Her father, a lecturer in chemistry, still likes to farm and he cultivates all kinds of beans, maize, and yams.

"So you had lots of good country chicken at home in Nigeria?" I ask.

She laughs. "No, no. My father likes to cook, but if he slaughters one of Mom's chickens for the stew, he has to pay her for it. My mom says this is her business and he has to pay. That's how it is."

She places the chicken pieces into a small pot with a little water, adds a bit of salt, a few grains shaved off a Maggi cube, some curry powder and thyme, a few slices of the onion. She removes the pot with the potatoes from the burner and places the one with chicken on the fire. She says it will take about fifteen minutes.

"But I don't want to be wasting your time," she says, as we stand waiting for the chicken to cook. Again, I remind her that not only is she giving me her time (along with her food), she is also sharing her knowledge with me. She says it makes her happy to talk about food and about her home.

In the mornings in her town, she says, people start the day with a drink of "pap," a nutritious beverage made with corn, guinea corn (sorghum), or millet. Then for breakfast, she normally takes *akara*, a kind of bean cake. This she makes with black-eyed peas, or cowpeas, which are soaked until it is easy to peel off the "bark." Then she grinds them to a smooth paste in a blender – she has a powerful one but if you don't or if you do but don't have electricity, you can use a mortar and pestle. To the paste you then add onion and a little salt, but no (hot) pepper.

"If you put pepper in and fry them, they will soak up the oil," she says. "So we don't put pepper in. We make the pepper sauce separately and put it on the *akara* when we eat it. The pepper sauce we make with so many different peppers. You wash them and add a tiny bit of water and grind them up in a blender. You like hot pepper?"

I assure her I do. "Then you will like *moimoi*. It is another kind of bean cake, but made with pepper." She says *moimoi* is made the same way as *akara,* with black-eyed peas. Except that for *moimoi* you add hot pepper when you grind the beans and onions to a smooth paste.

"In Nigeria we have so many more peppers than here," she says. "They grow so many different ones in the north of Nigeria, around Kano. But here I use the local peppers, the red ones to give it a nice colour."

This seems the perfect moment to ask her about alligator peppers. I've been hoping we would be having them in today's pottage. No such luck. She says alligator peppers are hard to find in Freetown and are far too expensive. So here in Sierra Leone mostly she cooks with regular hot peppers, a wide array of *Capsicum* species introduced to Africa during the Colombian Exchange.

In Nigeria, however, alligator peppers are still abundant. She says her grandfather, who disowned her father for converting to Christianity, is a herbalist. He swears that if you eat seven seeds of alligator pepper a day, everything you say will be true. Seven grains of paradise a day and you will be bound to the truth, unable to tell a lie.

The kitchen is filling with the tempting aroma of the chicken and spices and my stomach starts to growl. Dorcas removes the pot from the stove, and pours a little vegetable oil into a frying pan. Then she lightly fries the small pieces of green beans and adds those to the chicken mix, and does the same with the carrot pieces. Next she fries up the onions and spring onions, but she insists they shouldn't be overcooked, so she removes the frying pan from the gas burner and allows them to sizzle in the remaining hot oil. These she adds to the potato mixture (from which she's poured out most of the water) and puts that pot back on the stove. Into it goes the chicken and vegetable blend, then the rest of the Maggi cube, more curry, some ground-up crayfish, salt, and the hot pepper mixture (blended hot peppers) that she's prepared in advance.

"You boil and stir it all up," she says, as she does just that. "Some people add flour to this, but I don't. Some people like to add smoked fish too. They like smoked fish in Kogi State so much!"

And that, she says, is how yam pottage is made, even when it's not made with yams. Although I'm still a little disappointed about that, as soon as I taste it, my disappointment dissipates. It's simply wonderful.

As Dorcas prepares to head home, I ask her, "So if ten Igala women from Nigeria were showing me how to make yam pottage, how many different recipes would I have for yam pottage?"

She laughs. "Ten. Maybe even more."

After that, I am determined to find the wondrous, truth-inducing alligator peppers. I put the word out with Sierra Leonean friends that I'm on the hunt for some grains of paradise. It's not as easy as I had expected, at least not in the capital.

In Sierra Leone, the pepper is used almost exclusively as a medicine and for spiritual purposes. Like other traditional crops, it is becoming increasingly rare, and in cities the dried peppers can be found mostly in herbalists' stalls in markets. Fatmata Sharka, a friend and agricultural development agent who is a mentor to me on all things crop- and farm-related, warns me to be wary of the pepper. It is said to have spiritual powers; if looked after carefully, it can guarantee a happy home and marriage. But woe unto anyone who fails to take the requisite care of the pepper and inadvertently lets its tiny seeds, the grains of paradise, scatter in the house. They've been known to cause so much trouble the home can "burn up." Although this, so they say, can be countered by planting a succulent shrub called "never die" in the compound, which has the power to ensure that one's luck never dies.

It takes some days before Fatmata's hunt for the sublime pepper bears fruit, so to speak. We're both participating in a conference intended to counter the grabbing of her country's farmland by foreign investors, when she proudly presents me with an alligator pepper wrapped up in a scrap of brown paper. I cradle it carefully in my hand, cognizant of its purported power to wreak havoc on my life, and pull back the paper. I confess I am initially disappointed by its sorry appearance. It is a brown and wizened little thing that looks as if it has been retrieved from the bottom of an ancient sarcophagus.

But Fatmata instructs me to gently pry away the papery skin and fish around inside with my fingers, where I uncover dozens of tiny black grains. They look a little like poppy seeds, but are even smaller, almost as fine as ground black pepper. She warns me they are very hot, so I gingerly place one onto my tongue and brace myself for a fiery assault. As the grain dissolves in my mouth, it invokes not just a picante tingling but also an explosion of delightful flavour, a hint of the pepper's distant cousins, cardamom and ginger, with some citrus touches too. One by one, I consume and savour seven of the little grains of paradise.

Alligator peppers containing the tasty little "grains of paradise" have important spiritual and medicinal uses in Sierra Leone. (Saskia Marijnissen photo)

3

Green leaves and yams

When your yams are nice and white, you should cover them.

(Don't flaunt your wealth.)
– Sierra Leonean proverb

Africa's yams – not to be confused with the sweet potatoes North American grocers sometimes label as yams – are amazing tubers that come in all shapes, textures, and sizes. Some are immense woody things, big and clumpy as an elephant's foot or a tropical tree root. They may exhibit fascinating, even slightly alarming and gargoyle-like protuberances. Some are small and cylindrical. Some are large and cylindrical. Some are round. And there is absolutely everything in between. They may be covered with thin brown skin, or thick and hairy stuff that looks like it has been shorn from an orangutan. They can reach lengths of two metres and weigh in at fifty kilograms, the size of a small adult, or at less than a kilogram, like a super-sized potato.[10] Their flesh varies from white to yellowish to red and even purple.

Farmers in West Africa cultivate at least four yam species, which belong to the genus *Dioscorea*. The ancestral tendrils of two yam species stretch back across continents and centuries to Southeast Asia, from where they were likely brought to Africa by Portuguese boats in the sixteenth century.[11] Two others are native to Africa, which people there domesticated from wild forest plants as many as 10,000 years ago. The wild yams probably sustained hunting and gathering populations for tens of thousands of years before that. Wild or "bush" yams are still an important (and tender and delicious!) food in rural areas where forests have not disappeared, and where fallowed land returns to bush and small "tree-crop plantations" (mixed coffee, cocoa, oil palm, kola nuts, and many other useful vines and trees) replicate forest conditions. They are much appreciated in rural Sierra Leone. Throughout the long civil war, bush yams sustained many people as they fled for their lives through the forests for months – and sometimes even years – on end.

Unlike potatoes that are planted in mounded rows, yams are cultivated in individual hillocks of soil. Among some ethnic groups, a man's prowess – and thus his suitability as a prospective husband – was traditionally measured by the number of yam mounds he could hoe in a day.

More than 60 million people living in countries along the Gulf of Guinea coast, from Cameroon across to Côte d'Ivoire, derive the bulk of their daily intake of calories and important nutrients from yam dishes.[12] The tubers are rich in vitamins A and C and contain three times more protein than cassava. They store well and even better when dried and turned into flour. Across the forested zones of Central and West Africa, yams were once so prized and precious they were sometimes venerated, imbued with immense spiritual and religious importance, as Chinua Achebe wrote.

Dorcas had listed just a few of the scores of ways the great assortment of yams figure in local cuisines in Nigeria. Yellow yam, she said, could be boiled and served with onion sauce. Water yam was boiled and served with various sauces. Black yam – which in her Igala language is *ojedudu* and the Yoruba people call *amala* – could be peeled, dried, and then ground into a powder. When you cooked this one, Dorcas said, it would be brownish.

If you want to make *fufu,* there are still other kinds of yams suitable for this quintessential West and Central African specialty that has dozens of variations, such as *foofoo* and *foufou,* depending on who is making it and where and with what starchy ingredients. *Fufu* is so much more than just a food; its preparation is an art. In some places *fufu* is made of fermented and dried tubers, and this is mixed with water and stirred into a smooth, tangy paste. In other places it's made by boiling the tubers and pounding them in mortars.

Watching women brandishing wooden pestles, sometimes taller than themselves, to pound foods in a waist-high mortar (*Clunk! Clunk! Clunk!*), while dipping their hands into the mortar between *Clunks* to knead and shape the doughy contents, is, for me, as nerve-wracking as watching a tightrope walker defying gravity on a very high wire with no safety belt. It's also incredibly hard work that precludes the need for Pilates or Crossfit training; a daily routine of food processing with wooden mortars and pestles sculpts the finest of shoulders, torsos, and upper arms.

When the *fufu* has been pounded to a smooth consistency, it is then shaped into appealing balls. No matter how they are prepared, yam dishes are generally served with sauces and many of those are made with green leaves.

Trying to catalogue even a few of the myriad crops that nourish Africa, and how these are used to create the diverse cuisines on a vast and varied continent, is like an immersion course not just in cooking but also in botany and linguistics. Especially when it comes to the leafy greens that go into the hundreds, if not thousands, of different sauces, soups, and stews, which are the crowning glory over staple starchy dishes of tubers, grains, or plantains that have traditionally energized the people on the continent.

Some of the greens are cultivated, such as cassava and sweet potato leaves. Some are collected wild. Some are a bit of both. It would take years to sample all the leafy greens used in African cuisines, a whole encyclopedia to document them. To make things just slightly simpler, the scientists who devote themselves to studying the value and diversity of these greens have come up with an acronym for them – TLVs, short for Traditional Leafy Vegetables.[13] Some are used to make a sauce slippery or gluey, and some are the main ingredient, giving the sauce or stew or soup its flavour and substance.

It can be very difficult to procure many of the TLVs in Europe and North America, so African cookbooks catering to the diaspora often suggest using kale, spinach, collard greens, chard, or dandelion greens as substitutes. That there are so many potherbs available in Africa says a lot about nature's love of biodiversity in the tropics. That there are so few leafy greens available in the industrialized northern lands also shows the modern corporate food system has no great fondness for the messy multitudes of wild, uncultivated plants.

In anglophone West African countries, mixed green leafy soups or stews often go by the name of "palaver" or "trouble" sauce, made in a variety of ways with various leafy greens. They may contain any kind of meat or fish, diverse vegetables, hot peppers and other local condiments or flavour enhancers, and palm or other cooking oils. In Sierra Leone the sauce earns its name because the different ingredients are rivals competing with each other for attention, having words or "palaver" among themselves, says Rachel Massaquoi in *Foods of Sierra Leone and Other West African Countries*. After the sauce is cooked, and especially if it has time to sit overnight, its flavour improves because the antagonistic ingredients realize they're all in the same soup so they'd better accept it, forge a truce, and do their utmost to make the dish taste as good as they can.

In Cameroon, the nation's staple leafy sauce is *ndolé*, thick as a stew and flavourful as the majestic Mount Cameroon is high. It comes very close to being one of my all-time favourite foods. It has as many incarnations as there are cooks in Cameroon, but invariably contains bitter leaves, usually of *Vernonia amygdalina.* They are so bitter that after they've been sliced into tiny slivers, they have to be washed and wrung out – with all the energy you might expend when trying to remove an especially intransigent stain in a tablecloth. This is done several times before the shredded leaves go into the pot with the ground (raw) peanuts, tomatoes, onions, oil, peppers, garlic, and meat or fish – and these days probably also a Maggi cube or two. The *ndolé* is served with many starchy dishes, and preferably (speaking for myself) with a *miondo* or *baton,* a long slim "stick" made with fermented and pounded cassava steamed inside banana leaves. Cameroon – with over two hundred ethnic groups and at least a half-dozen agro-ecological zones – is known as an Africa in miniature. It has a cuisine so complex and diverse that it would require (and deserves) an entire book unto itself.

In Kenya, to crown a bowl of steaming starchy *ugali* made of cornmeal, the leafy green topping is called *sukumawiki,* Kiswahili for "stretch the week" because with its core ingredients of kale and other leafy greens, tomatoes, and onions, it is not excessively onerous on limited household budgets. In Nigeria, waterleaf (*Talinum triangulare*) is a nutritious and popular favourite. In several West and Central African countries, staple sauces made with sweet potato or cassava leaves are known as *saga-saga.*

The generic term for leafy sauces in Sierra Leone is *plassas.* With the help of Sierra Leonean women friends, I tried over the years to compile a list of greens that could be used to make *plassas.* It included cassava leaves, sweet potato leaves, pumpkin leaves, *craincrain* (bush okra, jute leaves from various species from the genus *Corchorus*), *pila* or *pillaah* (leaves from the plant that produces the delicious bitter ball, or *jakato*), cocoyam (taro),

sawa sawa (sorrel), a plant called "bitter leaf" that grows wild
all over the place and requires a lot of washing and pounding to
make it a little less bitter, okra, papaya (which also needs to be
treated like bitter leaf), and something called *kpoluhun,* which
has to be pounded like cassava leaf until it becomes black and
slippery. Sierra Leonean cook and food writer Rachel Massaqoui
bemoans the disappearance of a vegetable called *bologie,* which her
grandmother called "bush onions"; its leaves were combined with
bitter leaves to make bitter leaf sauce.[14]

Of all the TLVs I've tried, my favourite is the spinach-like
potherb that is called, rather unhelpfully for the inquisitive foreigner seeking a scientific classification, "grin," or "green" in the
Krio language.[15] Eventually, after much fruitless sleuthing in Sierra
Leonean kitchens, farms, and markets, I finally learned from Fatmata Sharka, agricultural extension officer and botanist-cook ex-
traordinaire, and the friend who brought me the alligator pepper,
that "grin" is a term used for several species of amaranths. Amaranths are one of the oldest food crops in the world.[16] They are
so valuable that they really deserve some fanfare and at least a few
paragraphs to honour them here.

There are some sixty species of plants in the genus *Amaranthus,* which originated in the Americas before spreading round
the globe. Only a few of the amaranths are food crops, and of
those some are grains and others are greens. Before the arrival
of Columbus in the Americas, grain amaranth was probably as
important as maize and beans to Amerindian populations.[17] It
was so precious that it was closely linked to the spiritual world
and rituals, and this led the Spanish conquistadors to condemn
it as a pagan food. As Amerindian cultures collapsed, so did the
cultivation of amaranth grains in the New World. But even as the
crop was losing favour as a grain in the New World, amaranths
were making their way across oceans to Asia and Africa in the
great migration of crops during the Columbian Exchange, and
inserting themselves into landscapes and into diets.

Yanah Kelfalla with "grin" leaves, Sierra Leone.

Amaranth greens are the most important potherbs for count-less people in the humid lowlands and drier savannahs of Africa. The leaves are exceptionally rich in protein, accounting for as much as a quarter of daily protein intake among some groups. They are rich in vitamin A-forming carotenoids, without which children can go blind. They also provide vitamin C, and accumu-late minerals such as iron and calcium. Rural women are the main producers of amaranth and indeed all the TLVs, which could, with the right promotion, do a lot to reduce malnutrition and poverty in Africa.[18]

At least this is the view of some researchers in Benin,[19] the sliver of a nation tucked between Nigeria to the east and Togo to the west. They found that in their country, people consume 187 different traditional leafy vegetables, of which only 47 are culti-vated and 140 still grow wild. The researchers observed the TLVs are largely known, grown, and harvested by rural women, whose immense knowledge and skills they applaud. They describe the women as not just homemakers but also "plant gatherers, home gardeners, plant domesticators, herbalists and seed custodians."[20]

There is only one thing missing from that list. Invariably, the women are also culinary experts, repositories of immense knowledge about how to cook the foods they cultivate and collect.

4

Time for terroir?

The Tokpa [in Benin] is not solely a food market; everything from brilliantly printed fabric to small but surely incendiary deminjohns of gasoline can be purchased. However, the exuberance of the food section and the variety of comestibles there speaks to the importance of food on the African continent.

– Jessica B. Harris
High on the Hog:
A Culinary Journey from Africa to America

Benin has marvellously complex cuisines. This may be because of the numerous greens and other crops that thrive in its varied ecological niches, but it is also a reflection of the country's cultural and ethnic diversity. And that, in turn, is a legacy of its remarkable history. It was seat to medieval African kingdoms and female warriors that Europeans dubbed Amazons, confusing them with a nation of female soldiers in Greek mythology. Even today, after centuries of Christian missionizing and Islamic influence, a significant percentage of Benin's population follows traditional religions, including the unfairly maligned Vodun or Voodoo, an extremely complex and sophisticated faith that stresses earth and ancestral spirits.

It would take many weeks to discover all of its culinary treasures, but during a short visit I am able to sample some Beninois specialities, thanks to the enthusiastic efforts of my kind host, geneticist, professor, and activist Jeanne Zoundjihekpon. Jeanne has devoted her career to defending biodiversity and family farmers in her country. It's not an even battle, given that her adversary is the leviathan of the world's financial and corporate machinery that promotes industrial agriculture and the corporate food system it begets and abets. But that doesn't seem to deter Jeanne, who exudes enough energy to fire up a whole city, or perhaps a nation.

It's late evening when I land in Cotonou, nearly braindead after a night of flying over an ocean and then a day soaring southwards over half a continent. Jeanne arrives at the hotel to welcome me. She bears food, lots of it in several baskets. The small hotel is new and has no functioning restaurant, so Jeanne has taken over its conference room and unloaded a banquet and the plates and cutlery to enjoy it. It looks to me a lot of food for just three of us: Jeanne, her assistant Brice, and me. There is fried fish, *attiéke* made from fermented and dried cassava, rice, and a sauce with vegetables.

I do my best to take note of the delicacies and what I am supposed to eat with what; apparently I am not to put the sauce on the *attiéke*. The sauce is meant only for the rice. The *attiéke* I am to eat separately with my hand, together with fingers full of the fish picked off its bones. But I am so sleepy after the long haul from North America that I fail to register the many fine points of this wonderful meal, my first on this whistle-stop culinary tour in Benin. What is clear, though, is that eating *à la Beninoise* is a fine art of mixing and matching diverse, delicious dishes, not easy for the foreigner to fathom at first go.

The next chance I have to *manger à la Beninoise* comes the following day in Pobé, a town about seventy kilometres north of Cotonou. I am travelling with Jeanne and three members of the national farmers' union to a meeting with smallholder farmers, following the narrow road known as Route Nationale 3 that runs almost parallel with the Nigerian border. As we drive through one village after another, I marvel at the ubiquitous roadside displays of giant glass jugs filled with what looks like white wine, which I assume to be local palm wine, harvested from indigenous palms. They glint in the sun like fabulous works of art in an exhibit celebrating liquid light. Eventually, I ask my companions how on earth the people in the villages can produce – let alone consume – so much palm wine.

They are polite. That is, they try not to laugh out loud. They explain that the villagers are not selling wine. Beautiful as it is, with the sunbeams splicing through the pale yellow liquid in the massive jugs, it is an explosive kind of beauty. What they are selling is gasoline. And yes, there are many horrific accidents in which people are burned to death, probably one a week. But that doesn't stop people from getting into the gasoline smuggling and peddling business. Each morning they head out on their motorcycles, dwarfed by a dozen or more empty plastic jugs hitched to their bikes, and make their way across the border into Nigeria where they fill the huge jerry cans with black-market fuel. Then they drive back across the border into Benin, the jerry cans bulging with gasoline, the motorbikes sluggish and heavy, overloaded beyond reason, safety be damned. Route Nationale 3 has become Gasoline Alley and illegal gasoline is the *business du jour.*

Family farming may be less lucrative and harder physical work, but it's a lot safer and more sustainable business, and it still employs – and feeds – most people in the area. That means there are many local specialties to be had and Jeanne has already decided on a shortlist I must try during my brief stay. In Pobé, after the meeting, she informs me I'm to sample *igname pilée,* or pounded yam. Yams, my companions tell me, are everything here in Benin. The "pounded yam" or *igname pilée* is made by boiling the yams, then mashing them in mortars and working them by hand while adding small amounts of the water in which they were boiled, to make the doughy substance easy to handle, smooth enough to be formed into satiny dollops. Sounds to me very much like the *fufu* I've eaten throughout West Africa.

We pull up in front of a modest little eatery that calls itself Bar Maquis Djagoun et Fils, tucked under some very tall trees on the edge of a mud road. Its menu is painted on a large signboard attached to the outside wall. Atop the list, as Jeanne foretold, is *igname pilée*.

Beside the names of different kinds of meat on offer there are helpful drawings of the creature that provided it. I deduce I can choose from rabbit, *agouti* (the rodent known as grass-cutter or Greater Cane rat), venison, and mutton. While everyone else heads inside, I jot down the other menu options in my notebook. Once seated with my travelling companions in the dark and relatively cool interior, I give their patience a solid testing as I try to find out what exactly each dish is and how it's made.

Lafun is a sun-dried and fermented cassava pulp that's milled into flour to produce a stiff porridge known also as *oka* to be eaten with soups. *Blocoto* is a rich sauce made with cow feet, cow tail, shrimps, palm oil, onion, tomatoes, hot peppers, and spices.

Then I want to know about the *fromage,* the cheese. Benin is a former French colony, and I've not been in any French West African country where French culinary specialties such as Camembert and Champagne could not be found in Lebanese or French supermarkets. The same is true of the cheesy product sold under the names *La vache qui rit* or The Laughing Cow from the giant French corporation, Fromageries Bel. Sold in shallow round cardboard packages on roadsides throughout Africa, it comes in individually wrapped wedges of a spreadable, creamy substance with no discernible flavour. I know from experience that it can withstand weeks of intense heat, inside a suitcase, without any apparent change to its texture or its blandness, which makes it a useful emergency ration for long desert trips. So, I wonder, is *La vache qui rit* the *"fromage"* they are referring to on the menu, or has a more genuine and flavourful French cheese somehow made its way onto local menus?

"The *fromage,*" I ask Jeanne. "Is that imported? I mean *real* cheese? From France?"

"No, no, no," says Jeanne, her hands waving about as if to brush away this Eurocentric question as you would an annoying mosquito. "It's real cheese but it's from Benin. It's Fula cheese."

The Fula, also known as Fulbe or Fulani, are a very large and diverse ethnic group found throughout West and Central Africa and as far east as Sudan. Traditionally they were pastoralists and experts on all things bovine. But cheese-making? I want to know more, but it's time to place our orders. There is some confusion, as we are six around the table and everyone is trying to find out what sauces are available to accompany the pounded yam, which it turns out is actually the only starchy dish available. The waitress isn't particularly forthcoming or helpful.

Finally, and never mind all the options advertised on the menu outside, it seems to come down to three choices of sauce to adorn a dish of pounded yam. There is sauce with fish and cheese, a sauce with the meat of the "grass-cutter" rodent and cheese, or a sauce with just cheese. Jeanne worries aloud that the cheese might not be appropriate for foreigners, famous as we are for our weak constitutions and digestive tracts. But I have made up my mind. I order pounded yam and *sauce avec fromage.*

It is an excellent choice. Several chunks of the delicious, slightly tangy cheese, reddish on the outside and white and air-bubbly inside, are swimming in a creamy sauce made from ground peanuts and seeds they call *sésame,* which come from an indigenous melon. And just to keep the poor foreigner completely befuddled, they refer to real sesame as *fonio,* which is actually a nutritious traditional grain cultivated in West Africa.

Using the fingers of my right hand, I pull off small chunks

of the smooth balls of pounded yam and dip each one into the sauce, drenching each handful with the creamy stuff and using it to scoop up pieces of the cheese at the same time.

How many ways are there to describe delectable? My happy food murmurs elicit laughter, which I choose to interpret as my companions' appreciation of my appreciation of their delicious cuisine.

Jeanne is telling me she has a friend, Béatrice Lalion Gbado, who has written a beautiful book about Fula cheese, *Le Fromage Peuhl*. She immediately gives her a call on her mobile phone to ensure I can get a copy before leaving Benin. And this is why I can now say the story of this African cheese involves women's intricate knowledge of the chemistry of curdling, fermenting, and processing milk. It also involves sophisticated knowledge of a widely distributed wild African plant (*Calotropis procera* or the sodom apple). Using grinding stones, women crush the leaves and stems of the plant and then knead the mush in a small amount of milk. They may repeat the process several times and may heat the leaf and milk mixture. The plant material acts like rennet and after it is removed and thrown away, the milk is left to sit, watched carefully while it curdles, separating into solid curds and liquid whey. The whey is used to enrich other dishes or given to calves. The white cheese can be stored or made still smoother by boiling it in the liquid whey. It is sometimes eaten as it is, or else "dyed" an attractive reddish-brown hue using the stalk or the bark of millet plants.

In recent years the price of cow milk has been rising rapidly, so farmers and cooks in Benin have increasingly turned to growing soy and processing it into soy *fromage* or tofu as a substitute for the original Fula cheese.[21] Either way, the *fromage* is an important component in Benin's cuisine. It makes for a fine snack the way it is or it can be fried or grilled. It can be added to sauces, complex ones involving vegetables and various kinds of meat or simple delicacies like the smooth one made with ground peanuts and melon seeds that I devoured with great gusto in Pobé.

Another day dawns and with it another chance to sample Benin's gastronomy. This time it is in Cotonou at a popular spot called Chez Mama Benin. As local legend has it, this eatery had its start with a woman who prepared and sold meals on the roadside. She recognized the huge potential of catering authentic Beninois meals to the growing urban population of professional people who worked downtown and would enjoy a comfortable indoor setting for lunch. Eventually, she saved enough to build a landmark restaurant to cater to them. Jeanne insists that I eat there, although she cannot join me because she's busy at the university. In her stead, her assistant Brice will accompany me.

Chez Mama Benin is nearly full when Brice and I arrive just after midday. The place is clearly popular; nearly all the tables are full and the clientele is solidly African. The server, a sullen and disinterested fellow, finally shows up and informs us that he will only serve us drinks. For food, we need to get off our backsides to make our selections; the day's meal choices are on display in buffet-style pans and kept hot under a glass counter at the far end of the restaurant. There are a half-dozen dishes available, all of them inviting, but I am very keen to try some Traditional Leafy Vegetables in this country renowned for its variety of TLVs. I settle on a sauce with small whole crabs, long green beans, hot peppers, and leafy greens.

Apparently this is not considered a suitable choice for my foreign palate.

"This one is too slippery for you," announces the server with a sniff.

"It's gluey," says Brice. "Made with okra."

I've never behaved well when told what is or isn't good for me, so I say, "It doesn't matter. That's the one I want." The server performs an exquisite Francophile shrug and tells me that the sauce will come with *pâte de maïs,* or corn porridge. He emphasizes this *pâte de maïs* is not fermented. I nod, as if I understand why he's telling me this.

Meanwhile, Brice chooses a leafy sauce with fish, which is served with *pâte d'igname sec*, a neatly formed ball of what looks, to me at least, like chocolate gelatine. But no, he explains, it's another dish made from yams. To make the *pâte d'igname sec*, Brice says, you first peel the yam and then dry it. As it dries, it changes colour, turning brownish. It is then ground into flour, or "powder," as he puts it, and that is mixed with water to make the *pâte*.

This is highly recommended for older people because it's "lighter" and "gentle" and "tasty." Fermented corn porridge, according to Brice, is considered healthier than the non-fermented one. The corn porridge that I'm taking is made from ground corn kernels and very rich, not advisable for the elderly or for diabetics. I'm intrigued by his solicitousness. First he was worried I'd find the sauce too slippery; now it appears he thinks I'm too old and unhealthy to be eating the rich, non-fermented *pâte de maïs*. Of course he could be right. When I suggest I simply switch side dishes, take a fermented corn porridge rather than the one that has not been fermented, both Brice and the server sternly tell me this *is not done;* okra sauce is *always* eaten with *pâte de maïs*. I am again intrigued, this time by the rigid rules that appear to govern mixing and matching of dishes in Benin.

After a trip to the sink on one wall of the restaurant to wash my hands, I dig into the tender bowl of corn porridge with my right hand, scooping up the thick and gooey sauce, and struggling to get it into my mouth without losing it on my lap. The sauce slips down easily. Brice was right; it is quite slimy. But I have decided to like it and so I do; it's fiery hot and underlying the peppery flush is a gentle suggestion of the crab and the ocean it came from. Fine Beninois Meal ... number three.

Had I the time, if I could stay for a couple of months, I could eat a different specialty every day, so varied are the recipes and dishes in Benin. Alas, I don't. So Jeanne has made a to-eat list for me. And she is determined I sample one more local delicacy before I leave the country. She won't tell me what it is, just says, mysteriously, that she has called ahead to order to be sure it will be ready when we arrive. We've driven inland from Cotonou, away from the eroding shoreline and rubbish-strewn beaches, past endless lagoons laced with thatch fishing nets and traps, towards Porto Novo, Benin's official and administrative capital. Jeanne's husband is from the area and the place we are going to is run by his brother Victor, an English teacher by profession but now fully devoted, along with his wife, to running a popular restaurant.

The Grill V, with the V standing for Victor, is airy, enclosed by a low wall, and protected from whatever falls from the sky – sunshine or rain – by a roof supported by pillars in and among the tables and benches. Jeanne greets Victor and finally reveals to me the name of the gourmet dish, something called *kpété,* a specialty of the Porto Nova area involving pork and sauce. Behind the high counter where Victor is chopping chunks of pork into tempting morsels, there is a large grassy open area, which serves as the outdoor kitchen. I watch as a woman dumps an enormous platter filled with pieces of pork into an even more enormous cauldron, *marmite* in French, settled on three stones over a plucky fire. When the pork hits the boiling water inside, steam billows forth like a miniature mushroom cloud. Once it's boiled, the pork is then grilled.

Victor's wife welcomes us and hands us individual plates of crispy, spiced pork pieces, with generous side dishes of a mustardy sauce and another peppery one. She then brings over several small bowls containing servings of *pâte de maïs,* this time fermented corn porridge, which comes wrapped in banana leaves. I partake heartily of the pork and corn porridge. When my pork and porridge are gone, they are automatically and immediately replenished. A never-ending meal.

"*Kpété* is delicious," I announce, licking my fingers.

"But you haven't had it yet," Jeanne says. "This is just kebab. Grilled pork. The *kpété* is the sauce. It's coming now."

This is unfortunate, since I've already stuffed myself on grilled pork and *pâte de maïs*. Worse, when the *kpété* comes, Jeanne explains it's made with pig blood and that's why it's pink. I'm not a terribly big fan of any food that is bloody. But I can't refuse. So, trying to hide my trepidation behind a congenial grimace, I dip a piece of meat into the sauce and place it gingerly onto my tongue. Tart. Tangy. Something I expect I could come to like a good deal, given enough time and an empty growling stomach instead of one groaning with too much of a good thing.

Later that day, Jeanne drives me to the airport for my flight out of Cotonou, and when – just moments before boarding is to begin – she drops me off at the departure gate, she pulls out one last culinary surprise for me. This one is a Beninois cookbook showcasing the flavours of the country, *Saveurs du Bénin et de la Sous-Région 4* by Valérie Vinakpon Gbaguidi.

From far away in North America, I find myself flipping through it, savouring the photos and conjuring up the flavours of the dishes it profiles. Even the names of the Beninois dishes are tongue-teasers. *Sembinou kpé* is a sauce made with the fruits from a leafy green, mustard, peppers, beef kidneys. *Sinri kpé* is a sauce made with hibiscus fruits, shea butter, mustard and other northern spices, wild onions, hot peppers, and Fula cheese. Without even tasting them, I love some of the dishes just because of their names. *Sauce xissi xissi,* made with basil leaves. *Sauce feuille yantoto!* And *Lègba koklo,* literally "voodoo chicken."

As I study this cookbook, I wonder why it is that none of these local delicacies – the Fula cheese, the green leaves, and heritage yams – have been accorded *terroir* status, or a certification such as Protected Appellations of Origin, the way so many European specialties – wine, spirits, and artisanal cheeses – have been, in recognition of their origins and their sense of place.

But that's not to say that Africa hasn't already shared its indigenous culinary wealth with the world, even without such recognition.

5

Africa's culinary gifts to the world

Rather than viewing Africans as active in their own history, a "Euro-centric" view of colonizers and the colonial experience has dominated writing about Africa the past 200 years, including culinary writing.

– Fran Osseo-Asare
Food Culture in Sub-Saharan Africa

The names that early Europeans gave to chunks of West Africa's coastline tell a graphic story of what the explorers and traders – and those who financed them – were after when they plied the coastal waters from the fifteenth to nineteenth centuries, all the while destroying each other's forts and vying for control of lands and new territory. Their presence in Africa was all about getting their hands on resources they needed to build empires and expand their economies. In what are today the nations of Benin and Nigeria, it seems the resources they sought were the Africans themselves. They labelled this section of the coast along the Bight of Benin the Slave Coast. The modern country of Ghana was known as the Gold Coast.

Félix Houphouët-Boigny, the president who led his country, the Ivory Coast (Côte d'Ivoire), to independence from France, didn't see the need to erase the colonial name for his nation. He remained very closely allied with the French throughout his thirty-three-year reign and never bothered ridding his country of the name of a much-prized (by the European traders) commodity – the precious tusks of elephants, which were rapidly wiped out by the global trade in ivory.

The portion of the coastline now belonging to Liberia, Portuguese explorers named after the alligator pepper that abounded there; they called it the Grain Coast after the grains of paradise. Move further north and you come to what are now the nations of Sierra Leone, Guinea, Guinea Bissau, Senegal, and The Gambia. This became known as the Rice Coast.[22] Grain Coast, Rice Coast – the Europeans must have been deeply impressed by the distinctive African crops, the alligator pepper and the rice that abounded along the west coast of the continent, to name whole territories after them.

Although today there is a tendency for many governments, the World Bank, and proponents of industrial agriculture to denigrate peasant farming as inefficient and unproductive, this was not always the way outsiders viewed what they saw in African fields and markets. The first Europeans to visit West Africa were greatly impressed by the bounty of the foods they saw. Portuguese explorers and traders moving along the African coast admired lands full of food and livestock – rice, millet, beans, cows and goats, chickens and capons (roosters castrated to improve the meat quality), many kinds of wine.[23] They marvelled at vast areas of croplands dotted with giant cotton trees and markets with small mountains of rice for sale. European explorers in West Africa were often amazed by the "lavish hospitality that was offered by rich and poor alike to guests and visitors," and they wrote extensively about the copious amounts of delicious foods and remarkable dishes on offer.[24]

There is an incredible and almost inconceivable diversity of food crops in Africa. This astonishing abundance translates into an equally astonishing array of dishes that mix and match these ingredients in complex and rich pastes or sauces and soups. It is only recently that researchers have tried to document the approximately 7,000 different plant species used by people in sub-Saharan Africa as sources of food, clothing, shelter, energy, medicines, and animal feed.[25]

Thousands of these plants nourish the continent – native grains, roots and tubers, fruits, vegetables, legumes, and oil crops.[26] Of these, however, just one or two hundred are cultivated widely to provide for most of the needs of urban people. The rest are known only by rural people, family farmers, pastoralists, forest dwellers, and by traditional medicine men and women. This knowledge of the plant kingdom is increasingly found only among the elderly or scientists specializing in traditional knowledge.

Africa has provided more than one hundred species of plants to global food supplies, including two that became the most popular beverages on the planet. Coffee (*Coffea robusta*), now the mainstay of so many of our days and a multi-billion-dollar global industry, was first recognized as a vitalizing drink in Ethiopia. That was back about 800 B.C.E. As one delightful version of this discovery goes, an Ethiopian herder noticed that when his goats chewed on the red beans they became perky, and in this way, a humble pastoralist discovered coffee's tasty and stimulating properties.

Over several centuries, coffee gained popularity throughout the Arab world and was also cultivated there. By the seventeenth century, coffeehouses had spread throughout Europe, but Europeans eventually tired of merely consuming the coffee and decided to get into the business of production as well. They smuggled coffee plants out of the Arab port of Mocha and established Dutch plantations in Ceylon (Sri Lanka) and in Java. After that, coffee conquered the world, but thanks are still owed to the people of Ethiopia who discovered it.

Africans also domesticated the kola nuts that provide the caffeine in Coca-Cola and the oil palm that eventually produced the oil that goes into about one in ten products on supermarket shelves. Africa gave the world tamarind that is used in Worcestershire Sauce, the hibiscus found in popular herbal teas, and the gum arabic added to so many processed foods.[27] The continent's farmers also deserve credit for developing and for sharing with the world a host of other food crops – pearl and finger millets, sorghum, watermelon, black-eyed peas (cowpeas), okra (gumbo), sesame, and one species of rice.

Some of Africa's food crops were spread to India and Southeast Asia and across the ancient world 3,000 or 4,000 years ago through Indian Ocean trade routes. Later, during the Monsoon Exchange between India and Africa about 2,000 years ago, Asian crops such as taro and bananas made their way to Africa. Once there, farmers went to work domesticating bananas to suit their needs and local conditions, from the highlands of East Africa to the coastal forests of West and Central Africa. Over two millennia, in an impressive feat of informal plant breeding, African farmers developed 120 varieties of plantains and 60 cultivars of bananas.[28]

The next big wave of foods and crops changing continents occurred during Islamic expansion in the seventh century. Asian rice, citrus, and sugarcane moved from India to the Middle East, the Mediterranean, Egypt, and East Africa. There are early historical references to African cereals from Mesopotamia, where Africans taken from East Africa worked sugarcane plantations and cultivated African crops such as millet, sorghum, and melons near Basra in present-day Iraq. There, in 868 and 869 C.E., African labourers staged a successful revolt against the appalling conditions of their servitude, capturing Basra and nearby towns and holding them for fourteen years of well-earned freedom.[29]

Then Christopher Columbus landed in the Americas, unleashing an unprecedented wave of intercontinental migration of crops between the Old and New Worlds. Some ecologists have argued this was the most important event since the death of the dinosaurs.[30] During the Columbian Exchange, maize, manioc (cassava), peanuts, tomatoes, and two species of chili pepper (*Capsicum baccatum* and *C. pubescens*) were introduced into Africa from the Americas.[31] African peasant farmers rapidly adapted the Mayan maize from Central America for cultivation in almost every growing region of the continent.[32]

About fifty different African food crops also made their way across the ocean to the Americas, many in slave ships. Once in the New World, they helped to create new cuisines, with African flavours.[33] No one is really sure just how the African captives managed to carry their culinary staples with them on the horrendous transatlantic journeys. Some stories passed down through generations of Maroons, escaped slaves in the Americas, relate how women being loaded onto slave ships hid grains of rice in their daughters' hair, so that they had something to plant when they disembarked. This means it was Africans themselves who introduced African rice to Brazil. Captains of the slaving ships also loaded their holds with foodstuffs to keep their human cargo alive, if only barely, and women captives prepared African dishes for those on board. Any excess was then offloaded when the ships arrived at their destinations in the Americas, coming ashore as precious seed.

In this way, Africans imported some of their favourite and most important crops to the Americas. Among them are the African eggplant (also known as Guinea squash and garden egg), sesame, okra, cowpeas or black-eyed peas (*Vigna unguiculata*), West African sorrel, also known as *krinkrin* or bush okra (*Corchorus olitorus*), guinea sorrel (*Hibiscus sabdariffa*), Bambara groundnut (*Vigna subterranea*), Guinea pepper (*Xylopia aethiopica*), the lablab bean (*Lablab purpureus*), sorghum, millet, rice, and yams. The forcibly transplanted Africans started to cultivate their crops in the New World in gardens, which fused African and Amerindian crops and created new cuisines.

The transatlantic slave trade depopulated Africa's agricultural societies and cast them into tragic disarray. Africa's loss was the New World's gain. The Americas profited immensely from the labour, knowledge, and crops the Africans provided to the plantation colonies.[34]

Like people in Southeast Asia, the Near East, interior New Guinea, and Mesoamerica, Africans were domesticating plants and animals thousands of years ago.[35] They were experimenting and innovating to develop the cultivars that best suited their tastes, needs, local market demands, climatic conditions, and soils.

The plants that Africans domesticated in ancient times are, through their diversity and origins, adapted to many tropical ecosystems, including extremely arid places. Scientists are now telling us what peasant farmers already know: crop and seed diversity are the continent's defence against global warming and famine.

Pearl millet, a true African jewel, is believed to be the most drought-tolerant cereal of all. It grows quickly during short rainy seasons and can be harvested after just a few months. Sorghum, perhaps the oldest of African cereals, was domesticated and bred over many thousands of years; today there are two dozen culti-vated species of this invaluable food crop. Sorghum matures more slowly than pearl millet, but it can do so even after the rains end and into the dry season because of its ability to access residual moisture in the soil.

Africa also has an impressive history of livestock develop-ment and animal husbandry. Africans domesticated cattle at least 8,000 years ago and perhaps more than 10,000. Over great swaths of time, as the climate of the Sahara Desert went from dry to damp, to lush to dry again, people migrated with their por-table food supply – their cattle – moving south to what is now the semi-arid Sahelian belt between Sahara and savannah. They developed the dwarf humpless cattle that are resistant to bovine sleeping sickness, which is spread by tsetse flies and can wipe out entire populations of non-resistant breeds of cattle.

About a millennium later, Africans domesticated the donkey as a transport animal. They also bred their own indigenous poultry species, the delightful and raucous (and very tasty) guinea fowl. Sheep and goats were introduced into Africa about 8,500 years ago, and were subsequently domesticated to tolerate all kinds of climatic hardship – drought, cold, and intense humid heat. When Indian zebu cattle were introduced to Africa about two millennia ago, pastoralists crossed this breed with their own longhorn ones to produce the hardy and drought-resistant breed known today as *ankole* in Uganda. As if all this were not enough, African pastoralists and herders were also developing and nurturing the forage and fodder grasses in the pastureland that nourished their animals.

Africa's great history of plant domestication, farming, herding, and complex food cultures is often overlooked, particularly by those drawing up the current blueprints for Africa's agricultural development that will shape the future of its foods and farms – the African Union's Comprehensive African Agricultural Development Programme (CAADP), the Alliance for a Green Revolution in Africa (AGRA), and the G7/G8's New Alliance for Food Security and Nutrition. These multi-billion-dollar schemes see no future in peasant farming and focus instead on commodity crops, a global food regime and market, and a corporate approach to agriculture that threatens not just Africa's family farms, but also the diverse crops that are its culinary wealth.

Peasant farmers have bred and still nurture forty different livestock species and close to 8,000 breeds.[36] Contrast that with the focus of the industrial food chain on fewer than 100 breeds of five livestock species. And when it comes to plants, peasants also vastly outscore corporate plant breeders. While peasants have bred

5,000 crops and donated 1.9 million plant varieties to the world's gene banks, those in the employ of corporations that increasingly control the world's food system work with a paltry 150 crops, and focus on just a dozen.[37] Not only have they whittled down the number of crops grown to feed the industrial food system, the corporate plant breeders have also bred about 40 percent of the nutrition *out* of our grains and vegetables.

Africa's approximately 33 million small farms still produce almost all the root, tuber, and plantain crops consumed on the continent, and the majority of the grains and legumes, mostly with little use of fertilizers and purchased "improved" seed.[38]

Which means that now, more than ever, is the time to showcase, promote, savour − and try to save − the diverse crops that are Africa's culinary wealth.

6

Wonders of the African world

Breakfast in the majority of African hotels involves condensed milk, instant coffee, Danish butter and European jams. Most of the rice consumed in Africa comes from Thailand, and the markets sell European vegetables and American and Asian grains and even imported meat. This is the main challenge that African agriculture must face today.

– Salone des Gusto Terre Madre[39]

In 1998, Henry Louis Gates Jr., chair of Harvard University's African Studies Department, travelled to Mali as part of a television series called *Wonders of the African World* produced for the BBC in the United Kingdom and PBS in the United States. Among the wonders he profiled in Mali were the Dogon people with their cliff-dwelling stone architecture, the great sweeping Niger River that sustains more than a 100 million people in West Africa, the magnificent ancient mosque in Djenne that is the tallest mud structure in the world, and the Sankore mosque in Timbuktu that dates back to 1327 C.E. At a reception at the residence of the American ambassador, Gates declared that in addition to all of these wonders he had discovered another in Mali – the San Toro Restaurant in Bamako.

The San Toro is unique in Mali, quite different from so many of the restaurants and hotels in the city that cater to international clients, which seem expressly designed to make visitors believe they are anywhere *but* Africa. It was easier to dine *à la française* and to find Lebanese, Italian, Thai, Vietnamese, or Chinese food in upscale hotels and restaurants in Bamako than it was to find an upmarket locale featuring Malian dishes. Menus in hotels catering to international clientele may include token gestures to local culinary cultures, such as a few locally grown tropical fruits and juices on the breakfast buffet table. But even if local dishes do appear on the menus, you may need to order a day ahead and the prices are often exorbitant.

And then there is the San Toro restaurant, the Bamako eatery that Professor Gates designated an "African wonder."

In 2010, I have the opportunity to spend the time I need in the San Toro to discover what so impressed him. I've spent part of the day at the Congress Palace at a local food fair, where I picked up *Recettes des mets Maliens*, a new recipe book published by the Ministry of Employment. A few far-sighted politicians, with a good deal of lobbying from some Malian activists, have realized that local food is an important creator of jobs, as are the farms that produce the crops that are the building blocks of the country's regional cuisines.

I head to the restaurant alone, armed with the cookbook and a bag full of reference papers and books about African crops and foods. I choose a small table in the rear of the place. It's a bit early for dinner so I have the restaurant to myself. Most people who dine out in the evenings in Mali tend to eat fashionably late. But I've never been fashionable and I am hungry.

This is not my first visit to the San Toro. In 2003, I spent an evening here with Miriam Makeba, the late and more than great South African singer known affectionately as Mama Africa. When I met her, she had just been named South Africa's goodwill ambassador to the continent. Earlier in the day this remarkable woman had done an interview with me for the BBC and sung a beautiful new ballad dedicated to her great-grandchild. It was her idea that we share a Malian meal in the evening. For this, the San Toro was the obvious choice.

Over dinner, she said the last time she'd been in Mali had been nearly twenty years earlier with her grandchildren and their mother, herba's daughter Bongi. "We sang here, the two of us," she said wistfully. "My daughter was still alive then." She said she was now a great-grandmother and would have loved to have her granddaughter with her on this trip to Mali, Senegal, and Guinea. But her granddaughter was also a performer, and didn't come along because she was recording. Makeba said that after Mali she would go to Guinea, where she'd lived in exile for fifteen years, after the racist regime in South Africa revoked her passport for her outspoken criticism of Apartheid. She told me her daughter had passed away and been buried in Guinea in 1985, so when she went back, she would be visiting the grave. I was so awed by her presence, poise, passion, warmth, and her life stories that I can remember nothing of the food we ate that evening at San Toro.

This visit to San Toro is different. Not only have I come prepared with a ton of reference material, I've also come with a mind that is finally fully opening to the wonders of African cuisines and the crops used to create them. Apart from the recipe book, I have a booklet that a Malian agroforester has given me, which catalogues the useful indigenous trees and shrubs in the region of Bamako, twenty-eight of which are important sources of food.[40] I also have excerpts from three books about the lost crops of Africa, indigenous and adapted crops that could be promoted and revitalized to address the problems of hunger, malnutrition, and poverty.[41]

A pleasant waiter, clad in a tunic of unbleached Malian cotton, welcomes me and hands me the menu, an attractive leather-bound booklet on rough, locally made paper and handwritten in a flowery script. It offers an entire page of drinks, all local juices or herbal teas, *infusions* in French. How is an overwhelmed foreigner to choose?

One juice on tap is baobab, made from the dried fruit of the elegant tree that graces landscapes from Cape Town to Cap Verde. It's an incredible plant of many names – monkey bread tree, bottle tree, the upside-down tree, Judas Fruit, to list just a few.[42] The baobab (*Adansonia digitata*) is God's answer to the hungry, the artistically inclined, the homebuilder, and the handyman. Its leaves are loaded with vitamin A and both its leaves and white flowers are standard foods in many parts of the continent. In Mali, people harvest the leaves and dry them for use throughout the year in daily soups and sauces. The small black seeds in the fruit are delicious when roasted. The hull of the fruit, which resembles a giant walnut, is used to make musical instruments and serving implements. Ashes from the pod are used in soap. The bark and rind can be removed in strips without harming the tree and then pounded to make rope, woven to make bark cloth, cord, baskets, mats, and even shoes. The strips of bark can also be flattened as roofing tiles.[43]

The majestic upper structure of the baobab makes it ideal for hanging beehives. About the only thing not particularly useful in the tree is its wood, which is spongy and soft, but even that can be harvested from dead trees and pulverized to make compost. Last, but certainly not least, the white pulp of the fruit makes delicious juice, rich in vitamin C. Just twenty-three grams of the powder provide a daily requirement of the vitamin and there are enough baobab trees to provide for the vitamin C needs of millions of people in semi-arid West Africa.[44]

Also on San Toro's tap is *oseille rouge*. My reference books, spread on the table in front of me, inform me that *oseille rouge* is made from the flower of an indigenous African plant known by scientists as *Hibiscus sabdariffa*. In Mali, the Bambara call it *dah,* which produces a cordial called *dabléni*. In Senegal, the Wolof people know it as *bissap*. It's a deep ruby red, and in the markets of Bamako, small girls peddle it sweetened with sugar and sometimes vanilla, frozen into tiny little plastic bags like popsicles. My kids absolutely loved it.

The menu also offers mango and *zaban* (or *saba*) juices, in season. *Zaban* is a much-appreciated wild fruit from a vine called *Saba senegalensis*. It produces a refreshing juice that's also medicinal; it can be used to treat headaches, earaches, stomach aches, wounds, and worms. As far as I know, I suffer from none of these at the moment, but I'm intrigued and decide to try the *zaban*. I glance around, ready for someone to come and take my order. The waiter is standing directly behind me and I can tell he's been watching me poring over papers and books. He offers me a bemused smile that I've seen many times in Africa. It means I'm behaving oddly, but he finds it rather endearing, the behaviour of a child or perhaps someone not quite right in the head, a stranger with inexplicable ways.

I flush, probably red as *oseille rouge*, and quickly close the books. I explain I'm trying to learn about the many ingredients in Malian cuisine and if he would be so kind as to help me out, does he recommend the *zaban* juice?

He shakes his head and says it's not the season; *zaban* produces fruit only in May and June. Perhaps, he ventures, I would like to try one of the *dégué*, beverages made from *lait caillé* (a ferment that tastes like something between cottage cheese and yogurt), mixed with various indigenous grains, sometimes with indigenous fruits and some sugar?

I'm flummoxed. Mali, like other countries in Africa and all over the world, is overrun with billboards advertising Coca-Cola, its offspring and siblings, its rivals, and now a new rash of "energy drinks" high on caffeine, sugar, and other stimulants. Who would imagine the country could – if so inclined – boast so many of its very own natural and local drinks that it would take me half an hour just to choose an aperitif? The brand new Malian cookbook in my hands offers recipes for no fewer than forty-two hot and cold drinks made from local grains, fruits, and leaves.

I ask him what he recommends and he suggests that if I'm looking for something truly refreshing, I consider the ginger juice made with lemon and fresh mint. I take his advice and then turn to the next complex task: choosing a meal.

The names of the San Toro's dishes are delectably descriptive. Entrees include *Soupe Bozo,* which I assume is made with fish from the Niger River. The Bozo people are a West African ethnic group, the veritable masters of the Niger River. They're expert fishers, accomplished swimmers, divers, paddlers, and boatbuilders. They're also said to possess the powers to commune with all the creatures that live in the Niger River, including the crocodiles and hippos that once abounded there.

Then there is *Salade Niébé. Niébé* is the French word for cowpeas, another indigenous African legume. The book on lost vegetables of Africa informs me that cowpeas are grown by tens of millions of family farmers in Africa and they feed more than 200 million people on the continent. They are an important source of protein and digestible carbohydrate.[45]

I decide to give all the starters a pass and flip the page to the grilled dishes on the menu. There is *Tangine mouton,* mutton made with ginger and lemon. Chicken in coconut. *Brochettes* (kebabs) of beef in ginger. *Capitaine Grillé* or grilled Nile perch. Mutton with "spices from the north" of Mali. There is also *saka saka,* Mali's version of leafy green sauces that are mainstays across Africa. The list continues.

Again, I'm struck by the number of choices of local foods and dishes in this country known more for famine and its need of food aid than feasts. And I have yet to choose a side dish, of which there are several on the menu. There is *attiéke,* with its origins in Côte d'Ivoire, made by peeling and grinding cassava and mixing this with a small quantity of previously fermented cassava pulp, and allowing it to ferment some more to remove all traces of cyanide, before it is dried and sieved, ready for steaming. Also on the menu are *aloko* (plantain slices browned up in oil) and sweet potato.

There is also *fonio*, not to be confused with the sesame that they call *fonio* in Benin. Real *fonio* is a kind of miracle food, the oldest cereal in Africa.[46] People across West Africa have cultivated it for thousands of years. Today farmers devote about 300,000 hectares to fields of *fonio*, which feeds three or four million people. Fonio is a grass that flourishes even in periods of drought, and it may also be the world's fastest maturing cereal. Although it's sometimes called "hungry rice" in English, that's a misleading term. People who eat *fonio* don't do so because they have nothing else to eat and are reduced by hunger to consuming the tiny brown grain. They eat it because they love it. It has been considered the food of royalty and chiefs, and a food for special occasions. In some places, *fonio* is still part of ceremonies of thanksgiving for ancestors.

It's one of the world's most nutritious grains, rich in amino acids vital to human health, which are often lacking in today's major cereals, such as wheat, rice, maize, sorghum, barley, and rye.[47] It grows well on poor and sandy soils, and with rampant desertification and land degradation there are plenty of those in the Sahel, the semi-arid band of land that stretches across Africa from Sudan in the east to Senegal in the west. Some varieties of the grain mature so quickly – in just six or eight weeks during the rainy season – that they are ready to eat long before other staple grains. So they offer a quick and sure fix for the annual "hungry season" when farm families are waiting for their other crops to be ready to harvest.

Superlatives fail when it comes to this grain. Yet a Malian friend, the late Mana Diakité, told me a few years ago that urban dwellers have been turning away from *fonio* and other nutritious indigenous grains such as millet and sorghum as they adopt Western eating habits and, influenced by imported notions of which foods confer status, turn to rice for their midday meals. However, he still ate *fonio* regularly because he said it was good in his diabetic diet.

He figured he wouldn't have developed Type 2 diabetes had he continued eating the local foods his grandmother and mother prepared when he was growing up – the *soumbala* instead of artificial flavour-enhancing cubes, whole grains, and fresh ingredients instead of processed foods from outside. Mana traced his diabetes back to the years he spent in the United States where he and his wife were both working and unable to find, let alone cook and consume, Malian foods.

"We bought fast food," he said. "That was a terrible thing. It doesn't have any taste, and you grow like a balloon." In the U.S. he and his family longed for foods like *fonio* and the traditional dishes he ate when he was young. When he couldn't get them, they haunted him. "I will die with their taste," he declared. Sadly, Mana succumbed to the side effects of his diabetes and passed away less than a year after we had that conversation.

I close the menu and put away my books and crazy swirling thoughts. When the waiter returns bearing my ginger juice, I ask him what dish he would choose for himself, as the *maître d'* of the San Toro. He says the mutton today is particularly tender, and prepared with wild dates (from another invaluable tree called *Balanites aegyptiaca*) and tomato sauce the way they prepare it in the north of the country. He is sure I would enjoy that. And do I have a choice for a side dish?

"*Fonio*," I say, and lean back with a sigh.

A female waitress, wearing a dress of unbleached Malian cotton with elegant embroidery embellishing the front, startles me back to the present. She deposits a woven basket filled with slices of a French baguette on the table. Like the language of the colonizers, baguettes were introduced by the French during the several decades they ruled here, after staking their audacious claim over a good part of West and Central Africa. Both language and bread have stuck.

The bread may not be a particularly good thing for the economies of former French colonies; the wheat and yeast have to be imported and usually are – conveniently for the former colonial power – from France. But the crispy and crunchy baguette recipe that the French bequeathed francophone Africa is considerably more palatable, at least in my view, than is the one for doughy, sweet, and gluey white bread that has taken hold in former British colonies in West Africa, and in North America too, come to think of it.

Munching contentedly on a slice of baguette, I contemplate the intricate and pleasing interior of the San Toro. The floor is stone, the tables and chairs crafted locally of dark heavy wood and leather. The mud brick walls are covered with plaster, whitewashed, and trimmed with shades of ochre and brown, echoing the magnificent motifs and colours of Mali's famous mud cloth, or *bogolan.* The dyes used to make *bogolan* come from leaves, roots, and also mud that Bozo fishermen scoop up from the bottom of the Niger River.

The walls are adorned with colourful woven tapestries and magnificent pieces of *bogolan*, bronze masks, baskets, and gourds. It is as much a gallery of art as it is a restaurant. It is clean, quiet, and quite simply beautiful, a showcase for the country's artistry, architecture, building materials, and style. There is no television, no piped-in music or Muzak, just a small stage under an archway. There, a lone musician has begun strumming melodies on a *kora,* a 21-string harp-like instrument made from a gourd, or calabash, covered with cowhide. The *kora,* like the traditional drums such as the *djembe,* has very deep and long roots extending back many centuries to the glory days of the Manding-speaking peoples and their civilizations in West Africa. The music is haunting, mystical. It blends seamlessly with the faint, lingering scent of *wusulan,* an incense used throughout the Sahel. *Wusulan* is made from an incredible range of plants, including frankincense, vetiver grass, and a host of secret scents and spices passed down from one generation of women to another. It is burned daily to exorcise homes and buildings of bad spirits and smells, as well as for all kinds of feminine and seductive reasons. But those are *"secrets de femme"* that unfortunately don't really have a place in this book about food, juicy as they may be.[48]

In the San Toro, it is possible to imagine a Mali, an Africa, that is not drowning in imported ideas and ideologies, processed food and drink, trinkets and material claptrap, and the effects of a globalization process often conflated with development – squalor, garbage, cultural dislocation, and environmental disaster. In Bamako I've been troubled by all these things, and the gaping disparities between rich and poor that have become so exaggerated they seem to resemble a new form of Apartheid, based on monetary rather than racial divisions. While a very few select and well-connected Malians in the Bamako 2000 subdivision have been building ever bigger mansions and higher walls, the vast majority of the population has been struggling to survive everywhere else in ever-expanding slums buried deep in mountains of rubbish and filth. Such disparities and flagrant inequities help pave the way for political turmoil, extremist movements, and conflict – as they did in Mali in 2012.

Maybe I am predisposed to like everything about the San Toro, having listened to Professor Gates declare it an African wonder. But no matter where I look as I await my meal, I keep discovering more original and appealing details. Salt and black pepper are not found in shakers but in little clay pots from which it is possible to take a pinch of spice (literally) to sprinkle on food.

When my meal arrives, it too is beautifully laid out. The waiter places a large pottery plate covered with a matching dome on the table in front of me. He then lifts the cover to reveal a generous mound of brown *fonio* and mutton, bathed in sauce. I dig in, savouring the lemony onions and meat as tender as a chunk of ripe fruit. I judiciously dip each bite very, very carefully into some fiery hot pepper on the side of the plate, for some added excitement in my mouth. The *fonio* is simply delicious, an impeccable complement to the meat.

For a few blissful moments I have no thoughts at all. Just let my taste buds savour their own moments of quiet ecstasy until I've polished off the works and my plate is clean. I ask for the bill, which comes to the equivalent of US$12. I add a tip, pick up my heavy book bag, and head out into the warm night. I have a meeting with Aminata Dramane Traoré, the creator and owner of the San Toro.

Aminata Traoré is a remarkable woman; an author and political activist, she served as Mali's Minister of Culture for three years. Tall, elegant, and imposing, she dresses in magnificent Malian robes from local cloth and wears only Made in Mali jewellery, often very large earrings and beads fashioned by local artists. She is a powerful advocate of women's rights and an outspoken critic of the World Bank and International Monetary Fund, of neoliberal economics, globalization, and of foreign interference in Malian and African politics.

On the evening I visit her after dining in the San Toro, it is quite late, and I have the impression even Aminata, who usually strikes me as indefatigable, is exhausted. She kindly receives me in her apartment on the second floor of the Hotel Djenne, which she also owns. Like her restaurant, the apartment is elegantly furnished and decorated in Malian style. She pulls off her black headscarf, settles back in her leather chair, and begins to tell me something of the history and philosophy of the Djenne Hotel and the San Toro Restaurant.

"When I built the San Toro there were people who laughed in my face," she says. "I think this is because, in the spirit of colonized people and of people who have been poorly decolonized, there is the notion that the West has a monopoly on progress and modernity." In her hotel and restaurant, she says, she wants to show there is an African modernity that can be imagined and developed, using objects and products that, while not exact replicas of artifacts of yesteryear, promote and build on that past.

"Today the world is upside down!" she exclaims. "What's been put into our heads is that what we have is no good, we don't know how to do anything, and to be modern we need to create the same décor as in the West."

She says her original purpose in building a restaurant was not grandiose at all. She needed to solve an unemployment problem, namely the one in her own extended family. She hired many of her relatives to staff the place. After that, her vision expanded to the entire neighbourhood. In addition to the San Toro, the Hotel Djenne, and the Hampaté Bâ Cultural Centre just across the street from it, Aminata largely funded and directed the reconstruction of a small local market in the neighbourhood, the Misira, as well as the paving with cobblestones of all the narrow mud roads in the area. The hygiene situation improved immediately, malaria rates dropped, the market is now home to artisans producing cloth, leather goods, baskets so complex and large they have evolved into magnificent sculptures, and vendors selling everything from herbal medicines to meat. All of this is in sanitary conditions, no muck or filth underfoot.

I want to know why there is no alcohol served in the San Toro; surely that's an impediment to drawing diners who might want a glass of beer and wine with their meals? She smiles, and admits that at first, some people thought this temperance must have something to do with "Muslim fundamentalism." But, she says, it was actually in loyalty to a culture and lifestyle. She never saw her parents touch alcohol, and has never touched it herself, not even traditional brews made of sorghum. The vast majority of Malians are Muslims and as Islam forbids alcohol, few people drink it. Besides, Aminata is in charge of quality control in the San Toro, and she isn't prepared to serve something the quality of which she can't judge. How, she asks rhetorically, can she vouch for a wine if she knows nothing about it?

Aminata says she personally found the prototypes of furniture, architecture, handcrafts, artisanal products — and recipes — that could be modified and styled to appeal to her and to clients of the San Toro and Djenne. "There is already creativity in our cuisine," she says. "Certain dishes people eat all the time and want to eat all the time. But just as in France there is a *nouvelle cuisine*, there is also a new Malian cuisine. We did research, looked at all our local ingredients and use them in all sorts of ways, find out everything that can be done with *fonio*, beans, salad, even doughnuts."

Her restaurant is meant to be a sanctuary, a place for people to discover all sorts of local foods and beverages, not to order drinks they can find in every other place on earth. "The San Toro is a concrete example of what I would like all of Mali to be," she says. It is not so much a restaurant as it is an extension of her home, of the Hotel Djenne, a place to which she can invite visitors and friends to come and eat and sit around the table to exchange ideas and to discover "another Mali." For me, it's been a fabulous place for discovering an awful lot about Mali's diverse foods, the plants and trees and the farms they come from, all — in their own small ways — wonders of the world.

7

Fine dining in Timbuktu

To understand African cooking, you have to understand Africa. But understanding this enormous continent is no easy task.

— Marcus Samuelsson
The Soul of a New Cuisine:
A Discovery of the Foods and Flavors of Africa

In a market in any African city at almost any time of the year, there are mountains of fruit for sale, even in the dry Sahel countries. Many are exotic species that have been introduced to the continent over time – mangoes, papayas, oranges, limes, lemons, grapefruit, guavas, coconuts, jujube or *ber* (*Ziziphus mauritiana*). But many others come from indigenous, native African species.

I request a little patience here as I try to list just a small sample of the fruits native to Mali, just one semi-arid country on a continent of more than fifty nations. As cumbersome as the Latin names are, they're essential in cataloguing the fruits, because local trees can have as many names in local languages as there are local languages in the region in which they are found, and that can be dozens, even hundreds. At various times of the year in the markets of Mali you can find the following indigenous fruits – cantaloupe, tamarind, jackalberry (*Diospyros mespiliformis*), baobab (*Adansonia digitata*), many kinds of figs and dates, the monkey orange (*Strychnos spinosa*), saba or *zaban* (*Saba senegalensis*), *prunier* or *marula* (*Sclerocarya birrea*). The *marula* fruit is the source of the internationally marketed Amarula liqueur from South Africa, the bottle of which features an elephant because elephants simply love to feast on fallen, fermented *marula* fruit and then lumber drunkenly about.

The list of indigenous Malian fruit continues. There are wild raisins (*Lannea microcarpa*), *prunier de mer* or ocean prune (*Ximenia americana*), *prunier noir* or black prune (*Vitex doniana*). And on and on.

Yet this is in a dry country, where biodiversity is far less pronounced than in the humid regions in the tropics where rainforests thrive. Mother Nature is downright shameless about her love affair with heat, rain, and humidity; the more there is, the more species she embraces.

Here in Mali there is plenty of heat, but rains fall for just a few months of the year. Because the trees, shrubs, and vines all have their own preferred season to flower and reproduce, fruit is available the whole year round. And when the dry season sets in and other plants tend to wither and shrivel under the hot attentions of the relentless sun of the Sahel, you can always count on finding another glorious fruit – watermelon.

Watermelon is one of the many crops Africans took with them to the Americas during the transatlantic slave trade. It flourishes even in the drylands of West Africa and when it's in season, when the annual drought is settling in, it's common to see small mountains of watermelons for sale on roadsides and in markets. With its spreading vines, it sucks up the water it needs to grow and fill the green melons with oodles of sweet, pink liquid and red flesh. You could almost stick a straw right into the melon and drink directly from it.

And in many parts of West Africa, it is still commonplace to drink fresh juice directly from the orange, no straw needed. Vendors, usually young women, set themselves up or move about on roadsides or in markets with large trays heaped with fresh oranges. You can order up an orange or two for the equivalent of a few cents, and watch while the seller goes to work sculpting it. Hands flying, she'll use a small knife to shave the orange peel off in neat spirals that fall away from the fruit, leaving it soft and pliable, easy to squeeze. The finale is the circular incision she makes at the top, creating a little lid for the orange and its juice. Squeeze, squirt, and swallow. Heavenly. No fuss, no muss, no chemicals, no processing, no plastic. Just pure, sweet, and genuinely *natural* juice.

I find myself thinking I would pay just about any amount for some fresh orange juice, indeed for anything to drink or eat, as I sit one day in a United Nations Development Program (UNDP) Land Cruiser at the Timbuktu port, some fourteen kilometres from the ancient city and years before the fabled town would be seized by terrorists making it off limits to casual visitors.

Timbuktu, to some around the world, is synonymous with the end of the world, or even some never-never land that is not of this earth. My grandmother, annoyed one summer day by the havoc we grandchildren created in her award-winning flowerbeds of phlox during a game of hide-and-seek, scolded us that she was of a mind to send us all to Timbuktu. This was around the time of the Apollo moon landing and that's how I pictured our exile in Timbuktu; we would be crammed into a small capsule and sent off way beyond the moon, sentenced to an eternity in outer space.

But of course Timbuktu is very much a part of Planet Earth. It's a sandy town of great historic importance, and, according to the Imam of the city's Great Mosque, one of Islam's most holy sites. In the fifteenth and sixteenth centuries, it was one of the greatest centres of scholarship in the world, host to Africa's very first university, with many thousands of international scholars and students who produced hundreds of thousands – or more – of manuscripts on Islamic scholarship, astronomy, history, politics, philosophy, mathematics, and medicine. One scholar in Timbuktu described the ancient city to me as a kind of Venice on the edge of the Sahara Desert, with branches of the Niger River extending into and around the city. It was a major trading hub, a meeting point for traders coming from forested areas south of the river and camel caravans that traversed the desert, taking African goods – kola nuts, gold, slaves, salt, and foodstuffs – as far as the Middle East and north towards Europe.

In recent decades, however, the Niger has been silting up and retreating, leaving the town of Timbuktu high and very dry. A narrow little strip of pavement links the town and its river port, where riverboats and a dilapidated "ferry" (a barge tugged by tiny river canoes using outboard motors) ply the waters, bringing vehicles and passengers to the city from the south bank of the river.

As the desert swallowed up the city and the river shrank, famine began to stalk the region. But worse was to come. In 2012, the ancient city was taken over by militant groups that declared the north of Mali a separate country. Some of these are extremist Islamic factions that overtook the secular Tuareg groups and set about killing and maiming local people and destroying some of the city's ancient tombs and shrines, declaring them un-Islamic, and causing immense hardship and suffering in the region. Later, when French and Chadian military linked up with the Malian armed forces to attempt to retake control of the northern half of the country, there were horrific reports of reprisal killings.

But none of this was even imaginable more than a decade earlier when the UNDP flew a group of journalists to Timbuktu to look at development projects intended to improve food security in the region. On the second day of the visit, several of us find ourselves sitting in a UN vehicle and wondering about our own food security. The Timbuktu trip is part of a conference the UNDP has organized in Mali. Participants include editors and journalists from the U.S., Japan, the U.K., several African countries, even a couple of celebrity CNN correspondents, as well as Nobel literary laureate Nadine Gordimer, the keynote speaker. The conference organizers are challenging all of us to examine how the world's media portray Africa. We are of one mind that it is not a pretty sight.

In one paper published that year, Africa's image in the Western media was summed up this way: "With the stroke of a journalist's pen, the African, her continent, and her descendants are pejoratively reduced to nothing: a bastion of disease, savagery, animism, pestilence, war, famine, despotism, primitivism, poverty, and ubiquitous images of children, flies in their food and faces, their stomachs distended. These 'universal' but powerfully subliminal message units, beamed at global television audiences, connote something not good, perennially problematic unworthiness, deplorability, black, foreboding, loathing, sub humanity, etc."[49]

The question the UNDP is asking the conference participants to answer is how we in the media can help change this. The organizers think it will help if we look at some good news about successful African development projects, which will in theory combat "donor fatigue" caused by an endless diet of negative stories about African famine and conflict, or about stolen or wasted aid. The idea is to encourage public support for development efforts and agencies. To prop up flagging donations and funding, every so often UN and aid agencies take international journalists on such tours, hoping that under their tutelage, the reporters will produce positive stories about their work and the people benefiting from it.

But, as some of the participants point out, when disaster and humanitarian crises strike, the same organizations fly in the same international media to point their lenses and microphones at the human suffering to alert the world, open purse strings, and shame governments in wealthy countries to fund aid efforts. These stories tend to garner more attention and interest than do the happy little ones about small successes. So some of the participants are asking who is really responsible for the negative images – the media or the aid agencies and charities themselves?

The discussion has already been raging for two days in the air-conditioned comfort of the Hall of Bankers inside the grandiose Chinese-built Congress Palace in Bamako. But we aren't going to get even a hint of what Malian reality looks like from inside those hallowed halls. So the UNDP has organized this outing to Timbuktu, herding us into two recently refitted DC-3 planes that fly us over the spectacular inland delta of the Niger River, over desert and stupendous rock formations to the northern town. The idea is to expose the foreign journalists, most of whom have not been to Africa before, to some real Malian sights and also a couple of positive stories.

The conference organizers have decided that one such story is to be found just outside Timbuktu at a UNDP-funded rice irrigation project with water pumped from the Niger River. There we find farmers in the rice fields, waiting to receive us. They earnestly explain how the project has benefited them with year-round rice production. But they are hard-pressed to say how it will be able to continue after UN funding runs out. It is not building on local agricultural know-how and resources, and it is heavily dependent on expensive imported irrigation pumps, seeds, fertilizers, and pesticides.

However, there is a more immediate problem preoccupying some of the journalists. The UNDP planners seem not to have given enough thought to basics – keeping their flock of international journalists watered and fed. It is already after midday and we have spent a good part of the hot morning standing at the edge of the rice field under a ferocious sun. We are all thirsty and hungry, and this adds up to ornery.

The field visit over, we pile into UNDP vehicles wondering aloud why the morning's schedule has made no provision for basic bodily needs. There is a cardinal rule when handling a junket for journalists when the purpose is to get good press: ply them with plenty of food and drink.

Knowing Timbuktu and environs a little (at least better than the others who had never been there before), I suggest we stop at the small market at the port that services the city and try finding something to eat or drink there, before driving all the way back to the hotel where the afternoon sessions are to continue. I assure my fellow passengers we will find some snacks and drinks at the port, perhaps some grilled meat or just some fresh oranges or baguettes and cans of imported sardines with which we could make an impromptu picnic, and soft drinks to slake our thirst.

"It'll be fun," I announce.

The group doesn't seem in the mood for fun. They're greatly minding the heat, even inside the air-conditioned Toyota Land Cruiser. And the Timbuktu port market, which I know from previous visits as a bustling little place filled with the enticing smells of wood smoke, grilling meats, and sauces bubbling away, is almost deserted. Most vendors have either closed up shop (done by putting wares under cloth wraps) or are asleep under bits of tin or cardboard they've cobbled together to form awnings offering a hint of shade. A couple of them are spread-eagled and fast asleep on their vending tables. A few women are seated in front of tiny piles of forlorn onions and tomatoes that could pass for findings from an archaeological dig. There are certainly none of the usual market treats, no *beignets* (doughnuts) sizzling in hot oil, no meat roasting on grills, no fresh fruit, no groundnuts, not a ready snack anywhere to be seen. Not even anyone with a cool-box full of soft drinks, which have invaded even the most remote corners of the continent.

I wander about, hoping at least to find someone making the green tea that in Mali is usually ubiquitous. Prepared in tiny tin teapots over a miniature charcoal stove, it is mixed with a lot of sugar and poured into small glasses that, in North America, might be more associated with shots of alcohol. The bitter green tea leaves come from China, with names such as "Gunpowder." Generally the tea leaves are used three times and drinkers are expected to take three rounds of the strong sweet brew. Between the caffeine and the sugar, the green tea does feel like a shot of gunpowder as it moves through the body and makes the heart palpitate. It's an effective way to suppress hunger pangs when there's no other food available, keep you awake when you might otherwise doze off, a powerful perk-you-up when you've got an afternoon of heavy discussions ahead. But there isn't even a tea-maker in sight.

I drift about the market for a bit, as if by going in circles and gazing hopefully at the empty stalls and the ashes in the abandoned grills I can conjure up a stopgap meal. Eventually, I ask the women vendors what is wrong, why there is no activity in the market. They tell me no one prepares food in the heat of the day, and the vendors will start to cook or grill again in the late afternoon.

I climb back into the air-conditioned vehicle, apologizing for my failure to procure anything to eat and drink. And that's when I spy the watermelons piled up on the sandy shore where they've been unloaded from a newly arrived riverboat plying the Niger River between Mopti and Timbuktu.

"We're in luck!" I cry. "Look, I'll just hop out and buy a few watermelons. I have a jackknife in my bag so we can cut them up."

The American woman beside me gently places a hand on my arm. "We can't eat watermelon," she says quietly.

"Why on earth not?" I reply. "Watermelons are the best thing you can eat when you're hot and thirsty."

"No, we can't eat any fruit," she says.

"But you don't eat the outer skin, so there's no fear of con-

tamination. You just eat the flesh inside and they're so refreshing."
I make to open the door and she grips my arm a little harder.

"You don't understand," she says.

"What don't I understand?" I'm sure I sound impatient,
because that's how I'm feeling.

"Someone may have injected the watermelons with water to
make them heavier, so they can charge more. And the water may
be contaminated. We were instructed not to eat any local fruit or
vegetables. They're not safe."

I really don't want to be impolite, but I am hungry and
thirsty and my temper gets the better of me. "That's ridiculous.
They don't sell them by weight. Do you see a scale there? They
sell them by piece. Just a few cents for a whole melon."

"The embassy warned us," she replies, maintaining her good
manners and her resolve. Her American colleagues are nodding
and muttering their approval of her tough stand on the innocent
watermelons, which two young women are now holding up by
way of invitation for us to come out of our air-conditioned sanctuary and buy. It is a great opportunity – not just to buy succulent watermelon but also to exchange a few words and minutes
with local people, market women in Timbuktu, off the talk-shop
agenda prescribed for us by the UN. And there would be something symbolic, I think, about Americans savouring the refreshing
juices of watermelon in Africa where it originated before being
transported to the Americas during the transatlantic slave trade.

But we miss the chance. We drive away. The American journalists and editors have come all this way to Mali, flown up to
Timbuktu to discuss the prevailing negative and ill-informed
image of Africa in the media, and merely had that image and the
fears it invokes stoked by their own embassy on their arrival in
the country.

That evening, though, the organizers got it right. They
treated us to some of the city's fabulous music and its delectable
cuisine, which, like Timbuktu itself, is a crossroads where sub-

Saharan Africa meets the desert and the cultures of northern Africa. When the Moroccan army invaded and plundered Timbuktu in 1591, it marked the beginning of the end of the city's scholarship and great intellectual pursuits, of the city as a wealthy centre of trade and learning. But it also ushered in new cultural influences that can be seen today in the elegant architecture on the sandy pathways of Timbuktu and also savoured in the cuisine, which is a mouth-watering blend from south and north of the Sahara. It's not unusual to taste a bit of the Sahara itself in the flat crispy loaves of *takoula*, Timbuktu bread baked in clay ovens, because it's almost impossible to keep the fine desert sand from getting into the bread dough. There are several kinds of bread, some made from semolina or rice flour, some boiled or baked in clean hot sand. The bread and porridges made from millet or rice are eaten with a host of stews and sauces full of meat and meat juices and lots of spices.

Unlike the famous Colonel Sanders, who relied on just eleven secret spices for his Kentucky Fried Chicken, in Timbuktu there are at least fourteen key spices that account for the city's savoury cuisine. These have been documented by Miranda Dodd, a young woman of Canadian and American parentage who lived in Timbuktu with her husband, a Tuareg prince, and their son, until the conflict drove them out in 2012.[50] They had been running the Sahara Passion hotel and restaurant and tour service, promoting the cultures, foods, and tastes of Mali's north.[51] It's not an easy task compiling such information and conveying it to the wider public. The traditional cuisines are complex and the recipes dwell not in cookbooks but inside people's minds. And the ingredients do not come in convenient packages with labels, but as small bundles of leaves or seeds with local names.

Some of the spices Miranda catalogued are unique to the northern desert region and others are used throughout Mali and around the world. They include salt (rock salt from the famous salt mines in Taoudeni in the far desert north of Mali), anise seed,

cumin seeds, bay leaves, hot peppers, cinnamon sticks, pepper-
corns (*alhorabi*), dried powdered onion, dried powdered tomatoes, dates, dried and fermented onion balls, *maray* (or *soumbala*
from *dawa dawa* trees), *kabay* (a kind of lichen), and a seed that
is called *wangaray maffay jay*, which, according to Miranda, has a
strong odour "as if from a coniferous forest."

It would have been great if the conference organizers had
included an entire session on the spectacular foods to be had in
Timbuktu and Mali; it would certainly have helped to promote a
positive image of Africa. They didn't, but to their immense credit,
the banquet they offered up that evening in Timbuktu was a good
start.

We gathered for the event on the large patio of a local
hotel, sitting cross-legged on mats and carpets or reclining on
intricately patterned pillows of leather. The sun was making its
rapid descent towards a horizon etched onto the desert dunes
by low-slung mud buildings and graceful desert palms. The heat
of the day was dissipating and I, for one, was ready for a hearty
traditional Timbuktu feast. First came the drinks, which were not
local juices or infusions. Rather we were served soft drinks – case
after case of Coke and Fanta and Sprite. There was no beer, as
alcohol is greatly frowned upon in the holy Muslim city. Then
came the *pièce de resistance,* the *Mischoui*, an entire sheep stuffed
with couscous and spices, and roasted in a deep pit dug into the
sand and lined with charcoal. It was tender enough that it needed
no carving. Instead we used forks and some of us our bare hands
to pull the tender morsels of mutton from the bones and the
couscous stuffing from its interior, and pile this delectable mix on
our plates.

As we ate, and then afterwards as we and our full bellies
lazed about on the carpets and pillows spread out on the concrete
floor of the outdoor restaurant, Malian scholars regaled us with
eloquent tales of Timbuktu's glorious history and intellectual
achievements. As the night sky filled up with stars, a group of

Tuareg musicians and singers serenaded us with haunting desert melodies and performed magnificent shoulder-shaking dances around giant Tuareg daggers laid out on the ground.

It was a magical evening. The cultural talks, the music, the flavours, and the wonderful food struck me as perfect antidotes to the negative media image of Africa that we were trying to overcome.

8

Food security grows on trees

I used to think that aid was all about helping people achieve a sustainable life; not to downplay their local food culture and to make them dependent on foreign aid.

– Esther Garvi[52]

A seed sown in the soil makes us one with the Earth. It makes us realize that we are the Earth.

– Vandana Shiva[53]

In 2008, the executive vice-president for overseas operations of the U.S. charity Catholic Relief Services addressed top American politicians, urging more food aid for impoverished Africans suffering from skyrocketing food prices. As part of his impassioned plea, he stated that the plight of some people in Africa was so dire they had resorted to "eating *anza,* a wild plant with bitter leaves, to supplement their diet."[54]

In response, Esther Garvi, an insightful and knowledgeable specialist from the Eden Foundation who was living and working in Niger to ensure food security through traditional crops and farming, penned a blog bemoaning the "prejudice" inherent in the comment on *anza* (or *hanza)*, which left her bewildered.[55]

"Are we really so linked to the top 20 species of the world that when we hear of people eating other foods we simply assume they must be starving?" she wrote. "I love *hanza*," she continued, extolling the nutritious virtues of the fruit and the seeds – called *hanza* beans – of this perennial shrub that grows in farm fields. The fruit is an important food source when other food stocks are running short, in the "hungry season" at the end of the yearly drought and into the rainy season, before annual staples are ready for harvest. From the fruit come the *hanza* beans that then undergo a sophisticated and intricate process to prepare them for consumption or for storage, so they can be an important and tasty source of protein throughout the year. She points out that no one eats *hanza* out of desperation. They eat it because it is a much cherished food and the *hanza* shrub, *Boscia senegalensis*, is a wild plant that is very much part of the farming system and diets in seventeen West and Central African countries.

It is during the hungry season that the genius behind the traditional farming system in the Sahel reveals itself, with its built-in insurance against annual famine in a harsh climate. The rainy season, when annual crops can be cultivated in the Sahel, is short, lasting from June through to October, although precipitation is becoming more erratic with climate change. The hungry season is the time when granaries with last year's harvest of millet, sorghum, and other staples are empty and the next harvest is still months away. This can be a very lean time of year in a very lean part of the world. And that's where the shrubs and trees come in; they are very much part of the farm. Scientists are now recognizing what the farmers in the Sahel have known for eons – food security grows on trees.

Farm fields are dotted with all kinds of valuable indigenous trees scattered in the fields of staple crops, the millets, sorghum, and maize that grow during the short rainy season. The trees growing on and around farms act as a grocery store, pharmacy, and hardware store rolled into one. They produce not just foods and medicines but also fibre, fodder for livestock, and havens for bees. As I learned from researchers and farmers over the years I worked for the World Agroforestry Centre (ICRAF), the international agricultural research organization that focuses on farms that involve trees – especially indigenous ones that have developed within a particular ecosystem – they also protect and nourish soils and pump nutrients to the surface to increase yields of other crops on complex farms that can, to the untrained eye, look like a haphazard and ill-planned bunch of small fields surrounded by wild and woolly bush.

Trees, like livestock, like all the annual and perennial crops, are vital to these holistic farming systems. They protect the soils from wind and rain erosion in this hot and dry region, swept each year by Harmattan winds laden with dust from the Sahara Desert and pounded for two or three months by torrential rainstorms that can cause almost instant flooding if there is not enough vegetation to shield the ground from the driving rain. Trees safeguard water supplies and watersheds, absorb greenhouse gases, and store carbon, keeping it out of the atmosphere. They are the greatest defence against the ravages of land degradation, global warming, and the southward expansion of the Sahara Desert.

They were always rigorously protected in sacred groves and "society bushes" where people go to mark special ceremonies and rites of passage for youth entering adulthood, to honour their ancestors and all the resources and knowledge they have bequeathed them. Traditionally, the trees in the farming system were not planted; rather, the seedlings of important species that popped up by themselves were protected and nurtured in the fields until they matured. They were viewed as gifts from the gods.

Scientists have coined a word for the ecologically and

diverse kind of farming that integrates annual food crops, trees, and livestock in a holistic system; they call it "agroforestry." There are as many kinds of agroforestry systems as there are different ecological niches in the tropics, but the prevailing system in the Sahel zone is called "parklands." It's a perfect name for a farming system that creates a landscape with a sprinkling of trees in cropland that is reminiscent of a manicured park. Scientists have also shown that the parklands system, even though it has been dramatically degraded in recent years, is a powerful buffer against famine. When stocks of the annual staple crops run out, or if some of them fail, the trees are still there. Some trees provide food, some enrich the soil, and some produce fodder for livestock. Some do all of the above and have so many uses and are so vital they're spiritually important, even sacred.

In 1997, researchers from ICRAF and their colleagues in Mali, Niger, Burkina Faso, and Senegal carried out a survey with farmers in four Sahelian countries to learn more about the trees in their cropland.[56] The researchers went directly to rural families to find out from them which trees were most important, and why. Lead researcher Edouard Bonkoungou said that during years of drought, people could rely on the variety of products they harvested from trees, such as fruit, nuts, and leaves. Even during good years when annual crops did well, tree products provided people with the ingredients for their favourite dishes, for nutritional security, and also for revenue. The pods and seeds from a single *dawa dawa* tree could bring in about US$270 in a year, which was about the same as the average per capita annual income at the time. And yet the tree was not at the top of the list; it appeared only as one of the fifteen "priority" trees in the four Sahel countries.

The iconic baobab tree topped the top-tree list in Niger and Senegal, coming in second in Mali and fifth in Burkina Faso. This isn't surprising, given the immense value of its nutritious fruit, leaves, and bark and dozens of other uses too. Another tree that placed near the top of the list of priority species was the tall and imposing Borassus palm (*Borassus aethiopium*). This elegant palm produces fruit, delicious fresh and sometimes fermented into a popular alcoholic beverage. Its fibre is used for baskets and mats, and the flowers from male trees are fed to livestock during dry periods when fodder is scarce. Young seeds from the tree are processed and used as a substitute for cassava. Various parts of the tree are used as medicine to treat sore throats, bronchitis, and other ailments.[57]

The thorny and scrappy *Balanites aegyptica* also made the top fifteen. People value this tree for its fruit, the same wild date that enriched my mutton dish at the San Toro. It provides valuable fodder, as well as oil used in cooking and, as a quirky bonus, to cure inflammation of the ear. It can grow in areas so dry that few other tree species would even attempt to put down roots. Balanites trees can be grown in rows to create a "living fence" that can be planted around precious fields and vegetable gardens to protect them from marauding livestock, an eternal problem for farmers in the Sahel.

Also high on the priority list was the mystical and sacred *balanzan* tree, or *Faidherbia albida*. Its leaves make very nutritious fodder for goats, sheep, and cattle. Most remarkable of all, it's a very effective fertilizer tree. Millet and sorghum yields are higher under the tree's crown than they are beyond it. This is because the tree has odd but very useful habits. It keeps its leaves during the dry season when other trees tend to shed their foliage to defend themselves against dehydration during months of intense and relentless sun. So when shade is at a premium for a few months every year, *balanzan* trees offer very attractive places for livestock to gather to enjoy some relief from the sun and drop their fertile fecal loads. Then, during the rainy season, the *balanzan* sheds its leaves. The leaf litter, rich with nitrogen, combines with the accumulated manure to fertilize the soil, while allowing sunlight to reach the crops growing under its arching branches.[58]

But the real high flyer on the list of invaluable trees, the one that topped the list in both Mali and Burkina Faso, was the shea tree, known as *karité* in French.

The first I ever heard of *karité* and the shea butter that comes from its nut was back in 1986, four years after I'd first set foot in Africa. Strangely enough, I didn't hear about it from one of the millions of farmers who nurtured the tree that produced the precious nut. Rather, it was the wife of an American ambassador who first spoke to me about the remarkable shea butter.

I met her at a soirée at the residence of an American diplomat in the capital of Burkina Faso, Ouagadougou. She came across as a quiet and solitary person, very different from her husband, who served as the American ambassador from 1984 until 1987. He was a tall, rangy, swashbuckling, outspoken Texan. He had been hauled out of retirement by President Ronald Reagan to take over the reins of American hegemony in the relatively small and little-known country. His assigned mission, he told me, was to take on Thomas Sankara, the young president who had come to power in a military coup in 1983, launched a revolution, and changed the country's name from Upper Volta to Burkina Faso, literally the "land of upright men." The ambassador assured me that while he "liked the guy," there was no damn way the U.S. was "going to have another Cuba in Africa."

I was very new to the diplomatic soirée circuit in Ouagadougou. I'd just begun to report for the BBC World Service from Burkina Faso, so had only recently been added to the invitation list for some of the receptions and cocktail parties in grand diplomatic residences. The food served at such receptions was rarely a big draw; it often involved finger foods that were stubbornly *not* African and generally not very exciting or even very good. The French diplomatic residence was an exception because very fine French wines and champagne flowed liberally, French cheese and charcuterie weighed down buffet tables, and a French chef generally prepared the meals. The French liked to showcase their fine food cultures, and why not? Unlike diplomats from fast food nations, they had one that deserved to be showcased.

But it wasn't obvious that the French forgave Burkina Faso for doing the same and flaunting their fine foods. President Thomas Sankara had just launched what may well have been the world's first locavore campaign under the slogan, "Consume What We Produce. Produce What We Consume." He was way ahead of his time; this was nearly two decades before local food movements really took off in wealthy western nations.

Sankara's "Consume Local" campaign involved all kinds of extraordinary acts. He launched a national Day of the Tomato to celebrate the abundance of this staple vegetable in the country and to encourage local processing and sun drying to reduce dependence on the ubiquitous little tins of imported tomato paste. He banned the importation of apples, saying it was time that Burkinabe consumed more of their own nutritious and plentiful fruit. He pointed out that countless tonnes of mangoes, pineapples, papayas, and indigenous fruit were being left to rot on roadsides while some people spent outrageous sums on expensive travel-worn apples from South Africa and France.

He wanted to celebrate Burkinabe foods and products, no matter what the occasion. In November 1986, French President François Mitterrand flew into Ouagadougou in a Concorde jet for an official visit with Sankara. Relations between the two men were tense. French presidents still seemed to expect the heads of state of their former colonies in Africa to be obedient, perhaps even obsequious, in their dealings with their former colonial masters. Thomas Sankara categorically refused to comply with the unwritten rules. He had been giving Mitterrand and other Western leaders a lot of grief with his anti-imperialistic and pan-Africanist rhetoric and policies.

At the banquet to welcome the French president and his delegation, Sankara impertinently criticized Mitterrand for allowing the Apartheid leaders of South Africa, men "with hands and feet drenched in blood," onto French soil. As if this were not affront enough, Sankara insisted on an all-local menu, except for the addition of a course of "Les Fromages de France" before the papaya mousse. No French wine. This was simply not done. The remarkable audacity of the Burkinabe president in confronting his high and mighty guest was captured in the 2002 play *Sankara et Mitterand* that recreates that evening in Ouagadougou.

Not even a year later, Sankara would pay the ultimate price for his effrontery to his French guests, to powerful leaders around the world whom he accused of imperialism and neo-colonialism, and to some influential figures in his own country. In October 1987 he was assassinated, allegedly by the man who would succeed him as president, working with the connivance of the French and a handful of other foreign secret services.[59] The Buy Local campaign died with him.

The Sankara years were an interesting time to be eavesdropping on the diplomatic community. A few, including the German ambassador, greatly admired and respected him as a beacon of change on the continent. But most expressed disdain for Sankara and his revolution.

The wife of the American ambassador didn't openly express any opinions on politics, at least not with me, unlike her brash and paternalistic husband who had told me that because Sankara was "like a son" to him, his job in Burkina Faso was to "set him straight." She seemed, at least on the occasions I met her, subdued and contemplative. The evening she spoke to me about *karité*, she had moved away from the chatty circles of diplomats and spouses on the patio. She had wandered over to the swimming pool, removed her sandals and was sitting at the pool edge dangling her feet in the water. As she fluttered them about, the water shimmered around her legs, spotlit from the pool depths.

I recall almost nothing else of our conversation, not how it began nor how it ended, only that she told me she was extremely interested in something called *karité,* or shea butter. She said it had enormous value in Europe, where tiny amounts were used in some of the most expensive French cosmetics, including a moisturizing face crème she used. She had already made contact with two agents selling the butter to Europe. She intended to invest in it; the cosmetic market in Europe was hungry for the stuff and there was a great deal of money to be made from shea butter.

Shortly after that, I asked our babysitter-turned-friend, Asséta Zango, what she knew about shea nuts or shea butter, if she had ever used it as a cosmetic. She laughed, incredulous, as if I'd just asked her if she'd ever met her own husband. She told me she cooked with it all the time. The next day she showed up at our house with a lump of shea butter and the ingredients for a full Burkinabe meal – onions, beef, smoked fish, hot peppers, tomatoes, and various condiments and vegetables I didn't recognize. The house filled up with the sharp aroma of the shea butter as it melted in the pot, then the pungent odour when the *soumbala* was added, and finally the tantalizing smell of the beef and peppery sauce as it simmered on the stove.

Asséta prepared several balls of porridge, or *tô,* made from *petit mil* or finger millet, dishing these up for us in separate bowls and immersing them in the rich sauce made with shea butter. She told me *karité* was the very best cooking oil to be had, but these days urban people were turning away from it in their quest to adopt more modern diets and impress others by purchasing more prestigious imported vegetable oils. It was this trend, the denigration of healthy local foods and products and the indiscriminate adoption of inferior imports, that Thomas Sankara had tried to reverse with his pioneering Consume Local campaign.

Long, long before Europeans "discovered" shea butter and began putting it into expensive cosmetics, soaps, shampoos, and pharmaceuticals, long before the late Anita Roddick and her Body Shop started selling it to enthusiastic consumers around the world, Africans had been happily producing, eating, using, and marketing shea butter. It was an exclusively African resource. Shea nuts come from a tree found only in Africa, a tree that farmers nurture in and around their fields. It grows in nineteen countries across the continent, and is especially prevalent in savannahs and in the semi-arid Sahel.[60]

Shea trees are vital resources to the people of the Sahel. The shea butter is an extremely nutritious cooking oil, but that's just the start. As I was told by a market woman one day in Banjul in The Gambia, it is an excellent antidote to the symptoms of colds and to stomach problems. You just cut off a lump of the butter and swallow it. Malian women told me they applied it to their hair and skin during the dry season to protect against hot winds that made skin so dry it practically peeled off and hair so brittle that bits of it snapped off.

It was a woman's resource and for many rural women, shea butter was their main source of income, as I was to learn in Mali in the village of Segou Koro, a small community of mud and thatch homes a stone's throw from the majestic, moody Niger River. Segou Koro is a few kilometres outside the ancient city of Segou, in the heartland of the Bambara Empire that flourished during the eighteenth and nineteenth centuries. Agroforestry researchers directed me there to meet some master shea butter makers.

The day I head out, the dry season and the heat are reaching a crescendo. The relatively cool weeks of the dry Harmattan wind are over. Now, as people count down the days until the first rains will fall in late May or early June, humidity is on the rise and the heat crashes over the region each morning shortly after the sun creeps over the treetops. The sky shimmers with the heat, bleaching it to a pallid sickly shade of blue. A mere footfall on a path or a bicycle tire on a rural road stirs up clouds of fine brown dust that clogs the nose and sticks to the skin. The only farming activities at this time of year are in communities close to the Niger River or where there are hand-dug wells. From these, buckets of water are drawn for sprinkling over thirsty vegetables in small market gardens. We are deep into the hungry season, when the trees in the parklands agroforestry farming system come into their own.

A large signboard on the outskirts of town welcomes visitors to the city of Segou, proclaiming it the city of *balanzan* trees, or *Faidherbia albida*, one of the top-fifteen species of trees in the Sahel. The *balanzan* look beautifully sculpted with their wispy crowns and crooked, angling trunks that make me fancy the trees are reaching out to embrace each other.

Such hauntingly lovely landscapes have nothing in common with the man-made industrial plantations of teak, eucalyptus, oil palm, or rubber trees in West Africa. Those are ruthlessly laid out with rigid spacing and in ramrod straight rows, like an army on parade that's been zapped mid-step and turned to immovable stone, stopped dead in its tracks. In contrast, the *balanzan* around Segou grow in elegant harmony with other important trees native to the region – tamarind, the lovely *dawa dawa*, and, of course, its faithful parklands companion, the shea or *karité* tree.

I've driven from Segou out to Segou Koro and am now making my way along the narrow dusty path leading into the village. It seems unbearably hot. But "unbearably" can be a relative term when it comes to heat. It increases exponentially as I approach the shea processing area where the fires are roaring and flames lick at the base of giant black cauldrons. Apparently undeterred by the heat are two women wielding giant wooden spoons to stir their contents. Rivulets of sweat trickle down their faces. The cauldrons are filled with boiling brown liquid, shea nuts bubbling and gurgling in their own dark juices. It looks very much like molten chocolate.

Aminata Touré and Mariama Coulibaly welcome me with broad smiles and enthusiastic greetings. When I introduce myself and tell them my mission, they say they'll be very happy to tell me anything I want to know about shea butter.

Aminata begins, saying she's been making shea butter for the past thirty-six years, since she was a small girl working at her mother's side. First, she says, you have to collect the nuts. The green shea fruit appear in May and June, when calories can be in short supply yet are desperately needed for the heavy work of preparing fields and planting annual crops. So as families head to their fields to plow and plant them, they snack on fresh shea fruits that abound on the trees.

The flesh is sweet, buttery, and refreshing, rich in sugars, protein, calcium, and potassium. The brown nuts, about the size of chestnuts, are collected and placed in depressions in the ground that may or may not be lined with clay or baskets. Then they are covered and allowed to ferment, stored until the time is ripe for processing.

The nuts can function as a savings account for rural women who have never set foot in a bank and wouldn't have the money to open an account even if they had. Aminata tells me they process the nuts when they feel they have the time, or when they need some quick income, and sometimes just because they've noticed prices for the butter are high in local markets. This year they've saved a few nuts until the hungry season, because food stocks are running on empty and so is the cash needed to purchase food to supplement meals, and to cover costs of health, schooling, and clothing for their children.

There are many variations of the process, but Aminata has her own recipe for perfect shea butter. It is complex, so I ask her to take me through it slowly, step by step, giving me time to write it all down. First, she says, she boils the nuts in the large pot, as she is doing now. Afterwards, you have to allow them to dry so you can remove the shells. Next you roast the nuts and grind them into a fine powder, which is mixed with water to create a thick brown paste.

The next task requires a good deal of upper-body strength. You plunge your right hand into the large bowl of thick and heavy paste, brown as the batter for chocolate cake, and with your hand and arm whip the paste until white butter separates and floats to the top. Then you scoop out the butter and place it in a large pot over the fire until it becomes a clear liquid. At this point, you pick out any remaining shell fragments, and may even strain the butter, before allowing the fat to cool until it can be shaped into a block of smooth, cream-coloured butter. Then the large block of shea butter, sometimes several kilograms, is wrapped in giant leaves and placed inside woven grass for storage and use at home, or for transport to market if it's to be sold.

Aminata says she always works together with her neighbour, Mariama. They agree the best shea butter is produced during Harmattan, in January and February, when temperatures are slightly lower. Mariama speaks of the importance of the tree and nut quality, of temperatures during the process, and how all of these can result in less-than-perfect butter, leaving it grainy or with a very strong aroma. Her knowledge of the tree, its fruit, nut, and oil, seems endless.

Both Aminata and Mariama say they would appreciate a press for cracking the nuts that would dramatically reduce their labour load. But without one, they will continue to process the nuts by hand, as their mothers and grandmothers did.

"It's better to work as a group," says Aminata. "The older, more experienced women can help organize and teach the younger women."

She is aware that Europeans have now "discovered" shea butter. Just the previous week, she says, some white men came from Bamako seeking to place an order for shea nuts they would like her to collect from her trees as soon as the fruit ripens at the start of the rains. They told her the order came from France, and she is wondering why it took *tuobabs* (white people) so long to notice this fine oil.

They tell me that shea and some other economic trees are permanent fixtures in their farms, and around them they sow millet, sorghum, and peanuts. To prevent the trees from shading out the annual crops, they might prune a few of the branches but are always careful not to harm the shea tree; it is taboo to do so. The annual crops around the trees provide their families their daily staple of *tô* porridge from millet, the shea trees give them butter, and the *balanzan* trees in turn feed the crops with nutrients. Mariama also has a few *baobab* trees she calls her own and from these the youngsters in the family harvest the leaves she dries for use in sauces throughout the long annual drought. The previous year the two dozen shea trees in her family's fields produced a bumper harvest of fruits. This, Mariama says, is because "God knows how to do these things."

It strikes me, I venture to say, that it isn't just God who knows how to do these things. I suggest that Aminata and Mariama should take some credit too. After all, I continue, they are both accomplished farmers who cultivate a wide range of crops. They are tree experts and expert processors, knowledgeable about local market opportunities. Both Mariama and Aminata seem to mistake my praise for an attempt at humour, and they oblige with laughter. But then they assure me anything they know how to do is thanks only to Allah.

Regardless of who could and should claim credit for their know-how on farming and trees, the uncelebrated fact is that the people of the Sahel have a lot of expertise. Over centuries farmers have developed a sophisticated – if largely unwritten – body of knowledge about the shea tree and a deep understanding of its variations and its uses. They select carefully and skilfully which shea seedlings to protect and allow to grow in their fields. They distinguish a great number of superior and inferior tree types, and even give them names.

In Burkina Faso, narrow leaves on a tree might distinguish it as a *tam daaga,* or a tree that produces small fruits without useful nuts.[61] Because the trees are valued for both their fruit and the nuts that give them the oil, people use different criteria to identify superior individuals. If it's the oil they're after, then they select trees that produce large nuts and plenty of them, and nuts with a lot of high quality oil. If they want a tree that will provide a lot of fruit to eat and to sell, they'll select for individuals that produce fruit with more pulp or sweeter flavour. None of this is left to chance; many farmers report they carry out observations on the production potential of trees for several years, to help them select which ones to nurture in their fields.

It's estimated the collection, processing, and marketing of shea products provides women in the Sahel countries with up to 60 percent of their income and that more than two million women are employed directly or indirectly by the local shea industry.[62] The tree, with its many uses, and the nut with its quality oil, merit a good deal more research that can help local producers benefit more from their resource.[63]

After my visit to Segou Koro, I meet with agroforestry researcher Edouard Bonkoungou to find out more about the valuable commodity. Edouard's father was a noted botanist and gardener during the French colonial period in his native Burkina Faso. Edouard himself is widely respected for his agroforestry and ecosystem management work over the years with international organizations. He catalogues for me some of the many virtues of shea butter. In addition to its culinary and cosmetic importance, he says it is one of the best sources of natural sunscreens, especially for the fragile skin of "northern" people. Mothers use the butter to massage their children's bodies. It helps heal wounds and eliminates skin irritation. Once upon a time, it was also used to fuel lamps. In addition, the dark residue left after the clear shea oil has separated and been scooped off is used to waterproof house walls and to polish clay floors. The wood can be used to fashion sturdy tools and strong mortars, and the roots and bark of the trees also have numerous medicinal applications.[64]

Recently, international buyers have begun to descend on the Sahel to cash in on this new commodity. In addition to its increasing popularity in cosmetics, soaps, and shampoos, shea butter is now widely used as an emollient in pharmaceutical ointments and as a substitute for cocoa butter in European confectionary.

But there is a problem. It is difficult for rural women to process the nuts to meet quality standards for the global market, which means buyers tend to come and buy the nuts and ship them off the continent for processing, so value-adding and profits accrue elsewhere.

Edouard is also worried about the fate of the trees themselves. Local people do not plant them and depend instead on nature to place the seedlings in their farm fields and in fallows. With the immense pressures on land and vegetation caused by climate change, land degradation and overgrazing, population pressure and the push for modern industrial agriculture, especially in the well-watered inland deltas of the Niger River, populations of shea nut trees and indeed the parklands themselves are under threat. The indigenous trees grow very slowly, spending the early years of their lives sending down very deep roots before they grow upwards and start to produce fruit.

"We know that the trees have been there," Edouard tells me. "We were born and we found them there and we don't see any active replacement by people in the villages. Some of the individual trees, we know them by name and when we see them dying it's emotional, because it's like a person, a living person you have known and there are no kids coming after that tree." Here he pauses for a moment, before concluding, "So we need to do some planting."

In recent years, some small co-operatives, women's groups, and small companies have sprung up across Africa to produce pure shea butter for regional markets, and some of their products can now be found in the large Lebanese-owned supermarkets in Bamako and Ouagadougou. Some are also exporting their organic and fair trade shea butter internationally.

In 2011, the Global Shea Alliance was founded as a non-profit industry association, which aims to "drive a competitive and sustainable shea industry worldwide."[65] But the full potential of this green gold to improve the lives and living standards of the majority of the women who make and sell shea butter has yet to be tapped. The invisible hand of the global market isn't known for its compassion, and it's unlikely to offer the women of Africa help with the training and processing facilities they would need to enable them to maintain control of and benefit from their precious shea resources.

The U.S. ambassador's wife was right. There *is* a lot of money to be made from *karité*. But it's not obvious that the money will flow in the right direction, to the majority of the people who most need it and deserve it, the women like Mariama and Aminata in villages throughout Africa's Sahel.

9

Rainforest riches

I'm in Kumba market, in South-west Province of Cameroon, looking at stalls laid out with a wide range of unusual looking fruits, nuts, dried tree bark and other products that I cannot identify, but I am aware that they are the products of the Trees of Life.

– Roger R.B. Leakey
Living With the Trees of Life:
Towards the Transformation of Tropical Agriculture

Shea (or shea nut) is just one of countless African trees that produce favourite foods and valuable oils. The rainforests of Central Africa are also full of food trees that provide the people with important nutrients and flavourful ingredients for their complex cuisines, as I'm learning as I make my way through the noisy market of Biyem-Assi in the Cameroonian capital, Yaoundé. My mentor today is Margaret Numfor, a teacher, avid cook, and connoisseur of all foods local, who has agreed to act as my guide as I struggle to familiarize myself with just a few of the foods that come from the remarkable forests of Cameroon.

Margaret comes highly recommended as an expert cook and

an authority on forest foods. She's brought along a friend, Edith, who seems just as enthusiastic about our mission to document a few of the non-timber forest products for sale here. These, says Margaret, are far more valuable to local people, and especially to women, than the timber would be when the forests are felled.

The concept of non-timber forest products is a novel one to me, although specialists have turned it into an important science that inventories all the diverse things you can harvest from a forest and its trees – from medicines to mushrooms, caterpillars to fruits, nuts and leaves, fibre and fodder, to useful gums and oils. It's not that there are no non-timber forest products in the temperate climes; in North America there are some well-known and lucrative ones, including maple syrup, honey, and a handful of mushroom species. But this pales in comparison with Africa's non-timber forest wealth, where it seems there is hardly a tree that doesn't have at least a dozen useful products, in addition to their wood of course.

An astounding number of people in the world, more than 1.6 billion, rely on forests for their livelihoods; 60 million live in and depend on rainforests in Latin America, Southeast Asia, and West Africa; and a startling 1.2 billion people in developing nations – equivalent to nearly a fifth of humanity – use trees on farms for both food and for income.[66] Governments and global development institutions may not always recognize the importance of trees to food security and nutrition, but it is well known by local forest producers, farmers, and consumers.[67] When the forests disappear to make way for agriculture, or because of logging or industrial development, so do countless cherished foods and other valuable things the forest provides.

Margaret and Edith have pledged to show me just a few of the edible non-timber products that come from Cameroon's rapidly disappearing forests. We've not even left the roadside to enter the maze of the market but already they are talking a mile a minute, propelling me towards a grill where a woman is roasting some familiar foods; there are plantains and cocoyams, known here as *macabo*. But there's also one that's unfamiliar to me. It's a purplish fruit that Margaret identifies as a "plum" in pidgin English and "bush butter" or "African pear" in English. In French it's known as *safou*, across the border in Nigeria, the Yoruba call it *elemi,* and the Igbo know it as *ube*. To scientists, it's *Dacroydes edulis*.

Margaret helps me choose a *safou* fruit from the grill, which I do for a very reasonable 25 CFA francs (at that time, worth a few pennies). It's an oblong fruit with a purplish blue-hued skin. Following her instructions, I peel back the skin to reveal avocado-green flesh and bite into the warm fruit. It melts in my mouth, a smooth texture and buttery flavour all its own, but with something borrowed from avocado too. It's a popular snack, roasted or grilled on roadsides, but it is also often boiled as a tasty complement for plantain dishes or *fufu* made of pounded tubers. Margaret says the fruit comes in many shapes, sizes, and colours, and confirms it is a very important economic and culinary resource in Cameroon, exported throughout Central Africa.

Its delicious fruit pulp is nearly half edible oil, rich in vitamins and a range of amino acids. The kernel makes an excellent source of protein for sheep and goats. The flower attracts bees, making it useful for apiculture. The bark yields a resin that is used as pitch for mending earthenware and calabashes. The resin is also used to treat parasitic skin diseases, while the pulped bark is used to heal wounds. The list of the tree's medicinal properties is long.[68] And its delicious fruit has what it takes to go global. These days in Cameroon you can also find *safou* chips and even spreads made from the nutritious fruit.[69]

My grilled *safou* finished, Margaret and Edith urge me on. We move into a congested section of the market chock-a-block with leafy greens. Margaret tells me the greens are also from the forest, known as *eru, okazi,* and *koko* (among many other names), which come from a forest vine (*Gnetum africanum*). Untallied tonnes of the leaves are exported every day from Cameroon to Nigeria, in vans crammed with the greens inside and out. Margaret says the *eru* is cooked until the leaves become soft and then they are mixed and cooked some more with "waterleaf" (*Talilum triangulare*), a very popular green rich in calcium and vitamins A and C. Largely because of its enormous popularity and the loss of forest habitat, *eru* has been listed as threatened by the International Union for the Conservation of Nature.

Next we make our way past mountains of tubers and navigate a path through displays of fresh fruits that give way to displays of plant products and parts that may be used as spices, condiments, and/or medicines. The small stalls, underneath tin roofing, stretch away in the shadows as far as I can see. Margaret and Edith are talking rapidly; there is no way I can retain all the information they are dispensing, let alone all the names and uses of the countless plant products before us in the hectic marketplace, nearly all of which have their origins in forests.

They point at a dizzying number of barks, nuts, seeds, and vegetables. One they say can be used as a medicine or in "black soup"; it is charred with other ingredients to produce a charcoal black condiment to mix with pork or fish. There are small bags of mixed spices, which are used to prepare *M'bongo tchobi,* a favourite black-sauced dish of fish or meat originating with the Bassa people in Cameroon. There are five forest spices needed to make the sauce; the main one is a dark tree bark that gives the sauce its colour and its name.

Margaret picks up a black thing the size of a hazelnut, and tells me it's *fulo* or bush onion. It has a powerful and wonderful aroma, and she says it imparts that to *achoo* soup, "the yellow type of pepper soup." They both agree the bush onion is far better than the Maggi flavour cube by Nestlé, and while young women may be using it less, you can hardly go into the house of a woman their mothers' age without finding *fulo* is the spice of choice.

The bush onion is also medicinal; a good *achoo* soup made with the flavourful gem is, Margaret says, a perfect antidote for constipation. "It really cleanses the bowels," volunteers Edith.

Margaret picks up a piece of bark used to spice up all sorts of dishes. She calls it "tree garlic." I sniff deeply, again and again. It's redolent of garlic, evocative of freshly dug soil and deep verdant rainforest, and it's hypnotic.

I am recording our entire tour, but even so, I know the recording is filling up with unanswered questions as Margaret and Edith continue tossing out names I'll never be able to spell. To make things still more confusing and complicated, each of these many, many food products has names in one of the many, many languages, of which there are some 230 in Cameroon, in addition to the official French and English. Still, if the purpose is to show me the bounty of the forests and woodlands that help to feed and heal a nation, spicing up and enriching its cuisines with nutrients and fabulous flavours, the tour is certainly succeeding.

They escort me deeper into the market, hammering me with names and uses for dozens of different mushrooms, wild peppers from the forest, pods, leaves. When I can get a word in, I suggest to them that Cameroonian cooking must be extremely complex. They laugh.

"For foreigners, our cooking looks complex," says Margaret. "For us, we are so used to it, we cook as fast as we like and we don't even take much time cooking. Because we are so used to our spices that we just cook without any effort."

I ask them if Cameroonian consumers would be willing to buy the condiments if they were pre-ground and processed and packaged for sale in supermarkets. "No," says Edith. "People don't like the pre-ground condiments because you can't be sure of the quality and the quantity of each one in the mix, so that doesn't taste as good. It's best we prepare them ourselves. We have grown up to see our mothers use them so we have also learned how to use them."

But they are worried, they say, by the rising prices and decreasing availability of many of these local delicacies and treasured condiments. Nearly all of them come from forests, many collected and sold to middlemen by forest-dwelling Baka people. And as the forests go, so do the ingredients that make Cameroonian cuisines so extraordinarily diverse, delicious, and nutritious.

While in Yaoundé, I also have the good fortune of meeting another expert on forest foods and non-timber forest riches. Her name is Odelia Ngala of Cameroon's Ministry of Agriculture, and she's passionate about forest foods, a great friend to the people who know and depend on them. At the time we meet in her office, she is finishing her thesis on the foods, medicines, oils, and spices from the forests of Cameroon. She rattles off a long list of food products that come from trees, making my mouth water as she describes how a little of this vine and that nut could be tossed into the pot to make a delectable pepper soup.

Many, she says, are also medicinal and among some forest-dwelling peoples, they have a word for the forest that translates as "farmers' pharmacy." The problem is the true full value of the many non-timber forest products has never been calculated, largely because their value is for villagers, particularly women, for whom urban elites and politicians often have little regard. She estimates that if the true monetary value of all the foods and medicines from the forests could be estimated, it would be exponentially greater than the value of the timber they contain.

But, she continues, the government and foreigners tend to miss the forests' non-timber products and see only the trees they can fell for timber. "If I were to rank the problems in Cameroon," she says, "I think the disappearance of the forest would be one of the main problems. Because when you stand on the side of the road and see the number of trucks carrying timber to Douala, at times I just stand and look and I'm confused. Because the trucks just keep on passing every minute."

Soft-spoken but passionate, her voice quavers when she tells me she has been interacting for years with forest-dwellers. "For them, the forest is life." She says if the forest disappears, the people of the forest zone will not survive.

But all is not lost, at least all not *need* be lost. There are solutions. Enter the tree tamers, who see the salvation of the foods and forests in the domestication of the trees. The idea is to bring the trees out of the forest and onto farms, using basic horticultural techniques that allow farmers to select and reproduce varieties of the valuable trees the way they have developed the legion of cultivars of other plants farming peoples have domesticated over the millennia.

The intricate process of crop domestication beautifully illustrates the ingenuity and genius of human beings down through the ages. Domestication involves intense powers of observation, calculation, intuition, patience, and knowledge of soils, climate, precipitation, plant physiology, human needs, and local markets. Since the beginning of human time on this planet, people have discovered wild plants with useful products and traits. Then, somewhere around 10,000 years ago, they learned something else about the wild plants (and animals) that helped to sustain them: they learned they could bring them out of the realm of wild things and cultivate varieties with traits they sought to reproduce. In this way, our human forbearers took wild creatures and bred them into domestic livestock, poultry, and also the furry pets many of us love today.

Through selection and planting over countless generations, they developed seeds that could result in plants with particular traits – larger fruits or leaves, fruits with thicker pulp or bigger seeds, early or later fruiting, resistance to drought or to flooding or certain pests, whatever served their needs and conditions. With their painstaking work of selecting and crossbreeding plants, farmers around the world continue to produce an immense wealth of agricultural diversity.

10

Taming the trees of life

Thinking like an ecosystem also means seizing the advantages of your unique place on earth and using plants to help each other, planting trees and shrubs, for example, that rise to different heights and grow well together.

– Anna Lappé
Diet for a Hot Planet:
The Climate Crisis at the End of Your Fork
And What You Can Do About It

Although we as a species have come a long way when it comes to domesticating useful species to feed ourselves, many agroforestry and agro-ecological agriculture specialists think the work has only just begun. Roger Leakey is one of those who thinks domestication of the "trees of life" is the answer for many of the problems confronting Africa and the planet. Leakey has spent much of his career promoting tree domestication, taking the trees out of the disappearing forests and cultivating them on farms. He says the potential is simply enormous, in his book *Living With the Trees of Life: Towards the Transformation of*

Tropical Agriculture. So far, human beings have tapped very little of the genetic diversity and value of the plant life of the planet through domestication. Of a quarter of a million higher plant species on earth, about 20,000 have edible parts. And yet human beings tend to focus on just one hundred domesticated food plants. Another thirty species have been domesticated for non-food products such as rubber and timber. And we cultivate about 15,000 species as garden ornamentals.

This leads Leakey to ask whether we as a species think aesthetics are more important than food. Perhaps in the past, this has been the case. But he believes many of the most pressing problems of the day and many that are particularly acute in Africa – hunger, environmental degradation, and climate change – can best be addressed by turning our attention to trees that can be taken out of the forests to produce fruits, vegetables, nuts, and condiments that are rich in micronutrients.

This builds on traditional knowledge of crops and foods in Africa, and it can involve any one or a combination of basic horticultural techniques that entail "vegetative propagation," or cloning superior individuals – taking cuttings, grafting and also marcotting or air layering. Marcotting is a technique that requires removing a strip of bark from a tree branch and suspending a bag of rooting medium into which the branch will put out roots, after which that section of the branch can be lopped off and planted.

Farmers can use these techniques, Leakey says, to propagate planting material for the trees in small greenhouse structures they can fashion themselves with nothing more than a wooden frame covered with plastic. In this way, they can replicate a superior "mother tree" they know, capturing and copying any genetic traits they may value, be it larger fruit, sweeter fruit, larger nuts, higher oil content in nuts, early or later fruiting, and so on. According to Leakey, by domesticating valuable trees in this way, new cultivars can be developed that deliver a "quantum leap" in quality and yield improvement.

Another proponent of such domestication is Nigerian scientist, I.O.O. Aiyelaagbe. When I met him back in 1998, he was chief researcher at the National Horticultural Research Institute in Ibadan. He wanted to talk to me about several precious trees that provided cherished foods for the people of not just his country but for the whole humid coastal lowlands of West and Central Africa.

He rattled off several tongue-twisting names, both local ones used in Nigeria and also scientific ones. He said the fruits of these trees were important because, just like their cousins in the drier Sahelian region, they came into bearing between peak seasons, at the end of the dry season when annual food stocks were running out but before the new crops could be harvested. "Therefore they act as a stopgap meal for people," he explained to me. He said the products from the trees were important for national economies, traded widely as they were across borders throughout the region.

I wanted to know why these trees did not figure large in foreign-funded agricultural development schemes. He replied they were extremely well-known and appreciated *locally*, but it was difficult to promote them because of the avalanche of advertising for imported foreign foods and seasonings made by multinationals. By that he meant the onslaught of messaging on billboards, radio, television, and sometimes even using mobile vans with louspeakers that promoted imported processed foods as superior to anything local and traditional.

My meeting with Aiyelaagbe took place at a conference in Cameroon of agroforestry specialists, who were looking at which trees to domesticate to improve their value and prevent their disappearance along with the forests in West and Central Africa that were being ravaged by logging, mining, and clearing for agriculture. As they had done in the Sahel, the researchers had asked farmers in Cameroon and Nigeria to name the tree species they would most like to domesticate. The list the farmers came up with was very long. Working together, researchers and farmers then produced a more realistic list of five priority tree species they could start to domesticate.

In number five spot is *Garcinia kola* or bitter kola, which is officially considered a threatened species.[70] Along with other kinds of kola nuts, it has been used as an additive in soft drinks. But in Africa its nuts are chewed as a stimulant and they have immense spiritual and cultural significance across West and Central Africa. It is also valued as a purgative, and for its anti-parasitic and antimicrobial properties. It's used to treat bronchitis, throat infections, colic, head or chest colds, liver disorders, and even as a valuable chewing stick for dental care and hygiene. Recent studies have shown it to be an effective treatment for osteoarthritis.[71] And for good measure, scientists are working to confirm what African herbalists already know. They found that in male rats at least, kola nuts are an effective aphrodisiac that can enhance sexual activity.[72]

Ranked in fourth place was *Chrysophyllum albidum* or star apple, which has received almost no horticultural attention, despite its importance as a fruit available during the dry season when other foods are often scarce.[73]

Then there is *Ricinodendron heudelotii* or *njangsan,* named the third highest priority tree for domestication.[74] *Njangsan* is a tall, imposing tree that can attain heights of forty metres. Sometimes known as the African nut tree, it is found at forest edges and in secondary growth, with a remarkable range stretching clear across the continent from Zambia to Senegal. Its fruit contains small brown kernels, about the size and shape of peanuts, an ingredient in many local dishes and cuisines. These nuts are nutritious, rich in proteins, lipids, carbohydrates, calcium, and iron. More than half their weight is oil that can be used in cooking or even as a medicinal product. They are processed into powder or paste and used in a multitude of fish, meat, and vegetable dishes across the continent. They have an earthy cocoa odour, adding a nutty richness but slightly bitter flavour to a sauce while also thickening it.

In Cameroon, agroforesters working with farmers to domesticate it have been having great success. Martin Djana Nga, a village chief and cocoa farmer not far from Yaoundé, tells me it's a wonderful addition to his cocoa agroforest. The chief is proud of his twenty hectares of cocoa, which are in full fruiting glory, laden with beautiful red pods almost ready for the picking. Interspersed with the cocoa are indigenous fruit trees, some mature giants that grew there naturally and that his father protected and nurtured while he was alive. Some are younger domesticated trees that were produced in the community nursery, under the tutelage of agroforestry researchers. He tells me he's planted 170 domesticated trees of various species that will produce fruit for years to come.

"Even if I am already dead, this will help my children and grandchildren," he tells me. "In years to come I will make a lot more from this land because cocoa only produces once a year, and with all the fruit trees I have, there will be production all year round. So in January and February when I am waiting for my cocoa, I can sell fruit, and that will really help me."

We pause under a magnificent, majestic giant of a tree, where small *njangsan* fruits are piled, ready for collection and cracking. The value of the *njangsan* from just this one tree is around US$300 a year, and Chief Djana Nga imagines aloud the value all of the young domesticated *njangsan* trees in his cocoa agroforest will soon produce. But it's not just the prospect of increased income that makes his eyes light up. "My wife puts *njangsan* in sauces and with fish," he says. "And I have that, and a glass of palm wine to go with it, I am a very happy man!"

Like so many other of these "trees of life," the African nut tree itself seems to have a million and one uses, from drum making to cloth dyeing, to curing elephantiasis or preventing miscarriage.[75] So it's no surprise Cameroonian and Nigerian farmers told researchers this is a priority tree: domestication would allow them to build on its genetic potential to improve the products harvested from it and the income it generates. And not to forget the fine dishes that *njangsan* enriches. And it ranked only third on the top-five list.

Coming in at number two on the list is *Dacryodes edulis* or *safou*, the purple-skinned, green-fleshed fruit I had so enjoyed in the Yaoundé market. Topping the tree popularity poll in the region, Number One on the farmers' list of trees for domestication is the bush mango or *dika* nut (*Irvingia gabonensis*). To the uninitiated it may come as a surprise that the seed from the bush mango would rank so highly in the estimation of farmers in Central and West Africa. In markets, it is an innocuous thing – yellowish or brownish flat seeds that have no easily discernible smell or appeal. Rich in protein and oils, their main use is as a thickener for sauces and "draw soups" that slip easily down the throat, much the way okra does.

Cameroonian women tell me soups made with bush mango seeds are wonderful with pounded yam, cassava *fufu*, corn *fufu*, pounded cassava, or cocoyam. As are soups made with kernels from the bush mango's cousin, called "bitter bush mango" or *Irvingia wombulo*, which are also used to thicken soups.

The bush mango fruits, which not surprisingly resemble small mangoes, are delicious when eaten fresh. But they are not the valuable commodities the dried kernels of bush mango and bitter bush mango are. Both are traded widely through Central and West Africa. In southern Cameroon, for example, the seed is said to be the most important legal non-timber forest product.[76]

A new and potentially enormous market is developing for the bush mango kernels on the other side of the ocean. In North America, however, it's not to augment nutritional security but to help an obese continent shed pounds. Scientists have turned their attention to the effect of bush mango seeds in diets and found that they can be used to manage obesity and to reduce cholesterol.[77] *Irvingia gabonensis* is now becoming another new darling of the multi-billion-dollar weight-loss industry in the United States. While there is still a fair amount of scepticism in Cameroon itself about these claims, diet gurus in the United States are all abuzz about the African mango diet and its supposedly miraculous weight-loss powers.

"An all natural weight loss supplement with many additional benefits," crows African Mango Mart, just one of countless websites peddling dietary products from bush mango. "Appetite suppressant, burns excess fat, shed inches from waistline, improve metabolism, reduce cholesterol."[78]

Whether this new popularity will be a good thing for the bush mango and for the people of Africa, whose resource it is, will depend a lot on how the tree is cultivated and who markets the seeds as demand grows. It is important that control of the resource remain with smallholder producers and that global markets and giant retailers do not seize control of the value chain and push for monoculture and plantation agriculture – as has been the fate of Africa's oil palm.

11

Red and rich and much maligned –
Africa's palm oil

Among the Ibo, the art of conversation is regarded very highly and proverbs are the palm-oil with which words are eaten.

– Chinua Achebe
Things Fall Apart

Throughout the years we lived in West and Central Africa, much of what we ate was smothered in the red palm oil that local people coax laboriously from the fruit that grows on indigenous oil palm trees from the species *Elaeis guineensis*. Mary Fukuo, my Ghanaian friend and guide to everything Ghanaian while we lived in Tamale, introduced us to "palm butter soup," cooked up with her own mix of spices and vegetables and, of course, the rich, red palm oil. The soup she poured generously over silky smooth balls of yam *fufu*.

Sometimes, when she could get them, she added giant forest snails to the soup. The big snails were flavoursome and nutritious, if a little leathery. We ate Mary's palm butter soup just about every Sunday for a year. The Sunday meals induced a marvellous state of lazy stupor that led to a delightful afternoon nap, during which my digestive system quietly worked away on the starches and the creamy soup. My husband said the *fufu* reminded him a little of the delicious German potato dumplings, or *Kartoffel-kloesse,* that his mother made.

One day a normally genial and gentle Dutch woman came by to pick up her children who had spent the morning playing at our house, and found them and mine tucking happily into black-eyed peas swimming in red palm oil and hot pepper, one of my all-time favourite dishes, a Ghanaian speciality known as "red-red." She seemed horrified and delivered a strident lecture about the dangers of consuming palm oil. It was known, she declared, to cause heart attacks. Palm oil was terribly unhealthy. Studies had shown this. And so on.

This was perplexing. As far as I knew from Ghanaian doctors, in the early 1990s heart attacks were not yet a major issue in Ghana or indeed anywhere in sub-Sahara Africa where people were eating traditional foods, of which red palm oil was one. Back then, health problems associated with Western lifestyles and diets – coronary disease, obesity, and diabetes – were still relatively minor issues that afflicted demographic groups in Africa that were living and eating more like Westerners, consuming more imported and processed foods. And on the flipside, as far as I knew, the Westerners for whom coronary disease was a major killer were generally not dining on red palm oil from Africa.

So why was she convinced that if I continued to give my small children dishes cooked in palm oil, I was writing them a prescription for cardiac arrest and imminent death? She, like many of the expatriates in northern Ghana, purchased refined and imported cooking oils in supermarkets in the capital, Accra, or ordered their cooking oils, along with a huge variety of foods and household goods, by the container-load from European cata-logues. I started fretting that I should be doing the same even as I was becoming increasingly suspicious of the nutritional fatwa that had been placed on palm oil of any kind. If it were as bad as this woman claimed, wouldn't people living in the palm oil belt across the Central and West African coast have died out ages ago?

Something smelled a little oily here.

This was around the time that other vegetable fats – soy, corn, canola, peanut, all produced widely in North America and part of the vertically integrated food chain that large corporations increasingly controlled – were being touted as healthy choices. Advertisers and even many nutritionists were telling consumers that processed and refined vegetable oils in margarine were healthier than other more traditional fats, such as butter and lard. Breeding of the ancient rapeseed in Canada had produced canola in the 1970s; by the 1990s this cultivar was set for genetic modification and very wide-scale cultivation in North America.

Around the same time, coincidentally – or perhaps not – palm oil was suddenly being demonized as a health hazard, particularly by the American Soybean Association.[79] A few media headlines based on dubious studies or skewed interpretations of their results can be very effective in instilling fear of just about any foodstuff, useful tools for reducing sales of competing products. But why would Africa's palm oil be vilified this way? It was hardly competing with margarine or peanut oil sales among North American consumers.

But then I got to thinking that perhaps the health warnings weren't aimed at Africa's red palm oil at all. Maybe the purpose was to warn consumers off palm oil coming from Southeast Asia, which was creating competition for American soy and other oils from major North American and European crops such as corn, canola, and peanut. Southeast Asia's industrial palm oil has nothing in common with the rich, red, locally processed oil from the palm fruit that proliferates in West African markets and which comes from native trees growing on farms and in forests. The Asian version is highly processed into "refined bleached deodorized palm oil" – officially known as RBDPO – for the world commodity market.

Then, without the public really noticing, the bad press and hype suggesting that palm oil was a crime against the heart began to dissipate, just around the time that some very, very large multinationals moved heavily into the palm oil business. Corporations incorporated palm oil into their food chains, quietly slipping it into an astonishing range of processed foods and cosmetics. Today, one in ten products on supermarket shelves contains industrially produced and processed palm oil, and half of all processed edibles contain the oil in some form.

It turns out that Africa's indigenous palm oil never deserved the bad rap. Increasingly, science has been recognizing that the locally processed red oil from the fruit of wild trees is very nutritious, even medicinal. In traditional diets in Africa, red palm oil continues to be an important source of energy, lipids, calcium, and phosphorus.[80] It has a remarkable number of health benefits.[81]

The tree itself is invaluable. In the humid lowlands of West and Central Africa, native oil palm is an important component of family-run tree-crop plantations, agroforests that are just a few hectares in area. It is also found in what remains of natural forests or growing abundantly on land left to fallow and revert to bush.

The indigenous oil palm has a tall thick trunk capped with a frill of palm leaves and it dots the landscape on even degraded lands, growing happily in association with all sorts of other beneficial trees. Apart from its use in sauces and soups served over staple grain or tuber dishes, the oil is added to many kinds of dough made from cassava, rice, plantains, yams, and beans. Its red fruit can be boiled and roasted with a sprinkling of sugar. Then it tastes much like a date. Simply scrumptious.

Once the red oil has been removed from the fruit, the grey-black kernel – the size of a small almond – is removed and crushed to produce its own oil, this one completely clear and ideal for making soap. The pressed cake left over after extraction of the red palm oil can be used as fodder to feed goats and sheep

A palm tapper in Sierra Leone.

that family farmers may be raising.

The tree's fronds are used as thatch for roofs. And last but not least, stands of oil palm provide the region with one of its great delicacies – palm wine, which can be drunk fresh or distilled to make powerful schnapps. Tappers clamber up the trees like the unsung acrobats they are, using hoops made of woven fibres that encircle their backs and allow them to brace their feet against the trunk as they literally walk up the tall trees. Once at the pinnacle, they insert spigots into the tree and suspend plastic jugs there to collect the milky sap.

Some hours later, the tapper zips back up the tree to retrieve the jug now filled with palm wine, which continues to ferment quite rapidly. Drunk fresh to accompany a mid-morning snack of boiled plantains, the tangy palm wine is just about delicious and potent enough to elevate the imbiber's spirits and sense of well-being to a height exceeding that of the palm tree. Heavenly stuff.

In Sierra Leone it's known as *poyo* and I've become a fan. But following the advice of friends, I drink it only in rural areas where we buy it directly from the tappers to ensure it is freshly harvested and pure, not diluted with unsafe water or adulterated with risky chemicals as is much of the *poyo* sold in cities.

Sierra Leonean connoisseurs are prone to wipe their mouths after a large, satisfying slug of palm wine and with a smile big as a palm frond, repeat a well-known refrain, "From God to mouth, from God to man." And woman, of course.

The remarkable oil palm originated in Africa, where it has long been an important resource. Palm oil was part of the food supply in Africa well before recorded history and was widely traded across the continent. It has been found in Egyptian tombs dating back to 3,000 B.C.E.

The Europeans "discovered" Africa's oil palm when they explored the continent in search of wealth and resources. During the transatlantic slave trade, red palm oil was used to provision slave ships. Later, during the British Industrial Revolution, the oil was used to lubricate machines and to make candles. By the twentieth century, European colonists had set up large plantations of the tree in Central Africa and Southeast Asia. The lucrative palm oil industry in Asia was based on planting material that originated from just four specimens of the African oil palm tree that were taken to the Bogor Botanic Gardens in Indonesia in 1848, in a rather blatant case of bio-piracy. For more than a century, breeders and industrialists worked with this planting material, struggling in vain to improve yields of the oil palm, which remained poor in Southeast Asia.

Then in 1980, researchers from Unilever decided to make

off with yet another African resource, the pollinator of oil palm, a weevil known as *Elaeidobius kamerunicus,* and introduce it into Unilever plantations in Malaysia.[82] This helped the oil palm industry take off in Indonesia, Thailand, Papua New Guinea, the Solomon Islands, and India.

Monoculture plantations became the industrial norm, with just one or two varieties planted over thousands, even hundreds of thousands of hectares. Driving through such a plantation is dizzying, even hypnotic – row after regimented row after regimented row of trees, like visiting a mega-city populated only by clones, millions and millions of them. Genetic monotony is not a natural or healthy state of affairs.

Having not just tamed but also harnessed the African oil palm and its production for the economies of scale that funnel more and more profits *up* the value chain to the moneyed investors and corporations that control it, industry has been intent on making palm oil the world's most produced and internationally traded edible oil. Precious forests and peat lands in Asia have been slashed and burned and valuable farmland has been seized as palm oil plantations have expanded. This in turn led to a new wave of negative publicity for palm oil, this time for environmental reasons. To try to head off mounting criticism of industrial palm oil, in 2004 palm growers, oil processors, traders, consumer goods manufacturers, retailers, investors, and a few non-governmental organizations (NGOs) formed the Roundtable on Sustainable Palm Oil, "dedicated to promoting sustainable production of palm oil worldwide." However, the Roundtable has been strongly criticized by many NGOs and environmental and farmer groups, which see it as a green- and white-washing body for the palm oil industry.[83]

When concerns about climate change led to a proliferation of biofuels made from plants, this also fuelled the rapid spread of palm oil plantations throughout the tropics. The European Union and governments in China and North America set targets for the use of biofuels, and palm oil that could be converted to biodiesel became an even hotter commodity. Giant areas of forest and peat-land are still being cleared in Southeast Asia to make way for oil palm, causing haze and pollution problems that are crippling regional economies, harming health, and decimating forest lands.

Using palm oil to try to tackle climate change, as environmental groups have pointed out, is counterproductive. Burning and clearing forests and peat-lands, which emit massive amounts of methane gas when disturbed, are anything but an effective way to reduce carbon emissions.

In 2004, Malaysia and Indonesia accounted for about 83 percent of palm oil production and 89 percent of global exports of the commodity – refined and ready for use in food, hygiene products, and cosmetic industries. Malaysia, however, which had been developing its oil palm plantations to drive rapid economic growth since the 1960s, didn't have much land left for expansion of the plantations. New oil palm plantations went up in Indonesia and in 2007, Indonesia overtook Malaysia as the world's largest producer.

The palm oil rush could not be stopped with so much money behind it – and so much money to be made from it. Corporate behemoths such as Sime Darby, Olam International, and Wilmar International, as well as a host of European, American, and Asian investors and speculators, fanned out around the world looking for vast new lands to convert to oil palm plantations. They found them not just in Asia but also on the much-abused continent of Africa, which financial speculators were calling the "final investment frontier." Even before the financial crisis of 2007 and 2008 had ended, a new scramble for Africa was underway, this time for its fertile land.

In Cameroon, foreign investors from Asia, the U.S., and Europe rapidly secured enormous land banks for palm oil estates, often in fragile forest areas that had been carefully preserved because of their incredible wealth of biodiversity. The same was true in Benin, Côte d'Ivoire, Gabon, Liberia, Nigeria, the Democratic Republic of Congo (capital Kinshasa), and the Republic of Congo (capital Brazzaville).

Sierra Leone was part of the foreign rush for resources and land. Investors converged on the country, taking out long-term leases (fifty years, renewable for up to one hundred) on vast tracts of arable land (from 100,000 to 350,000 hectares) slated for giant industrial plantations. By 2013, it was estimated that one-quarter of Sierra Leone's arable land had been leased out to foreign investors.[84]

It is an ironic tragedy that much of the grabbed land in Sierra Leone and other African countries is being cleared for oil palm. The industrial plantations result in the destruction of local vegetation and farms, and the foods that have until now been cultivated on the land. And that includes indigenous palm trees that provide the nutritious red palm oil that is a staple and a valuable source of nutrients in the region. The locally processed oil is a mainstay of diets, an excellent source of vitamins E and K and beta-carotenes, which the body can convert into vitamin A, important for eyesight, among other things.

So it seems odd that governments, development agencies, and even researchers intent on improving nutrition in Africa appear to be turning a blind eye to the immense potential of the native tree, its nutritious red oil, and the promotion of the mixed farming systems in which it grows. The Bill & Melinda Gates Foundation, for example, is funding work on "biofortification," breeding higher levels of micronutrients into key staple crops in Africa, including cassava, sweet potatoes, maize, and yams.[85] HarvestPlus, the group carrying out the biofortification work, says its aim is to reduce "hidden hunger," the malnutrition caused by a lack of micronutrients such as zinc, iron and, yes, beta-carotene, the same nutrient that red palm oil provides in abundance. The reason these are lacking in people's diets, they maintain, is because of poverty and because staple crops don't contain enough of them.

But really, it could be argued that if Africa were not drowning in cheap, refined and bleached, and nutrient-poor palm oil from Asia, there would be little need for cassava or maize crops biofortified with micronutrients. It is perplexing that biofortification researchers are breeding orange maize and cassava with high levels of beta-carotene when traditional diets that were high in such nutrients are being eroded by the advent of modern industrial diets.[86]

12

Bamboo wine and mansions in the bush

I could tell that he missed the village, that he missed seeing those palm trees the men climbed, with a raffia belt encircling them and the tree trunk.

– Chimamanda Ngozi Adichie
Purple Hibiscus

In 2012, I had the privilege of working for several months with Sierra Leonean human rights and environmental activists. We were doing a study of how three large land deals with foreign investors setting up oil palm and sugarcane plantations were affecting communities on the land leases. As part of this, we attempted to do an inventory of all the food resources that people had cultivated and harvested from their farms, surrounding woodlands and waterways before losing their land to the investors.[87] The list tallied 117 different plant, animal, and fish resources that had once sustained them.

Yet the billionaire investors and corporations that had leased out the land for half a century or even longer seemed to have taken no notice of the importance of the multiple resources that had always sustained the local people. They tended to denigrate or even dismiss the agro-biodiverse family farming and local industries that their investments and plantations would eliminate, apparently oblivious to the bounty such farms might harbour.

As they are in much of Africa, farms and villages in Sierra Leone are thriving little industrial centres. In the communities we visited, we watched as cassava was peeled, grated, pressed, fermented, and roasted to produce *gari*, which has dozens of uses, including as an instant porridge. Women use oil from palm kernels, herbs, and also burned, blackened cocoa pods to produce soaps. They gather around wooden mortars to pound peanuts, rice, and spices into pastes or pieces. Blacksmiths toil away to fashion machetes, shovels, and other farm tools. Industry and productivity everywhere you look.

Much of it is strenuous physical work, though, and there is a very real need for processing equipment and technology, which would ease the heavy workload, especially for the women who wish for presses for palm nuts, graters for cassava, hullers for the rice. But it isn't obvious that large-scale mechanization, huge tractors, and other tremendously expensive farm machinery would solve problems in this setting. They would need extensive maintenance, easily accessible spare parts, and require a lot of costly fuel. Mechanizing family farmers with large farm machinery could snare them in the debt trap that has wiped out so many family farms in North America and Europe.

Industrial agriculture and the corporate food system already contribute about a third of the greenhouse gases on earth, accelerating climate change that so threatens food production.[88] The proponents of "modern" industrial agriculture in Africa – involving capital-intensive and heavy mechanization, consolidation of small farms into immense plantations, the reliance on "improved" or genetically modified seeds from agrochemical corporations, chemical fertilizers and pesticides, and large-scale irrigation – maintain that this is the way to assure future food production in the face of climate change. Some very powerful and moneyed groups have combined forces to push policies to promote industrial agriculture, including the World Bank Group, the Bill & Melinda Gates Foundation, and the governments of the United States, United Kingdom, Denmark, and The Netherlands.[89]

Critics say that, on the contrary, industrial agriculture will merely accelerate and exacerbate climate change and increase dependence on unsustainable use of fossil fuels, large amounts of toxic chemical inputs, and massive irrigation. They point to a spate of recent and urgent "wake-up" calls by scientists for a complete paradigm shift to agro-ecological intensive agriculture,[90] and the many ways this can be done on smallholder farms with some fairly simple agroforestry and agricultural techniques.[91] This would help close the "yield gap" – the difference between current yields and attainable yields using available technology on family farms.[92]

The UN Special Rapporteur on the Right to Food has warned that farmers around the world need to wean themselves off fossil fuels.[93] Africa's farmers won't need to do that, if they are allowed to keep their land and their farms.

Perhaps one of the reasons Africa's smallholder farms – and the foods they produce – have generally not been given their due respect is because it can be difficult for a northern foreigner to grasp how a family farm in the tropics works, to figure out just what's what in those fields and woodlands. Family farms in much of Africa are extraordinary for their complexity and diversity, at least where they have not been reduced to mere fractions of an acre that are cropped continuously because of land scarcity and population pressure. Usually only small areas are cultivated each year, often with a dizzying number of unfamiliar (to the foreigner) crops growing in no discernible (to the foreigner) pattern, where trees may dot the fields or be so numerous they resemble a forest, when in fact they may be a "tree-crop" plantation involving all sorts of perennial crops. They may also be fallows.

Customary land tenure can make it even more complex. On much of the continent, land has traditionally been held communally and shared out according to individual needs, and it is often in the custody of traditional rulers but informally "owned" by families who have used it for generations and have thus developed usufruct rights. Boundaries may be known only to the users of the land and their neighbours, who have (mostly but by no means always) managed to get along and avoid major conflicts, despite the fact that all of this is unwritten and there are no title deeds. No real estate market. No buying or selling. No fences.

For those who believe that all of nature's gifts can and should be monetized and privatized, this is anathema. The World Bank and the American version thereof, the Millennium Challenge Corporation set up under President George W. Bush, believe that land should be privatized and turned into a commodity that can be bought and sold, used as collateral, speculated upon for profit. Their critics say they are betting against the small farm and gambling with the future of Africa's food.[94] Nevertheless, there is a powerful push for privatization of land in many African countries, although so far traditional land tenure combined with some contradictory colonial laws putting land in the hands of the state remain the norm on much of the continent.

That is not to say that land reform isn't necessary; social activists have been calling for it for years. Women produce more than half of the food in Africa, and need to have access to and secure tenure of land they farm. So do the youth who desperately need employment, incomes, and a food-secure future. Knowing that your land is not about to be expropriated by more powerful figures in society – politicians, corporate elites, traditional rulers, foreign investors – is an incentive to land-users to invest long-term in the land with agroforestry, by planting slow-growing tree crops and reducing the environmental ravages caused by slash-and-burn agriculture. But at the moment, much of the work on land reform appears designed to rapidly privatize land so it can be easily acquired by foreign investors.[95] If that happens, family farms will be condemned to extinction even before they've been recognized as the basis for rural livelihoods and economies, social stability and, of course, magnificent foods.

To grasp how family farms are laid out, how they function and what marvelous edibles and drinkables they produce, the unschooled foreigner needs to do a lot of walking, looking, asking, and listening. That's what I'm doing in the heat of a Sierra Leonean afternoon, as I trek along behind a group of agricultural extension officers and farmers from the small village of Yaamu, not too far from the hard-luck diamond town of Koidu.

We are moving through what looks like unkempt bush – messy, unplanned, and chaotic. Rural households work several kinds of agricultural systems at the same time. They have their "upland farms," the fields where rice and all manner of vegetables, beans, tubers, and grains are cultivated after fallows are cleared, usually by burning. After a few years, they leave these to fallow again, sometimes for up to twenty years or even longer if land is plentiful. After that, they may again clear the fallow to make way for an upland farm.

Upland farms are distinct from the rice fields in the lowland "bolilands" that flood each year during the rainy season. Some of the rice paddies are nestled in inland valley swamps, flanked by trees, and around them are small plots of other crops here and there in and around the village. There are also dense "home gardens," or backyard plots where households cultivate an astonishing assortment of vegetable and leafy green crops, and sometimes fruit trees and medicinal plants as well.

At the end of this lesson in farm geography and this walk in the heat, I've been promised a reward, something over and above my actual quest to get to know the lay of a smallholder's land in eastern Sierra Leone. Our ultimate destination is a particular tree in a particular farm field, where I've been told we'll find "bamboo wine" on tap.

Bamboo wine is a delicacy that comes, not from bamboo, but from raffia palms, another generous and giving tree that grows wild throughout West and Central Africa. The tree is like a building supplies store where everything is free for the taking. Every part of the raffia palm is used – its leaves, branches, fruits, and roots. From it, rural people harvest the materials needed to make thatch and twine, baskets and furniture. Topping it all, the raffia palms produce bamboo wine and lots of it; a tapped tree can produce about ten litres a day for about three months.[96] Unfortunately, the tapping also caps off the life of the tree, eventually killing it. For this reason, tappers generally choose only old trees.

Today, two tappers from Yaamu are leading us down garden paths towards the promised tree. We've gone past backyard gardens, where groundnuts and vegetables are growing around various shrubs and trees, through well-managed tree-crop plantations where cocoa and coffee grow underneath large shade trees that also have multiple products and uses, and we've now moved onto the upland farm. We're well into the dry season and this field, planted with more than a dozen vegetables and grains, was harvested months ago. In its centre stands an A-framed thatched hut, about the size of a family tent one might see in a North American campsite. The agricultural extension officers tell me the family who cultivated this upland farm camped in the hut during the farming season. The word for such farm huts is *mansion*.

Past the little *mansion* of thatch, at the far end of the farm clearing, stands the tapped raffia palm. We watch while the lead tapper climbs a ladder propped up against the tree. The ladder is fashioned from a hefty pole of bamboo into which footholds have been carved. The second tapper follows him up. Both men perch precariously up there on the frond-like branches while they sample the tree's brew from the large yellow plastic jug that has been collecting the wine since dawn.

The rest of us mill about below, waiting. Someone pulls a carrot-sized cassava tuber from the ground and peels it with a pocketknife before offering it to me. I'm curious about possible cyanide content, which I understood was a risk of eating raw or poorly peeled cassava. But they assure me this is sweet cassava, safe to eat uncooked, unlike the bitter cassava variety that contains cyanide. I take a bite. It's crunchy and delicious as a garden-fresh carrot.

The group is becoming quite boisterous and laughter reverberates in the farm clearing. Most of the banter is in Mende, the language of the main ethnic group in the east and south of Sierra Leone, with a little Krio, the nation's *lingua franca*, thrown in here and there. They are teasing the tappers; the two men appear to have settled in comfortably way up in the tree for a good long drinking session. They certainly aren't hurrying down the bamboo ladder with the jug of wine. There is speculation that if they drink much more, they will just tumble out of the tree.

When they finally do decide to return to earth, the group quickly organizes a couple of plastic cups – no idea where they came from – and the bamboo wine tasting begins. The clear liquid is tart, but also smooth on the tongue. It seems very light, but perhaps deceptively so. After a few sips, I can't decide whether the slight dizziness I feel comes from the raging afternoon heat or the bamboo wine. Either way, it seems wise to head back to the village, to get out of the sun and to stop imbibing that heavenly nectar extracted directly from a tree.

In one afternoon, deep in rural Sierra Leone I've lerned so much and experienced two very big pleasures. One is the camaraderie and good humour that abounds among my hosts. The other is the natural delicacy, bamboo wine. My next mission is to learn more about another interesting food that was brought to my attention that day in the upland farm.

13

Miracle melon soup by Angela & Co.

Among my people in West Africa, cooking is an art form we naturally start to learn from a very tender age … By the time a child is old enough, she is able to cook any meal merely by sight, smell and taste.

– Rachel Massaquoi
*Foods of Sierra Leone and
Other West African Countries*

While we waited for the tappers to descend the palm tree with the bamboo wine that afternoon, I kicked at a cluster of pale green melons, about the shape and size of ostrich eggs, which were scattered about in front of the little farming *mansion*. I asked my companions – farmers and agricultural agents – what they were.

"*Egusi*," came the reply.

"*Egusi*?" I inquired. "Is it a gourd? Like a calabash you can use as a bowl or a serving implement?"

"No, no, no. It's not a calabash. You eat it," said one of my companions.

"It makes a fine, fine soup," said another. He breaks open

one of the *egusi* gourds and withdraws large white seeds that, to my eye, could be mistaken for those from any squash or pumpkin.

This is in early 2011. At this point I've been kicking around Africa for a long, long time. I've visited more than half the countries on the continent and lived in seven of them. I've gone from being addressed as "Mademoiselle" when I first landed in Niger, to "Madam" or "Aunty" when I was raising my children, and have now become "Mami" or "older woman" in Sierra Leone. And in all this time, I've never heard of *egusi*, a principal player in many West and Central African dishes. Maybe I just never asked the right questions.

I now know, but only because I stumbled across it in that abandoned upland farm in Sierra Leone and then belatedly started asking questions, that *egusi* (*Citrullus colocynthis*) is sometimes known as the "miracle melon." It's a highly nutritious crop native to Africa.[97] *Egusi* seeds are composed of nearly 50 percent edible oil and another 30 percent pure protein. Like so many indigenous crops, *egusi* melons are extremely versatile and a mainstay of cuisines in parts of Africa. The seeds can be used to produce cooking oil, roasted and eaten as snacks, or ground up like peanut butter. They can also be compacted into patties as a meat substitute, or soaked in water and fermented and dried to produce a heady condiment known in much of coastal West Africa as *ogiri*. *Ogiri* can also be made with fermented sesame seeds, another indigenous African crop. Raw *egusi* seeds are often ground up to form a paste used to thicken and flavour stews and soups. They can also be ground and mixed with honey and water for a high-protein baby food, even a substitute for breast milk if none is available.

Egusi plants spread and cover the ground as they grow, helping to suppress weeds, so farmers often intercrop it. It is also easy to cultivate because of its resistance to pests. And as I saw in the field near Yaamu, the *egusi* melons can be left in the field for a long time without rotting.[98] Once the seeds have been harvested, they store very well so there is little post-harvest waste or loss.

Egusi is another of the "lost" crops of Africa that scientists say could provide much more than just food. *Egusi* has the potential to improve the quality of life throughout the continent if it were promoted to improve nutrition and food security, contribute to diverse agro-ecological farms, and drive rural development from the farm up.[99] A miraculous melon, indeed.

But at the dawn of 2011, I know none of these things. Nor have I – at least to my knowledge – tasted *egusi*. It is Angela, an accommodating young extension officer in Kailahun, who offers to teach me how to prepare *egusi* soup. This starts with a trip to the market in Kailahun.

Once a thriving trading hub for cross-border trade between Sierra Leone, Guinea, and Liberia, Kailahun was decimated during Sierra Leone's civil war, which began very close to the town when the rebels marched across the border from Liberia.

For all that, however, and for all the destruction, Kailahun – like Sierra Leone itself – is spunky, resilient, and renewing itself. Despite the crumbling and broken buildings, naked power poles, and pitted roads of mud and rock, homes are being rebuilt, farms revived, and the market is full of foodstuffs. Traders come and go with trucks laden with fruit, cocoa, coffee, and produce bound for large commercial centres in the country, although they may find themselves stuck for days at a time in muddy quagmires that swallow the dirt roads during the rainy season. Small churches echo with the sounds of prayers and inspirational hymns. Calls to prayer from the town's mosques serenade dawn and dusk. There are posters all over town advertising locales that broadcast, with the help of generators and satellite television, the much-loved football (soccer) matches from the English Premier League and the Champions' League that have become something like an additional religion for the masses in so many parts of the world.

Under the weight of the mid-afternoon heat, the Kailahun market is subdued and sluggish. Angela is anything but.

She moves at a relentless pace through the warren of stalls. Her diminutive height is an asset; she doesn't have to duck to avoid bumping her head on the rickety sticks overhead, which support bits of cloth or plastic and sharp-edged metal roofing sheets for shade. Before we've purchased a single grain of rice or *egusi* seed, I've knocked my head twice on these ceilings.

We agree it is wise to buy plenty, enough for a meal of *egusi* soup to feed at least a couple of dozen people. Inevitably when there is a large meal being prepared, numerous unexpected visitors will appear. I'm sure this will be the case in the small guesthouse where we are staying. It doubles as a regional office for a development agency and it is always difficult to tell who actually works there as secretary, extension officer, watchman, driver, and who is just there to visit someone who works there. It goes without saying that any food there is will be shared with everyone who happens to be present.

The market is a showcase for the rich assortment of local farms and fallows and forests. Angela is patient with me as I quiz her about what is on display. There are slices of dried bush mango seeds or *dika* nuts from the tree *Irvingia gabonensis,* the nutritious condiments used to thicken stews and soups, which grows in the humid lowland forests (or what's left of them) from Cameroon across to Senegal. In Sierra Leone they are known as *boboi* and *An-gbare,* among other local names.

There are also finger-sized mahogany-coloured slivers of nuts, which Angela identifies as *tola* or *kpei* (*Beilschmiedia mannii*), another important food that comes from wild trees. *Tola* nuts are ground to a fine brown powder, which imbues a stew or sauce with an extra layer of flavour. The *tola* powder is also for sale in the market, sold per "cup" (the tiny tin from Peak evaporated milk is used as a standard measure for this). These days one of these tiny tins of *tola* can cost nearly US$2.50. It's likely to become still more expensive because the wood from this tree has long been popular in international markets and exported from

West and Central African forests. In Sierra Leone, it is known as "African teak" and logging is decimating its population. This is tragic for a tree that has more uses than you can shake a *tola* stick at.

The database of Plant Resources of Tropical Africa expounds on the numerous non-timber uses of this immensely valuable tree: "The pounded bark is eaten with rice as an appetizer. The fragrant leaves are pounded in water, and after pressing through muslin the liquid is drunk. In Liberia the flowers are commonly used to flavour rice and other food. The fruit is eaten and is an ingredient of sauces. The seed is a popular food commonly sold in West African markets; it is roasted and ground before consumption, and added as a condiment and enrichment to soups, rice, and vegetables. The seed yields an edible oil. *Beilschmiedia mannii* is planted as a shade tree for coffee in Liberia. A decoction of the bark and leaves is used as a lotion to treat headache. Pounded fruits are used to treat cough, bronchitis, intercostal pain, rheumatism, and dysentery, whereas a decoction of the fruit is used in the treatment of diarrhea in calves."[100]

Although I'm keen to buy and try the *tola,* Angela insists we don't need it for our *egusi* soup today. She pauses in front of a wooden table full of small piles of hot peppers, Maggi cubes, and some tiny bags of very tiny shrimp. She says the shrimp are caught in local streams and rivers and add flavour to soups and stews. But when I suggest we buy some, the market women around us suddenly launch into a furious discussion in Mende. Finally, Angela turns to me and relays the message from the vendors, who think this is not food for white people. If I eat these shrimps, she warns me, I'll erupt in black spots. They advise me to buy a shrimp-flavoured Maggi cube instead. I give up and give in. Maggi it is.

The only chicken for sale in the Kailahun market doesn't involve any parts of the fowl that I consider edible. There are gruesome little piles of chicken feet on one table, meaty pink chicken tails on another. Angela says these amputated chicken bits come from America. She won't eat them, but women hard-pressed for money do sometimes buy the imported chicken scraps, unable to afford local meat or fish to put in their sauces or soups.

But I've told her that for our *egusi* soup, money is not an issue. So we cut no corners, spurn the imported chicken bits that are exuding an unhealthy smell in the heat, and then splurge on smoked fish for 15,000 Leones (about US$3.75 at the time).

This is what we purchase for the *egusi* soup in the market.

2 cups of *egusi* seeds for 3,000 Leones (about US75¢)

1 handful of hot peppers for 1,500 Leones ($1.25)

1 shrimp-flavoured Maggi bouillon cube for 1,500 Leones (25¢)

9 cups of white rice for 9,000 Leones ($2.25)

4 "eggplants" that look like purplish green unripe tomatoes for 2,000 Leones (50¢)

4 bitter balls *(jakato)* for 2,000 Leones (50¢)

1 tiny plastic bag of salt for 500 Leones (12¢)

1 tiny can of imported Chinese tomato paste for 1,000 Leones (25¢)

1 handful of okra (gumbo) for 500 Leones (12¢)

3 onions (imported ones from Holland, no local ones available) for 600 Leones (15¢)

3 bags of charcoal for cooking for 1,500 Leones (about 38¢)

Grand total? Just over US$10 for everything. For me, this seems remarkably inexpensive, given that we intend to feed twenty or more people. But again, it's an exorbitant sum if you are on a more typical Sierra Leonean budget with an income of less than a dollar or two a day that has to be stretched and squeezed to feed, clothe, and school a large family, as are two or three million people in this country.

Back at the guesthouse/office – a small bungalow with a backyard of gravel and grass – Angela sets to work unpacking the food. She is immediately joined by a willing group of volunteers, young women who seem to materialize out of nowhere. When it comes to cooking in Africa, especially when it's traditional food that has to be prepared from scratch, helping hands are nearly always available and welcome. But it is quickly becoming obvious to me that Angela doesn't consider *my* hands very useful. I have tried to help, picking up the pestle, ready to pound the *egusi* seeds into a paste in the wooden mortar. But I make only a few ineffective and poorly aimed strikes before Angela gently removes the pestle from my grip.

So I've been relegated to the steps, observer status only. Two young men arrive bearing a charcoal stove, a locally made and very practical device, a step up from the traditional three-stone hearth. The charcoal stove consists of two hollow metal boxes with a shallow compartment for the charcoal, over which the curved-bottom pots will be placed.

Angela starts by peeling the eggplants. She is bent double to do this, with the effortless ease of a yoga master happily holding the pretzel-like pose of an Intense Forward Stretch. In the same position, she then carves the eggplants into thin slices that fall into a plastic bowl to soak in salt water. This, she says, will make them cook well.

Another young woman, whom I gather is the sister or daughter of one of the development agents, takes over the pounding of the *egusi* seeds in the mortar. Another arranges the charcoal in the small stove, fanning it with a plastic bowl to encourage its quiet combustion. Then Angela goes at the bitter balls (*jakato*), cutting them in half and rinsing them in a bowl of water, along with peeled and chunked onions, and two handfuls of hot red peppers.

I feel as if I'm trying to monitor three simultaneous tennis matches. The young woman pounding the *egusi* now scoops the whitish paste into a bowl, and, using a bucket of water that a young man keeps refilling from a neighbourhood well, she meticulously washes out the mortar. Then she puts the onion chunks and hot peppers into it and goes to work pounding those.

The pestle and mortar resonate like a base drum. She pauses long enough to squeeze the water out of the eggplant slices that Angela has left to soak, and then tosses those into the mortar too.

Next Angela turns her attention to the smoked fish, a fresh-water species she calls "bony fish." She deftly peels away the skin and pulls strips of the flesh from the bones. She plops them into a pot along with the Maggi cube. She covers it and says it will need to steam for a while.

Meanwhile, someone else mixes the *egusi* paste with water until it is milky and thick, then sieves it to remove the "bran." In a second pot, where water is boiling already (when did that get put there?), she now mixes the *egusi*, and the mixture of pepper, *jakato*, and onion and leaves it all to simmer.

Then she drains the water off the fish (into the grass and gravel of the backyard) and removes the remaining large bones, breaking up the flesh into smaller pieces and adding them to the *egusi* and vegetables along with the *jakato*.

Now it's like trying to watch six tennis matches simultaneously. Or maybe it's more like an orchestra playing a symphony without any need for a conductor or musical scores. Everyone seems to know their part; there is no discussion or dissension about how this or that should be done, or indeed what should be done. The harmony in the outdoor kitchen for this impromptu meal makes me wonder if the adage about too many cooks spoiling the broth doesn't apply here the way it does in my house, where just two people in the kitchen – my husband and myself – cannot manage more than a few minutes of trying to share tasks without discord.

I've given up trying to compose a detailed, step-by-step recipe for the meal they are preparing. Angela tells me she's already boiled the okra and then pounded and added it to the rice before it was tipped into a very large pot of water for cooking. The okra, she says, makes the rice smooth and easy to swallow. The tomato paste from the tiny tin is the last thing to go into the *egusi* soup, which now simmers away and imbues the outdoor kitchen with an aroma that makes my stomach grumble impatiently.

Their skills and dexterity at preparing food without all the amenities of a modern kitchen are, to me, amazing. For me, a kitchen means running water, countertops, and level surfaces for mixing and cutting. Even with a cutting board and the sharp blade of the knife aimed away from my hands, I can pretty much count on taking off a slice of skin on one of my fingers about once a month in my North American kitchen.

I've spent countless hours watching African women cutting up onions or tomatoes or tubers that they hold in their hands while hacking into them, blade towards the palm of the hand, and never seen one inflict a wound. I wonder if it has something to do with the way meals are prepared. In more traditional outdoor kitchens, or under a thatch awning or in small cook-houses required during rainy seasons, women tend to do most of the food preparation while sitting on small stools. They work quickly and efficiently but never appear harried or hurried.

Preparations now complete and sauce bubbling away in one large pot, rice in another, Angela and the others have begun to wash all the utensils using a bucket of water and a large bowl into which they pile the cleaned dishes and knives and spoons. From somewhere, they have come up with large metal platters and bowls that they lay out on a table on the back veranda, ready for serving.

The late afternoon sun suddenly disappears behind angry storm clouds swollen and bruised indigo by pent-up vapours. Moments later, a tree-bending gale blasts through. We seek shelter on the back porch. Lightning thrashes the horizon and torrential rains pummel the earth. Steam oozes out of the pots on the stove. When the storm has passed, as quickly as it rolled in, the air is delectably cool. The sun reappears for a few minutes before setting, and Angela and her competent team of cooks dish up the *egusi* soup and rice on a half-dozen large platters.

Four of these are spirited out to the front porch of the house, where a dozen men have gathered to play checkers and to banter about soccer and politics, favourite themes in the country. Two of the plates remain out back with us, the women.

No one asks me for my verdict on the *egusi* soup, but I offer it anyway. "Absolutely delicious!" I say, savouring the rich medley of flavours in the soup soaking into the hearty country rice. The hot pepper gives the whole meal a powerful kick, a culinary exclamation mark.

"Beats anything I've eaten in five-star hotels in Africa!" I add, reflecting on my one culinary experience at a five-star hotel on the continent, the utterly forgettable fare I'd had in the Mount Kenya Safari Club.

Angela and the other cooks smile at my enthusiasm. But they don't respond. It dawns on me that none has a clue what I mean by a five-star hotel.

When we've emptied the two plates, Angela smiles and says, "So now you can cook *egusi*!"

I don't want to disappoint her, so I nod my agreement. But I couldn't put that meal together on my own, using those utensils in the outdoor kitchen, if my life depended on it.

14

A history shaped by rice

Perceptions of a continent populated by hapless farmers and herders in need of European instruction are inaccurate and fail to do justice to Africa's deep botanical legacy ...

– Judith A. Carney and Richard N. Rosomoff
In the Shadow of Slavery:
Africa's Botanical Legacy in the Atlantic World

Never dump your old pot just because you have bought a new one.

– Kenyan proverb
The Wisdom of Africa
Pete Lewenstein, editor

Sierra Leone may be best known around the world for its diamonds, and, more particularly, the so-called "blood" diamonds that fuelled its civil war and later inspired a Hollywood film. But the loom upon which much of Sierra Leone's history has been woven is not diamonds at all – it's rice.

Although rice is typically associated more with Asia than it is with Africa, it shouldn't be. Two separate species of rice evolved in two very separate parts of the world. One, *Oryza sativa,* comes from Asia. The second rice species, *Oryza glaberrima,* was born and bred in West Africa.[101] Farmers in the bend in the Niger River, between the ancient towns of Segou and Timbuktu in what is today Mali, domesticated the precious little grain about 3,000 years ago, working with the wild ancestor *Oryza barthii* to transform it into *Oryza glaberrima.* From there, the crop spread and became a major staple food across a huge expanse of West Africa.[102]

The people of the region became expert rice cultivators and their knowledge of the crop and its many varieties was profound. They knew which soils tolerated which varieties. They developed a rice variety with a wide canopy that shaded out weeds. They produced cultivars that floated and could grow in deep water, others that would thrive in different latitudes, seasons, swampy areas and drier uplands, and some that resisted local pests and diseases. They developed varieties that matured early and others that matured late. They took advantage of the smorgasbord of genetic variability contained in the tiny grains and harnessed it to improve production, reduce risks of crop loss, and assure their own food supply. They bred the crop to suit their needs and they knew how, when, and where to plant each seed variety.

The early European explorers greatly admired the technical prowess of the African rice growers – their sophisticated systems of dikes, their skills at transplanting, and their intensive cultivation practices. At some point, probably in the sixteenth century, the Portuguese introduced the Asian species of rice to the farmers on what they dubbed the Rice Coast, today the nations of Guinea and Sierra Leone.

The West Africans' expertise as rice farmers turned out to be a poisoned chalice. In the early 1700s, the nefarious effects of globalization and the spreading tentacles of European capitalism were about to be felt in the hinterlands of West Africa, and nowhere more so than in the area that is now the Republic of

Sierra Leone. Unbeknownst to the people living there, who were farming their rice and mixed crops and generally minding their own business in villages surrounded by forest, across the ocean big ideas were being hatched that would soon put an end to their well-being.

Colonists had acquired vast land holdings in Georgia and South Carolina and they were looking for a crop that would transform them into wealthy plantation owners. They decided on rice. But they were land barons who needed knowledgeable and skilled rice growers to do the hard work on their plantations. The rice magnates turned their sights on the people of the Rice Coast.

There was already a slave-trading castle on Bunce Island in the mouth of the Sierra Leone River, about twenty kilometres upriver from the present-day capital, Freetown. The tiny island – about a half-kilometre long and a hundred metres wide – had the ignominious distinction of being the main slave trading operation for the Rice Coast. It was controlled by the London firm of Grant, Sargent and Oswald. The principal partner, Scottish merchant Richard Oswald, developed a close relationship with Henry Laurens, a wealthy rice baron and slave-trader in South Carolina. They rebuilt the fort that the British had established in the 1600s and put together a fleet of boats to cruise up and down the coast in search of slaves for shipping west from Bunce Island. In the last half of the eighteenth century, these two men orchestrated the mass export of human beings from the island to the Americas. During the 1700s, an estimated 100,000 Africans were chained up and shipped from the Rice Coast to the Carolinas, to sugar and tobacco plantations in the West Indies, and elsewhere in the Americas.

In South Carolina and Georgia they fetched premium prices because of their expertise in rice cultivation. Their knowledge and their labour in rice paddies transformed South Carolina in the eighteenth century into the richest state in the North American colonies and Charleston into a fashionable and wealthy city of slave-owning plantation owners.[103]

Many of the descendants of the slaves in the Carolinas, the Gullah people, still use words and names common in what is today Sierra Leone. Some, however, made their way back to their homeland long ago, in the late 1700s. They were former slaves whom the British granted freedom in exchange for their loyalty during the American War of Independence. After the war, they were ferried from New York to the British colony to the north, to Nova Scotia in what would become Canada, where they were to be granted land.

The land they were given in Nova Scotia at Birchtown was as rocky and infertile as the North Atlantic climate was inhospitable, causing suffering and death. Eventually, their leader, Thomas Peters, went to London to negotiate the return to Africa for those who wished to go. In 1792, close to 1,200 of the Black Loyalists were granted passage back to Africa, where they founded Freetown for the newly created Sierra Leone Company. This tragic cycle of human suffering was shaped largely by rice and African prowess at rice growing and breeding. This was poignantly documented in Lawrence Hill's 2007 novel *The Book of Negroes*.

There's a saying in Sierra Leone that if you haven't eaten rice today, you haven't eaten. On average, each person in Sierra Leone eats over a hundred kilograms of rice each year. And once upon a time, Sierra Leone produced enough rice to feed not just itself, but also to export to neighbouring countries. But then came the discovery of diamonds and a rush to dig them, and later the oppressive kleptomania of the government of Siaka Stevens. Local rice production could no longer satisfy the growing population. Stevens established the one-party state and seized control of the country's diamonds in the 1980s, leading Sierra Leone into steep political and economic decline, despotism, and military rule.

There were also "structural adjustment programs" or SAPs, recipes for austerity from the World Bank and International Monetary Fund, which were supposed to ease economic malaise.

Instead, as these financial institutions eventually admitted, they merely exacerbated it. Political stagnation, social inequities, corruption, and collapsing infrastructure led to extreme disenchantment that fed into the vicious conflict that began in 1991 when rebels marched into the country from neighbouring Liberia. The civil war was caused by deep-rooted injustice and a deficit of democracy, but it lasted as long as it did because of diamonds, which kept warlords in money to procure weapons.[104] By the time peace was restored in 2002, tens of thousands of people had died and the country's infrastructure and agricultural sector had been decimated.

Slowly, in the years that followed, agricultural production picked up again. By 2011, and with locally grown rice leading the way, agriculture – most of it smallholder – was contributing about half of the country's gross domestic product.

Local varieties are known as "country" rice in Sierra Leone. They are generally pinkish brown and much richer in flavour (and vitamin B and protein)[105] than the imported Asian and American white rice that fills African markets. But when it comes to Sierra Leone, it seems that eating local isn't always an easy thing to do. At least that's what I'm finding as I set out to hunt for country rice in the capital, Freetown.

I start with upmarket restaurants, thinking the establishments that attract foreigners might wish to showcase local produce and foods. First on my list is the string of bars and restaurants along Lumley Beach. The beach is a magnificent jewel in the west of Freetown, ten kilometres of white sandy beach blessed with warm and generally tranquil water safe for swimming. For the most part, it's protected from the worst of the garbage run-off and sewage that collects along much of the city's coastline. The beach is a magnet for expatriates and well-heeled Sierra Leoneans who frequent the beach bars and restaurants, the casinos and clubs set up along the strip. Many are Chinese and Lebanese owned. There are a couple of upscale hotels and garden restaurants that serve no Sierra Leonean dishes at all.

The waiters along the beach find my requests for local "country" rice quite amusing and even surprising. They explain patiently to me that the only rice on their menus is "English" rice. They laugh when I quip that no rice is produced in England so there can be no such thing as English rice.

Safi, a very helpful and efficient waitress in a Lebanese eatery, admits that at home she eats only country rice because it tastes much better and is far more nutritious. But, she explains, the people who frequent Lumley Beach bars and restaurants generally don't like local dishes. Indeed, there is no Sierra Leonean food on the menu, apart from the fresh shrimps, barracuda, red snapper, sole, calamari, or lobster that local fishermen bring in from the waters beyond the beach. Eventually, it becomes a well-rehearsed routine. Each time I order a meal, I ask for country rice on the side. And each time Safi laughs and tells me there is only English rice.

Next, I tackle the upscale bars and restaurants clustered around Man o' War Bay, a stone's throw from Lumley Beach. These also appeal to the affluent development and diplomatic crowd. They also draw business people, the men (and they are mostly men) involved in the mining and agricultural sectors as foreign investors flock to the country to get their hands on minerals, oil, and farmland. They come from everywhere – Belgium, Canada, China, Germany, India, Lebanon, Malaysia, The Netherlands, South Africa, the U.K., the U.S., Switzerland, Vietnam, you name it. Many are of a swashbuckling breed that have a particular fondness for fragile, post-conflict countries like Sierra Leone, where laws are flexible, politicians particularly malleable, and where diamonds, gold, murky business opportunities – and young women desperate for income – abound.

Southeast Asian, Lebanese, Chinese, Indian, and British owned, these restaurants and hotels also serve only white rice. No local cuisine to be had. Then it is up the steep mountain road that winds its adventurous way to the exclusive Country Lodge. With its spectacular panoramic view of Lumley Beach and the golf club far below, its tennis courts, swimming pool, gym, and fine-dining room decked out in gilded bric-a-brac, there isn't much country flavour in the Lodge at all. And yes, they have no country rice.

Nor is there any local rice a little way down the mountain-side, in the Mamba Point bar and restaurant. It's a drinking and eating spot that draws UN experts, youthful NGO development workers, and high-flying (and sometimes bottom-feeding) tycoons in equal measure in its air-conditioned bar with the immense flat-screen television tuned nearly non-stop to sports channels, especially ones broadcasting live soccer matches from England or Europe. There is a sushi bar off to one side.

When I ask for country rice in the Mamba Point, the con-genial waitress laughs. You'd think I'd just asked for a plate of braised Brontosaurus ribs and not a plate of the nation's home-grown staple. I ask her why she finds it so amusing that I want Sierra Leonean rice. She informs me that clients don't like it. I ask how she can be so sure they don't like it if the restaurant doesn't offer clients the choice. She shakes her head and laughs some more, as if I am trying to be funny and her job is to indulge her customer's offbeat sense of humour.

Eventually, once I move away from Lumley Beach and the lofty locales of Freetown and venture onto main thoroughfares, I do find a few small eateries that specialize in local food. There are also countless individual vendors on roadsides, selling rice (mostly imported) and various sauces, grilled fish or beef, interesting sand-wiches in which doughy rounds of bread are rubbed with a hint of sardines or filled with sweetened condensed milk. Or slath-ered with industrial-grade mayonnaise that comes from giant jars, which roadside vendors place in the hot sun, day after day after day, to satisfy the growing mania for the stuff. I am initially surprised that this doesn't make people sick until someone explains to me that store-bought mayonnaise contains pasteurized eggs, lemon, and vinegar – so refrigeration is to maintain its flavour and colour, not food safety.

The menu at the Balmaya Restaurant on Motor Main Road offers fresh mango juice, *olele* (a spicy steamed dish generally made from ground cowpeas, fish, hot pepper, and palm oil) and a daily "African dish" at international prices, which its well-heeled clientele can certainly afford. At midday, the place is chock-a-block with United Nations, business, and development people.

There is also the Bamboo Hut, my personal favourite, because it is modest, inviting, expertly managed and run, and it serves wonderful Sierra Leonean dishes – cow foot soup, beans, cassava chips, and – at last – country rice! It is homey and welcoming; it feels like eating at a friend's house.

At least it did, when it was open. When I returned in 2013 to get some thoughts from the Bamboo Hut staff on why so few formal eating establishments showcase local cuisines, I find it has been shut up tight, another victim of the project to turn the narrow Wilkinson Road into a massive four-lane boulevard.

It isn't just in Freetown restaurants that cater to elites and expatriates that local food is hard to find. In Koidu, the epicentre of the country's diamond-mining operations, the hotel-bar-restaurant-casino that caters to those on the glittering end of the diamond deals is on the outskirts of town. It's set behind very tall walls topped with razor wire. I've spent many hours in the restaurant observing and eavesdropping on the larger-than-life clients that this Wild-West diamond town and hotel complex attract.

At the hotel's restaurant, a middle-aged Lebanese woman tends to the bar, but most of her attention is on the television that is permanently tuned to Arabic stations beaming soap operas around the world. The waitresses are Sierra Leonean. The menu is quite limited – you can eat chicken with chips or rice, steak with chips or rice, beef brochette (kebab) with chips or rice. Not quite spam with spam, but not all that far off.

None of the drinks are local. There is not even any Star beer, which is the closest thing to local beer you can buy in the country. While not locally owned, Star is at least brewed in-country by the Sierra Leone Brewery, a member of the multinational Heineken Group, headquartered in Amsterdam. The soft drinks all come in cans, imported, no locally bottled soft drinks or fruit juices on tap. Even the bottled water is imported from Lebanon.

On one visit, I inquire if the rice is local.

"No," says the sullen young waitress.

"Where is it from?" I ask.

"I don't know. It's white rice. It's not local." She says this with what comes across as pride. Perhaps others have inquired before me to ensure that it *isn't* local?

"How about the chicken?" I ask. "Is it local?"

"No."

"The beef?" I inquire, hopefully. "Is it local?"

"No," she says, drawing out the word on an exasperated sigh. "Madam, nothing is local here." I can't tell if she thinks this is a good thing or bad thing.

This reminds me of a conversation I once had with a waitress in a pancake house in western Canada. Before ordering, I asked if the maple syrup was real (no), if the fruit was fresh (no), and then if the whipped cream was a hydrogenated vegetable oil in a spray can or real cream, which came from a real cow. Spreading her feet and heaving a sigh, the waitress informed me, "Look lady, *nothing* is real here."

Like the waitress in Koidu, I couldn't tell if she was genuinely tired of my tedious demands, or somehow equally perturbed that nothing was fresh, local, or real, and happy to find a customer who cared the way she did.

Why don't Sierra Leone's capital and its larger urban areas offer more restaurants to showcase its own foods and dishes, the way Asian, Latin American, European and Mediterranean, some Middle Eastern, and other countries do? Is this a legacy of colonialism? Is it because so many of the restaurant and hotel owners are Chinese, or Lebanese, or European themselves? Is it because there is a tendency for some *nouveau riche* who can afford to dine out to try to rub out their own reality and replace it with an imported veneer that portends to be superior and urbane? Or is it because those who frequent the upmarket restaurants and bars simply want a meal out to be foods they wouldn't get at home?

I don't have an answer to those questions, but I'm guessing it may be a little of all of the above. Thankfully, it's still easy for me to get very good local food at friends' homes.

15

Cooking with Thelma

We often rightly worry about the loss of one's language because of its potential to endanger the identity of a group of people. However, we should also apply our anxiety to the disappearance of traditional foods ... they not only nourish us physically, but they sustain, protect, feed and personalize the people that cook them.

– Rachel Massaquoi
Foods of Sierra Leone and Other
West African Countries

Thelma Turay is indefatigable. She's slim, trim, and has the loping stride of a much taller woman. I tower over her by several inches but I can't keep up. She moves with grace and practiced ease through the congested labyrinth of the market in Makeni. It's a blistering afternoon and we're on a shopping expedition to buy the ingredients for a home-cooked meal of country rice and a sauce that Thelma intends to make with the amaranth leaf called *grin*.

I am having trouble trying to imagine what this town would have looked like just a decade earlier, when it was in the vicious grip of rebels and the terror they spread. At that time it was the headquarters for the notorious leader of the Revolutionary United Front, the late Foday Sankoh who died while awaiting trial before the UN-backed Special Court for Sierra Leone.

But today, peace is more than a decade old and Makeni is rebel-free. It is pulsating with the noise, bustle, honking traffic, and congestion of any rapidly growing African city. There's been a flood of foreigners converging on the area to work in massive iron ore mines and on the Addax Bioenergy sugarcane plantations. A new luxury hotel has gone up on the outskirts of town to house the influx of flush expatriate bosses, overseers, and consultants. It belongs to one of the country's wealthiest men, a partner in Addax Bioenergy, an oil industry mogul and former Managing Director of Sierra Leone's National Petroleum Company. A spanking new paved road has just gone in, smoothing the ride for clientele heading to his exclusive hotel complex.

Not so here, where the market is expanding and consuming much of the city centre. Roads, alleyways, and paths are piled high with goods spilling onto thoroughfares already crammed with vehicles and motorbikes.

Everywhere you look, someone is trying to sell something, as if a giant discount big-box store has had its walls pulled away and a hurricane has blasted through, scattering stuff everywhere. A quick sample inventory list includes electronics, mobile and smartphones, plastics, cooking wear, every counterfeit brand of jeans that Asian factories can knock off, black-market soccer jerseys from just about every team on earth, shoes, sandals, flashlights, tools, luggage, furnishings, pirated DVDs, religious paraphernalia, cartons full of plastic bottles filled with soft and energy drinks, and, yes, even kitchen sinks. It is a labyrinth of plenty of everything, fashioned into a functioning daily market by human beings whose livelihoods depend on what is known hereabouts as "small, small business." The big business is the manufacturing, most of which is in China.

In the parts of the market devoted to food, local produce is piled, displayed, and arranged wherever you try to step. Following Thelma, I carve a slalom path on tiptoe to avoid the neat towers of tomatoes, meticulously arranged in pyramids like miniature red cannonballs. We pass little tables and baskets filled with beans of all shapes, sizes, and colours, a veritable kaleidoscope of pulses. Fortunately for me, local people have made things simple for English speakers, categorizing the many different peas and beans as black-eyes, broad, big, small, and pigeon peas (or *concho*). The broad beans are especially appealing; they're smooth, glossy as polished gems, each one a unique miniature mosaic in all shades of brown, beige, and grey.

Have I already said it is very, very hot? I've emptied a one-and-a-half-litre bottle of water and am still parched. No one else in the market seems to share my misery or my constant need for liquid. The only times I've heard complaints about temperatures in Sierra Leone are when the temperature plummets to just below twenty degrees Celsius. It does that for a few days in December or January. It is not unusual on these rare, not-hot-and-humid days to see people don a winter wardrobe – fake fur winter hats, ski jackets with hoods pulled tight. These are often items tossed off during spring cleanings in northern lands, donated to charities, then sold to dealers and bundled up as frippery for shipping to Africa by the container-load. Second-hand clothing and shoes fill markets and clothe much of the continent. Africa's textile makers, weavers, dye makers, and tailors have paid the high price for these cheap castoffs, with lost markets and jobs. Thelma and I move through an entire section of the Makeni market, large as a mini-shopping mall, which is devoted to stalls selling second-hand clothing in various stages of disrepair.

The heat is on because we're into the month of May. The wind from the Sahara, the Harmattan, has long since turned tail and headed north, changing its name to Sirocco as it blows its desert dust north into Europe. Here, close to the West African coast, the annual rains have already begun and the humid air sizzles with heat, hammering it home. I am wilting, drenched with sweat. My head pounds. Thelma, however, looks fresh and sprightly as a daisy. She is wearing a long multicoloured peasant skirt, a beige shirt, a pair of blue canvas running shoes, and a white sunhat – a smart outfit she's put together from the aforementioned second-hand clothing in the market.

She moves quickly down the narrow mud paths made even narrower by the spreading displays of fresh farm produce. It's all delightfully orderly in a delightfully disorderly way. The food market offers a panoply of diversity, odours, and flavours from an exultation of vegetables, spices, fruits, greens, beans, and tubers that family farmers grow in abundance in and around their villages. But what I'm seeing today is vastly diminished from the diverse bounty of just a few years ago. Sierra Leonean food writer Rachel Massaquoi grieves for the "vanishing vegetables" of her youth, of traditional diets.[106]

In her book, she tells the story of an epiphany she had at a supermarket in Canada, where she now lives, when she spied vegetables shaped like green spirals for sale in the produce department.[107] They looked familiar to her, like the *gbuhing* she had grown up eating in Sierra Leone. She stood beside the display of vegetables, smiling at everyone who passed, hoping someone could tell her more about the curly greens. Eventually, a woman noticed her interest and told her the greens were fiddleheads, which come from wild ferns that grow on muddy riverbanks and are harvested before they unfurl in the early spring. Rachel Massaquoi then bought the (Canadian) fiddleheads, which evoked powerful memories of years ago, when she had learned from her grandmother how to prepare the Sierra Leonean equivalent, the *gbuhing*, for her cocoyam leaf sauce. Today, she writes, the fiddleheads have all but disappeared from the Sierra Leone diet.

Favourite African foods may be vanishing from markets and diets, but there's no shortage of imported foodstuffs. I wander over to a rickety stand in the Makeni market, on which flats of eggs are balanced precariously. Underneath the table, I spot some large yellow cartons from which the eggs have come, labelled "Confidence" brand "Farm Fresh White Shell Eggs." The "farm fresh" seems a curious claim; they've made their way here from India. That's quite a hike – across oceans and then inland to the Makeni market in Sierra Leone – for any egg claiming to be fresh off the farm.

Thelma reaches past the flats of eggs and picks up a tiny tin of tomato paste. At first, because its colours – green, red, and white – are the national colours of Italy and also because most of the tomato paste in Africa's markets once originated there, I assume that this too is from Italy. But on closer inspection I see this tomato paste was packed by PFT Co. Ltd., Africa Road, in a Free Trade Port in China, for the Watanmal Group in Hong Kong.

I drop the tiny globe-trotting tin of tomato paste into a cotton bag, along with three onions Thelma selects from a small pile on a wooden table. Large sacks underneath the table reveal the origins of the onions. They are Ladybug brand "*onions, oignons, zwiebeln, cebbolas*" from The Netherlands.

We move on. The mud path underfoot is paved with the ragged remains of discarded plastic bags. To avoid contributing to the relatively recent scourge of the plastic bag, today I've provided Thelma with two large cotton bags for our groceries. One side of the bag says "cotton yes" and on the other are the words "plastic no." Not that anyone is reading it, but it makes me feel better in that way that individual actions, insignificant as they may be, can help to pacify in this age of guilt. In this age of plastic.

Our two cotton bags are now filling up – with little plastic bags. So far, we have bought a bit of salt (in a tiny plastic bag), a few tablespoons of freshly made peanut butter known here as groundnut paste (in a tiny plastic bag), and some dried hot pepper (in a tiny plastic bag). The only items not in plastic are two smoked fish and some chunks of beef. These are wrapped in bits of heavy brown paper torn from a bag that once held cement.

Thelma says we now need to buy some cooking oil. In a country practically swimming in the stuff, there doesn't seem to be any local red palm oil around. But she assures me peanut oil will be fine, and she has the woman vendor pour a little into a small plastic bag. I want to know where the peanut oil comes from and the woman points to a large drum underneath her stall. It is not from Sierra Leone at all. Rather, like the onions, the oil comes from Holland. Last I heard, peanuts don't grow in Holland. So who grew the peanuts that were shipped to Holland, processed for their oil, and then shipped out to African markets to undermine family farmers? Who knows?

Next, Thelma turns her attention to finding African egg-plants. About five hundred years ago, the small white and some-times green vegetable (*Solanum* species) from Africa made its debut on English dinner tables. Greengrocers in London intro-duced the strange new vegetable they had picked up along the West African coast, calling it "Guinea squash."[108] Its delightful ellipsoid shape and its size eventually led to an appropriate new name – "egg-plant."

Then a new Asian vegetable showed up in British kitchens. This one was purple and irregular and not even vaguely reminis-cent of an egg, although it was botanically related to the smaller African egg-shaped vegetable. For reasons best known to the cooks and greengrocers of the period, the original eggplant from Africa more or less disappeared from Europe, and the flashy but not-at-all-egg-like purple interloper stole the name and the culinary show. Centuries later, the purple eggplant has gone from strength to strength in cuisines around the world, while the delicious little African version has remained a well-kept secret of African farmers and cooks.[109]

Thelma explains to me that in Sierra Leone two indigenous vegetables fall into the larger category of eggplants. One is the garden egg or (African) eggplant, which can't be eaten raw. The other is *jakato* or the bitter ball, which tastes delightful in a slightly bitter kind of way, whether it's raw or cooked, and I remember it as a flavourful ingredient in Angela's *egusi* soup. This short course in eggplants finished, Thelma eventually chooses and buys four bitter balls.

The next task is to find the amaranth leaves, "*grin*" in Krio. In the market area devoted to leafy greens, women sit next to plastic buckets and metal bowls bursting with the foliage, all neatly tied into bundles, all for making leafy sauces. The women vendors sprinkle their verdant wares regularly with water to keep them fresh, and in the glare of the afternoon sun, the droplets of water glisten like diamond studs. Thelma buys two hefty bundles of *grin*.

Now, at last, it is time to find some country rice. Thelma is an expert on rice – not just on buying and cooking it but also on growing it, which is how I first met her a couple of years earlier. I'd been preparing media reports on the land deal that gave Addax Bioenergy control over more than 50,000 hectares of land for sugarcane and ethanol production. The Environmental, Social and Health Impact Assessment for the project claimed the land in question was "scared" [sic] by tobacco production and largely unproductive, so no great loss to the thousands of people who grew food crops on it.[110] Seven European development banks and the African Development Bank, using public funds, financed the deal that they viewed as a positive development for Sierra Leone.[111]

Thelma humbly begged to differ. She had been working in the area with women's farming groups before Addax Bioenergy took over the land.[112] She'd taken me by the hand into a small concrete building where the women stored their rice. She wanted to show me the tonnes of rice women farmers were able to produce with their own seeds, without any imported fertilizer or pesticides on the land said to be scarred and unsuitable for food production. But now their land had been taken for sugarcane and

Thelma's farming groups wouldn't be growing their rice, vegetables, and cassava there anymore.

This is why she has moved to Makeni, where she now works with other women's farming groups around the town, planting vegetables, raising chickens and goats, and cultivating country rice. She asks me what I prefer, country rice that is parboiled or country rice that is not.

I confess that I'm not clear on the difference. Over the din of the market, Thelma explains that the parboiled rice has undergone an intricate process to lock in nutrients and make it more resistant to pests. First, the rice is threshed, a laborious and taxing job done by thrashing the harvested rice stalks with sticks. The husk rice – without the hulls removed – is then soaked in hot water in a large drum overnight. In the morning, the drum is put over a fire and the rice steamed until it becomes fluffy. It is then spread out on the ground (or a concrete drying floor if there is one available) to dry before it is hulled, either in a mortar with a pestle or in a mill (if one is available). Thelma says just three cups of parboiled rice will produce as much cooked rice as four cups of regular country rice, and it stores much better. So the parboiled rice, sold at the same price as the regular country rice and the imported Asian brands, is a better deal and more nutritious. We take four cups of parboiled country rice, and with that, our shopping is done.

The tally for the fixings for our dinner? About 40,000 Leones, or US$10. Thelma could never afford all these ingredients for a single meal. That would use up a large chunk of her monthly salary.

Thelma lives in a one-storey green bungalow of painted mud bricks topped by a rusty tin roof. Several other families share the small house, renting individual rooms. She rents just two, one for herself and one for her niece and two nephews who are staying with her in Makeni. She leads me through the dark hallway and out a back door to the kitchen area, marked by a small thatched hut and a cleared area of packed earth. A large mango tree stands in the centre, its spreading canopy of dense foliage like a lacy, leafy ceiling.

Her niece and one of her nephews, both young adults, appear without being called. They stand there polite as you please while Thelma introduces them: Princess and Solomon. Then, without being asked, they head into the house and come back bearing metal-framed chairs into which Thelma and I sink. I soak up the blessed shade of the mango tree, and watch, amazed, as the kitchen materializes in front of me. Princess and Solomon troop back and forth between the interior of the mud house and the kitchen area, bringing plastic bowls, buckets, a waist-high wooden mortar and a pestle tall as they are, knives and spoons, and a charcoal stove made of metal with a clay interior over which a single pot can be placed.

They take command of the bags we've lugged from the market, removing all the small plastic packets and laying them out in a giant plastic bowl. Once again, I'm politely excluded from the preparations. Thelma issues the odd instruction on the making of the meal, but mostly she and I just watch and talk as dinner takes shape.

By now, the heat is easing slightly as the sun slinks towards the horizon, preparing to clock out at the end of its day. Out of the deepening blue, Thelma suddenly starts to tell me about a daughter I didn't know she had. From her handbag, she pulls a photograph of a smiling young woman. Thelma says it was taken when her daughter was a nursing student in Freetown, when she was about to graduate. She never did. She died in a tragic and suspicious fire there a few years ago. Thelma suspects the culpability of prominent people for the fire, in which five people perished, but she doesn't go into detail about how and why and I don't ask. I don't know what to say. What is there to say?

We sit in silence for a few moments watching Princess washing the produce in a bucket of water. Thelma says her niece and nephews are law students at the new Catholic university in town, and she feeds and houses them on her salary from the Ministry of Agriculture, which amounts to something just over a hundred dollars a month. No matter the financial difficulties this arrangement may cause these days, this is how things have always been done in much of Africa. Aunts and uncles are interchangeable with mothers and fathers; in fact, aunts and uncles are considered parents, and extended families the safety nets that governments rarely provide.

Princess and Solomon have assembled the outdoor kitchen and taken over the cooking without so much as a prompt from anyone. Princess sits on a tiny stool to work. She washes the leafy greens thoroughly in a large bowl of water, then twists and grasps them in a very tight bunch in her left hand. Holding this over a plastic bucket at her feet, she uses a large knife to shave off tiny shreds of the greens. These cascade into the bucket. A finely tuned dance of hands, knife, and leaves, enthralling to watch. Food as edible art.

Where I come from, I tell Thelma, this kind of willing helpfulness in the house is not necessarily the norm. While there are many exceptions, quite often Mom and maybe also Dad will do the shopping and the cooking and the kids may show up, between text messages and video games and sessions with whatever social media the parents have not yet discovered, just in time to eat. Some families or family members might run out to the nearest fast food outlet and skip the whole kitchen and cooking business altogether. Thelma's listening and nodding, but I'm not sure that what I'm saying means much to her, or if it's even possible in this setting to imagine such things.

Solomon holds a match to the charcoal in the stove and uses a plastic plate to fan it till it begins to produce white heat. He pours some peanut oil into a large aluminum pot, dumps in slices of onion, adds a little water, and places it on the charcoal. The outdoor kitchen is like a family processing plant – Thelma peels skin off the smoked fish and deftly plucks the flesh from the bones. The fish and beef go into the pot with the oil, water, and onions. The aroma of the cooking food floats lazily about in the cooling air of twilight. It awakens my appetite that has been snoozing during the crushing heat of the day.

Hot peppers are tipped into the pot along with the greens, the lid goes on, and the mixture is left to boil. Nobody is timing anything. There is no glancing at watches. Time here passes without being measured or monitored.

We talk about this and that; the young people are shy and don't speak unless I pose a question about their studies, what their plans are. They hope to finish university and find work that can support them and their families in years to come, no more, no less. Yet plans like these for young, poorly connected Sierra Leonean men and women are truly the stuff of dreams, as I suppose they are increasingly around the world.

While the sauce boils in the covered pot, Princess picks tiny stones and chaff from the rice. It is now ready for the pot and the stove. This is the original slow food. Because it's a one-pot charcoal stove, the sauce eventually comes off to make room for the rice. Thelma dispatches her nephew down the road to a neighbourhood vendor to buy some packets of cold water to drink with our meal. Normally, I know, they would drink the tepid water that comes from the well in the neighbourhood, but Thelma probably suspects (correctly) that I am wary of water that doesn't come from a deep drilled well and besides, the cold water would be a treat for us all.

Even the water is sold in plastic bags, and I'm not convinced that it's any safer than the well water. Following Thelma's example, I use my teeth to tear off a tiny corner on the square plastic package and hold it gently to my mouth. Hers doesn't spill. Mine does, but the cool water on my lap is welcome.

When the rice has cooked – and I'm not sure how Princess knows when it has without peeking under the lid – she removes the pot. She does this with her bare hands. Normally, they would all eat together, from a single bowl. But in deference to the stranger in their midst, they spoon out a small mountain of rice into a plastic bowl then douse it with sauce and hand it to me, along with a spoon. They do the same for Thelma. Princess and her brother fill a large plate with rice and sauce and share it, eating with their right hands. The rest, Thelma tells me, is to be shared with the others living in the house. Anything left over from that will be breakfast for Thelma and her wards.

The country rice, soaked in the rich and flavourful leafy sauce, is deeply and satisfyingly delicious, spicy enough to tango with my tongue, and I use almost these words to convey my enthusiasm for the food. This seems to please all three, and this in turn increases my pleasure as I spoon the country rice dripping with delectable green sauce into my mouth. And I ponder, not for the first time, how fortunate I've been to have had so many African mentors and friends over the years, who have helped me appreciate their foods and the markets that supply them.

16

Shopping lessons with Mary

Knocker, sticker, shackler, romper, First Legger, Knuckle Dropper, Navel Bone, Splitter Top/Bottom Butt, Feed Kill Chain — the names of job assignments at a modern slaughterhouse convey some of the brutality inherent in the work.

– Eric Schlosser
Fast Food Nation:
The Dark Side of the All-American Meal

Mary Fukuo was my lifeline while we lived in Tamale. We'd become friends years earlier, when she and we were living in Burkina Faso, but in Ghana she quickly became far more than that. She was my guide, social advisor, personal protector, and, as they say of a dear woman friend in Ghana, she became my "sister." It was Mary who had introduced me to the joys of red palm oil and the palm butter soup she created with it.

She was also my translator. She spoke several indigenous languages, in addition to French, German, and Ghana's official tongue, English, inherited from the country's former colonial power. Yet her multilingual prowess is not at all uncommon in

Ghana or for many parts of Africa, where so many people juggle half a dozen languages, or more, without even noticing that their linguistic talents are dazzling to those of us without them.

Mary was determined that I quickly master the fine art of living in northern Ghana. And that included getting to know my way around Tamale's Aboabo market and the vendors, so that I would not pay *obroni* or "white man" prices. She would get indignant and extremely agitated when someone tried to coax a few extra cents out of me because I was foreign and new, an *obroni*.

She marched through the market like a mother hen with places to go and business to do while her baby chick (me) tagged along behind, quite helpless on her own (true). She chatted away with the market women, offering long and convoluted greetings in a confusion of tongues, and even hurling playful insults and exchanging snippets of local news and gossip as she paused to buy, before charging on through the network of market stalls while my basket filled up with fresh produce.

The baskets were locally made, intricately woven with vetiver grass dyed all shades of colourful. The handles were bound in leather. At some point between then and now, China appropriated the design – if not the quality – of those northern Ghanaian baskets; it now markets inferior facsimiles of them around the world. But back then they were produced almost exclusively by local women's groups, while the leatherwork was done by men.

Mary inevitably took the basket from me when it got heavy, placing it on her head. There seemed to be a notion in Ghana that we pale foreign women were weak and fragile, unable to perform normal chores on our own. Perhaps this was because so many of us couldn't cope very well with the heat, complained incessantly about the lack of water and electricity, and were unable to carry anything on our heads except a sunhat. Nor could many of us get a fire going over a three-stone hearth and whip up a meal for twenty from scratch (including slaughtering, plucking, and preparing a chicken or two). In Tamale, I often did feel feeble

and unskilled, with my formal schooling and skill sets developed
in and for a very different place and a life with all manner of
props on which my survival depended.

Mary liked to distribute her business among as many market women as she could, and always bought from a dozen or so
regulars, one vendor for tomatoes, another for hot peppers, a different one for yams, and so on. This meant a lot of extra talking and also walking from one section of the market to another.
After a few weeks under Mary's tutelage, I began to acknowledge
that what had looked initially like chaos in the market was in fact
highly organized and even structured, something I would notice
over and over again in subsequent years in Africa.

Everything had its own distinct place in the market; those
selling tomatoes formed a cluster, as did those selling spices or fish
or the *gari* made from fermented, roasted, and grated cassava. It
had only seemed chaotic because initially I had been unable to
decipher the patterns and order that were all there, unwritten and
thus invisible to newcomers overwhelmed by the hustle and bustle
of local markets. Over time, I got to know where to go for fresh
produce, fish, lovely wax prints, and also imported ingredients –
Maggi cubes, Nestlé NIDO milk powder, Nescafé, canned tomato paste, sweetened condensed milk, margarine, mayonnaise, and
other consumables the multinational food industry had concocted
to withstand months of hot sun without spoilage, to cater to a
tropical market.

I soon came to marvel at the intricacies and complexities
of the markets, especially the remarkable supply chains that were
anchored on countless small-scale farms. There was a complex
network and rotation of satellite markets in rural towns, which
kept producers and vendors busy going to different little markets
every day of the week, in a functioning local food web. They were
marvels to me. They were farmers' markets, supermarkets, and
department stores all rolled into one commercial and social hub.
And all in the great – hot – outdoors.

But … there was still a big but. There was one part of the market in Tamale with which I just could not seem to come to grips. That was the section devoted to red meat. Just to get to the building where meat was sold, you had to navigate your way across a large muddy area and through an outdoor display of smoked cow legs and hooves, hides and heads. The charred body parts were laid out on the bare ground and to me it looked like an unearthed bovine graveyard. Even in the heat, it made me shiver. I couldn't help but imagine that accusing eyes were staring out at me from the ghastly sockets in the smoked cow skulls.

Inside the low-slung hall where the fresh meat was sold, things weren't much better for this faint-hearted foreigner. It was hot and loud. Butchers and customers shouted at each other over the cacophony of the hacking and ringing of machetes slamming into bones and concrete counters. The din sounded to me like the trading floor of the New York Stock Exchange (at least the way it's been depicted in movies; I've never been to the New York Stock Exchange). Butchers energetically hacked away at carcasses with cutlasses and their counters were piled high with intestines and other innards. Blood and bone chips literally flew. A raincoat and earplugs would have been useful protective clothing for the place.

The more I was learning from and about local markets and the foods sold there, the more it was dawning on me how little I'd considered the origins of the food I'd eaten most of my life. Meat, for me, had always been something that spontaneously wrapped itself up in shiny plastic wrap before it lay itself down to rest on refrigerated supermarket shelves, as harmless, lifeless slices or filets or innocent red or white lumps. When fried or roasted or sautéed in the kitchen, these meats gave off mouth-watering aromas and later, on my palate, they tasted fine. Comforting. Satiating. No questions asked.

That is precisely the problem: no questions were asked. Growing up an urbanite in the gilded decades of industrial food, shielded from anything except the finished and packaged products in our stores, fridges, and kitchen cupboards, I had failed to ask any questions at all about the food I ate and where it came from, who produced it and how. As a child, I thought margarine a vast improvement over butter. I remember the excitement I felt when my mother first presented my brothers and me with glasses of a floridly orange juice-like product made from Tang crystals, which we were told was drunk by NASA astronauts. How cool was that?

My brothers and I used to fight like mad over the prizes – plastic figurines and other useless trinkets – that were tucked into boxes of breakfast cereals to make children nag their mothers to buy them. I turned up my nose when my mother produced real porridge from plain old oatmeal or other grains. I wanted colourful bits of reconstituted grains industrially processed and regurgitated to form letters and crunchy bits that snapped, crackled, and popped. These we slurped down, sometimes while singing the jingles the advertisers had implanted in our compliant and suggestible little heads. It's indicative of how effectively the advertisers managed to saturate our brains with their propaganda that I can still sing some of these jingles half a century later.

We didn't even notice this was happening, and, in my case, I almost never equated foods I ate with living things, either plant or animal. As it developed, the corporate food system strangled family farms and transformed farming into agribusiness, deftly excising the word "culture" from agriculture. Industrial agribusiness snuffs out diversity and sacrifices flavour and nutrition for storability and transportability, pumping out a very limited number of crops and from them a multitude of processed foods, or in the words of food writer Michael Pollan, "edible food-like substances" or "foodlike products."[113]

In the course of my own lifetime, corporate agriculture has taken over our major food crops in North America, whittled them down, hybridized and genetically modified them and sown them on farms as big as small nations. They have become links in a long and powerful industrial food chain that first encircled North America before expanding to garrotte the globe.

But growing up in a North American city in the 1960s and '70s, I was oblivious to all of this. And so it was that I failed for so long to make the connection between a hamburger or a steak or boneless chicken and an erstwhile moving and breathing creature that had eyes (big, sad ones in the case of a cow), ears, hearts, brains, and yes, lives, even if they were often pretty miserable ones cooped up inside Concentrated Animal Feeding Operations, or CAFOs, the benign euphemism for the sordid reality of industrial livestock rearing. Thousands of animals or fowl are locked up in horrifically confined spaces in giant buildings, medicated and fed and fattened until they're ready for the kill. Sort of like a prison camp, slaughterhouse, and excrement factory rolled into one. Millions and millions of animals and birds that spend their entire short and miserable lives on death row. Out of sight, and a far cry from the way family farmers in Africa (and elsewhere on the planet) handle their livestock, the few chickens, goats, sheep, and cows they may have.

It's very common to see a goat or sheep or a few chickens tied up and spread-eagled and bleating, or crowing on the carrier or crossbar of a bicycle or motorcycle, or perched precariously on the top of an overloaded van carrying passengers and cargo. After reasonably happy lives of free-ranging munching in fields or around family compounds or in the bush, these animals and fowl are simply taken to market for sale. It's a normal cycle of life and death for domestic livestock. It's the way family farmers on every continent have done it for eons. And it's still the way the majority of Africa's farmers rear their animals.

I've been present many times when sheep or goats are slaughtered for Muslim friends in preparation for a celebratory feast of one kind or another. Invariably, it is done with great respect and compassion, preceded by prayer, as prescribed by *Dhabiha* in Islamic law. Only healthy animals can be eaten and the killing has to be done in a way that causes the least amount of pain and anguish.

In Ghana, I started to learn, the hard way, that if you're going to be a responsible red meat-eater (which I hear my vegetarian friends and family members decrying as an oxymoron even as I write the words), you have to learn to look your meat in the eye, get used to the blood. My first lesson came with Spot. Spot was a fine specimen of a sheep that was offered to my husband on one of his working trips to Ghana's Northern Region. The kids named him to honour the large black spot on his white nose. They loved him.

Eventually, Spot grew into a good-sized ram and a Ghanaian friend suggested it was time he be given back to his maker, in honour of Eid al-Adha, the Muslim Festival of Sacrifice. I protested. My husband overruled, as Spot *was* his sheep. A Muslim cleric was summoned to our compound and we all went out to witness the ritual slaughter. My son and daughter, while initially upset and alarmed, were placated by their Ghanaian friends who explained this was a very special and even a sacred occasion. They maintained that by sacrificing Spot, we were showing great respect for both the sheep and for the Almighty. I think I was the only one who was unable to watch the subsequent quick death and carving up of Spot.

Until I moved to Africa, I'd been spared realities about meat and I had quite enjoyed my blissful ignorance. So that's my excuse, legitimate or not, for reacting so poorly to the smoked cow heads and the butchery in the Aboabo market. One day, hot and bothered and overwhelmed by the challenges of adapting to our new lives in Tamale, I let slip to Mary the revulsion I felt at the meat market. Besides, I said, for the life of me I just couldn't imagine what one would actually *do* with a smoked cow head.

She didn't exactly lose her temper, but she did stop and speak to me firmly and loudly enough to make people around us stop and stare. She began to rhyme off the names of some popular foods in Germany – pig heads, whole ones boiled and served on plates in pubs on *shlachttag*, literally "slaughter day." Steaming mounds of coagulated blood – *blutwurst* – served on a plate. Intestine soup, calf brain, cow tongue, tartare made of raw pork and topped with a raw egg yolk, and so on. Did she complain? Did she accuse Europeans of barbaric menus and disgusting food? No, she didn't. And she was tired of hearing European women going on about the disgusting market and its meats. Furthermore, she informed me, those heads and skins and hooves were absolutely delicious, true delicacies, when boiled up. Nothing was wasted here. Nothing!

I wanted to remind her that I wasn't German, nor European. I wanted to say that I was just as squeamish about some of the European foods that double as local specialties – from Scottish haggis to kidney pie to *foie gras* to pig heads on a platter, and to some of the fast food concoctions that are daily fare for millions of people at global chains. That is, I wanted to tell her that I didn't go for any of those revolting things either. I wanted to tell her my palate was humane and pure.

But of course this was not true. I am not and was not a vegan, not even a vegetarian. I love meat. Furthermore, I am no innocent when it comes to eating acts that others might construe as barbaric. I have never felt any qualms about boiling lobsters alive, with barely a thought for anything but the delectable flesh in the tail that I will smother in melted butter. Raw oysters make me groan with pleasure. As children we spent long summer afternoons roaming sandbars at low tide on the Atlantic coast on the hunt for razor clams. We then squeezed the tender white heads out of the clams and yes, bit them off. Alive.

Just as I once gulped down those clams, I now swallowed the defensive argument that was squirming about on my tongue. Squeamishness, as Mary had just made clear to me, is in the mind of the eater.

17

Bugs and food bugaboos

If Americans who ordered chicken wings were instead served a dish of deep fried grasshoppers, they would gag, even though many people in Thailand would line up for the delicious snack.

— Rachel Herz
That's Disgusting:
Unraveling the Mysteries of Repulsion

The squeamishness issue, what is edible and what isn't, what food makes one person drool and another gag, came up again in Tamale the morning after the very first heavy rainstorm of the year. It was in late May, and the rain came as a blessed relief after eight months of unrelenting sun that had baked the ground until it was hard as concrete. The first downpour of the rainy season always caused flash floods as torrents of blood-red water turned roadways into rivers before the moisture began to soften up and then soak into the earth.

The rains unleashed swarms of flying winged insects – termites, I was told – that hatched overnight by the zillions. In the morning, they littered the wet ground. Their little honey-coloured bodies were about the size of a coffee bean, but their four gossamer wings were large as those of dragonflies. Their abdomens were striped with gentle shades of brown and gold. Just hours after they emerged from their termite mounds to take their nuptial flights, these poor insects lost their capacity to fly and lay writhing and helpless on the ground. They continued to buzz and squirm for hours as they shed their wings, which had apparently become useless.

I didn't pay all that much attention to the population explosion of winged insects, although my daughter was fascinated by the broods of termites, studying and poking at the new playthings from the skies. She became even more interested when her friends went about collecting them in plastic buckets. She came racing into the house to get a large bowl and headed back out to join in the great termite harvest. Her Ghanaian friends showed her how to pull off the wings. Transforming them into a favourite delicacy was as easy as plopping them in a frying pan. No oil required. As they sautéed in their own oil, they smelled quite good. If I didn't look too closely, I could convince myself they were crunchy little nuts browning in the pan.

We poured them into a shallow bowl and once they had cooled a little, my daughter and her friends feasted on the termites. I knew I should give them a try. They were said to be high in protein, and someone even claimed they contained compounds that were natural anti-malarial agents. I looked hard at them, and swallowed a few times, but I regret to say I didn't partake. I did, however, manage to keep my aversion to myself so my food bugaboos wouldn't be passed on to my children.

Disgust, it seems, is the only basic emotion we have to learn and there's nothing like unfamiliar foods we never learned to eat to trigger the gag reflex.[114] A fair bit has been written about exotic and iconoclastic foods around the world, from cockroaches in Asia to the world's most expensive coffee, *Kopi luwak* from Indonesia, made with beans that have passed through the digestive

tract of a civet cat, and so on.[115] All cuisines have flavours and
ingredients that can most politely be described as acquired tastes
– insect tea, seal flippers, cheese made with mites. One person's
delicacy is another person's worst nightmare. Just as Mary said, everyone has their own distinct ideas about what is good to eat and
what isn't. Yum or yuck – it's all in the mind.

I was again reminded of this in March 2013, when the news
broke that U.K. border guards at Gatwick Airport had seized
ninety-four kilograms of dried caterpillars that a young man from
Burkina Faso was carrying in his luggage. Countless media outlets
ran with the story, from the *Washington Post* to the *Jordan Times*,
from Fox News to the *Winnipeg Free Press*. Some gave the story
catchy headlines that set a jocular, slightly mocking tone, like this
one from *The Independent* in the U.K.: "Monkeys in my pants?
No, just 94 kg of caterpillars in my luggage."[116] The article cited
an insect expert from the Natural History Museum who said the
caterpillars were likely mopane worms, the larvae of the magnificent Emperor moth of the species *Gonimbrasia belina*.

The British Government ran the story on its website, saying the confiscated caterpillars had been intended "to be used as
food." It earnestly reported that the discovery of the dried caterpillars at Gatwick was "among the largest of its kind at the airport." And it quoted a woman from Border Force who said the
luggage was intercepted thanks to "the vigilance of our officers"
who "stopped these dried insects from entering the U.K., and possibly posing a risk to our food chain."

This set me to pondering the risk that a few bags of dried
mopane worms might pose to the Western food chain, com-
pared with some of the other problems that have plagued that
food system in recent years. There was Mad Cow disease that the
U.K. was exporting in its contaminated beef for years after British Prime Minister Margaret Thatcher's Conservative government
permitted cow parts to be used in the feed for normally herbivo-
rous cattle. There have also been frequent problems with industri-

ally produced and processed meats becoming contaminated with E-coli and Listeria. These have led to the deaths of the human beings who consumed them, despite the fact they are supposed to meet the safety requirements of government agents and food safety agencies in the industrialized West. In industrial agriculture, animal feeds also contain cocktails of antibiotics and growth hormones. All of which might be construed as a somewhat larger threat than a few free-ranging caterpillars.

I'm not going to pretend that the idea of eating caterpillars appeals to me, any more than does the idea of any of a long list of creatures (or their body parts) that many of my fellow human beings consider true delicacies. But as Mary had made abundantly clear to me, and as I constantly tried to remind myself, just because something doesn't appeal to my culinary tastes doesn't mean it is not a perfectly good food, superior nutritionally and environmentally to many of the ones I consume.

Insects of all kinds – some 250 different species of them – figure in diets throughout sub-Saharan Africa.[117] But the mopane caterpillars are the most popular and economically important, accounting for almost a third of all the insects consumed on the continent.[118] They are said to be delicious; at a cultural fair in the city of Bobo-Dioulasso in Burkina Faso, a winning recipe in the culinary cook-off featured caterpillars and *soumbala* made from *dawa dawa* seeds.[119] They are also extremely nutritious. More than half of the caterpillar is protein, and the fat content may account for one-fifth of its weight, with nearly half of that being essential fatty acids. The worms are also a good source of calcium, zinc, and iron.[120] Today they are widely available dried and in large bags in supermarkets in the capital, Ouagadougou.

In parts of the Democratic Republic of Congo caterpillars are sometimes a more important source of protein than meat. The average household in the capital Kinshasa eats about 300 grams of caterpillars a week, and in some months caterpillars constitute more of the diet than do fish or game. According to a Congolese saying, "As food, caterpillars are regulars in the village but meat is a stranger."[121]

It takes only three kilograms of feed from leaves of the mopane tree to produce one kilogram of the caterpillars. Compare that with the ten kilograms of cattle feed needed to generate one kilogram of beef, and the 15,415 litres of water that requires.[122] The worms are an inexpensive and environmentally friendly source of protein for many millions of people in Africa.

In the mopane woodlands of southern Africa, some 9.5 billion caterpillars are harvested each year, worth about US$85 million.[123] Although overharvesting poses a risk to the species as its economic value rises, so far, the mopane caterpillar is not an endangered species. Indeed, when swarms of its adult self – the Emperor moth – go on feeding frenzies, they can defoliate and devastate valuable trees. So the eating of their larvae can be a healthy way to tackle a pest. However, to maintain a supply of the worms in areas where they have enormous economic and nutritional value, as they do in southern Africa, it is perfectly feasible to domesticate and farm the moth, as has been done with the silkworm in Asia.

The more I learned about the mopane worms, the more it seemed the media's handling of the seized caterpillars in Gatwick was an enormous opportunity lost. The incident could have been the ideal occasion to open a whole new can of nutritious worms, sparking a global discussion about the value of insects in combatting malnutrition and hunger not just in Africa but around the world.

The Food and Agriculture Organization (FAO) of the United Nations sees the practice of eating insects – or entomophagy – as a fine way of assuring food security for the growing human population on earth, especially given the threats climate change present to agriculture and global food production.[124] Insects are a highly nutritious and healthy food source, rich in protein, fatty acids, fibre, and mineral content.

Of course, not all insects should be eaten; alive they are also immensely important actors in the health of the planet and all the creatures that dwell on it.[125] Of 100,000 pollinators, a whopping 98 percent are insects. Without pollinators we are in deep trouble, and important ones such as bees and bats are already in severe and steep decline in North America.[126] Ninety percent of all flowering species depend on pollinators to reproduce, as do three-quarters of the hundred major crop species on which human diets are based. Insects also break down organic materials and wastes and prepare them for recycling into the ecosystem.

More entomophagy might also lead to more respect for and appreciation of insects, and this could be beneficial for both human beings and the edible insects. Some are in peril because of overharvesting, pollution, habitat destruction and degradation, and wildfires. Insect farming, which may seem a novel concept to many of us, is certainly not a recent one. The ancient Greeks and Romans dined on insects, and Roman aristocrats were gourmands when it came to beetle larvae, which they reared on flour and wine.[127] Bees and silkworms were domesticated in ancient times, because people valued the honey and silk they produced and wanted more control over these. The same is now being done for insects such as crickets, which make fine animal feed.

It shouldn't be an insurmountable hurdle to convince the world that bugs are nutritious and delicious and they should eat more of them, although I confess I've surmounted none of my own bugaboos about bug eating. Fortunately, much of Africa, and indeed nearly a third of the world's population, won't have to struggle at all to enjoy insects in their diets. At least two billion people on this planet, most of them in the tropics, already consume insects, close to 2,000 different species of them.[128] The most popular appear to be beetles, but caterpillars are not far behind, followed by bees, wasps and ants, grasshoppers, plant-hoppers, scale insects, true "bugs" of the Hemiptera order, termites, dragonflies, and flies.

Contrary to popular misconceptions, insects are not consumed as a last resort, as famine foods when all else fails. People eat them out of choice, because they like them. A Malawi cookbook from 1992 offers many insect-based recipes, which it calls traditional delicacies that are much sought after.[129] Among them is a recipe for barbequed palm weevils.

Palm weevils colonize palm trees of all kinds, oil palm, raffia, and coconut species, and are found in both rotting and healthy trees. Knowing when to collect the larvae is a fine art in the Democratic Republic of Congo, one that has been mastered primarily by women and children. It involves putting the ear up to the trunk of the tree to hear the burrowing and chomping weevils to decide if they are at the ideal and preferred developmental stage. Once they've been collected, the women wash and fry them, usually without any oil added because they exude their own as they cook. The weevils are reportedly delicious when spiced up with onion, pepper, and salt.[130]

Westerners may be the hardest nuts to crack when it comes to encouraging more entomophagy. In Western countries, the practice of eating insects is generally viewed with disgust and sometimes even associated with "primitive behaviour."[131] There is no simple explanation for this, but some speculate it has to do with the kind of agriculture that developed in the temperate and industrialized West. Industrial agriculture has greatly simplified nature, reduced biodiversity with its emphasis on monocultures and economies of large scale, so there is far less potential to harvest from nature. Urbanization, which until fairly recently was most extensive in the West, also puts people out of touch with nature, and with nature comes insects. It could also be that insects in the tropics tend to be larger and juicier than they are in more temperate parts of the planet. Whatever the reasons for Westerners' aversion to insects, they tend to view them more as pests than as food, and this negative attitude is being spread to others. Some Christian missionaries in Africa preach that the eating of winged termites is a heathen custom.[132] That's an odd twist, given that the Old Testament advised Christians and Jews to eat locusts, beetles, and grasshoppers, and there are mentions of insect eating in the religious literature of Christians, Muslims, and Jews.[133]

Industrial approaches to farming imported from the West also contribute to the erosion of edible insect populations. Using pesticides to combat common pests, such as the brown plant-hopper that attacks rice, can backfire. They can kill the predators that could keep the planthopper under control, and exacerbate or even cause outbreaks of the pest, while destroying populations of other beneficial and even edible insects.

Some also suggest that Western prejudice against bugs as food has had a negative effect on Africa because, as colonial shapers of policies and outlooks on the continent, their own disgust for entomophagy has resulted in a reduction in the consumption of insects and a loss of important nutrients.[134]

All of which makes me feel terribly guilty for my inability to give bugs a chance. They say that tastes are culture, and that means they can be learned and sometimes even unlearned. I'm afraid that so far, I've failed to unlearn my distaste for insects on my plate, or anywhere *near* my plate. But I haven't given up. And I like to think I'm making some progress when it comes to other new-to-me kinds of meat on African menus, at least some of them.

18

Meat means celebration

That evening, the aroma of crocodile in tchobi sauce and mango puree on toast embodied African legends. It is the aroma of forest breezes when the spirits fly from branch to branch and disturb the sleep of human beings.

– Calixthe Beyala
Comment Cuisiner son Mari à l'Africaine

In much of Africa, meat is still something to be enjoyed on only very special occasions, at religious celebrations and naming ceremonies, baptisms, or weddings. Average meat consumption per person in sub-Saharan Africa is the lowest on earth; in Sierra Leone, for example, it's just 7.3 kilograms a year.[135] Compare that with the meat-eating statistics from Western industrial countries. In the sausage-lovers' land of Germany, it's 88.1 kilograms per person per year. Cross the Atlantic to North America, the land of inexpensive burger joints, and it goes even higher: the average consumption of meat in Canada is 94.3 kilograms per person a year and in the U.S.A. a whopping 120.2 kilograms. Of fifty-three African countries, in only two – South Africa and Gabon –

does the average meat consumption exceed fifty kilograms a year. Fish is a far more common ingredient in African sauces and soups than are beef, pork, mutton, or goat meat, and even then, quantities used are generally modest and becoming more so as prices rise and supplies dwindle.

The large herds of goats, sheep, or cattle have traditionally only been found among pastoralists, who view them more as savings accounts than as a constant source of ready meat or income. Many rural and even some urban people may own a few goats or sheep, a chicken and duck or two, but these are primarily raised either for selling when income is needed, or for slaughter for religious or ceremonial purposes. As New York chef Marcus Samuelsson wrote in *The Soul of a New Cuisine* – his book celebrating the foods and flavours of Africa – it's difficult to come up with generalizations about a continent as enormous and varied as Africa, but one that can safely be made is that "meat means celebration."

Weddings also mean celebration. After we left Ghana and moved to Kenya, I had the opportunity to attend a colleague's spectacular wedding in his hometown of Addis Ababa. We were treated to a feast of Ethiopian culture – including a spectacular dance show in which the men and women performers appeared to have no bones at all – and Ethiopian food, a sit-down buffet for hundreds at the Hilton. The dishes were simply dazzling, a showcase of Ethiopia's fabulous and unique cuisine.

Its staple is *injera*, a very large pancake made with a sourdough starter from an indigenous variety of millet known as *teff*, although sorghum and wheat can also be used. The *teff* is pounded into a fine powder and sifted. The dough is then allowed to ferment before being poured into a large pan, traditionally over an open fire but today increasingly over a clay stove to reduce firewood consumption. Professional *injera* bakeries around the world are developing their own *injera* cookers, similar to large round waffle-makers.

Injera is a fabulous multipurpose food, acting as plate, eating utensil, and nutritious staple. You tear off bits of it and use them to scoop and soak up the stew, or *wat*. A national favourite is *doro wat*, a spicy chicken stew, while others are made with beef and fish.

The wedding menu offered all of these Ethiopian delicacies and more, including raw beef. Entire carcasses hung on the wall behind the servers, who obliged by carving off hefty slices of the red meat for diners. A banquet fit for a king, and my colleague, the groom at that glorious wedding, was dressed for the part in his exquisite tailored jacket embroidered in gold thread.

There is nothing inherently wrong with eating uncooked meat, not if you have a taste for it and do not have environmental, religious, or ethical reasons for choosing to live as a vegetarian or vegan. Raw meat features in many world cuisines. But if meat inspection and public health infrastructure are weak or non-existent, consuming uncooked meat can be risky. In Ethiopia, as we found out, raw beef can be a main course that leads to a dessert of *Zentel,* the medicine that treats a variety of worms.

At an outdoor restaurant where we ate in Addis, a friend drew my attention to the clutter of little boxes that littered the ground around our table. On closer inspection, we identified these as empty packages of Zentel tablets. A few weeks after our trip to Ethiopia, when we were all back in Nairobi, one of my travelling companions discovered she had smuggled a tapeworm back to Kenya. There was nothing for it but to kill the unwanted beast in her intestines with a dose of Zentel. But she said the tender raw beef she'd eaten in Addis had been worth it.

Most meat eaten in Africa – and I'm happy to say this because I'm one of those who hasn't developed a taste for raw meat – is well cooked. For some very special occasions, the entire cow, sheep, or pig may be roasted whole to ensure there's enough to feed a large wedding party or the throngs sure to be present at the enthronement of an important traditional leader, or just to share

Celebrating a wedding with food, The Gambia.

with neighbours and friends and the less fortunate.

During the Eid al-Adha Festival of Sacrifice in Mali, the holy festival for which we sacrificed Spot in Tamale, it's not unusual to see a sheep tethered in front of just about every home for a few weeks in advance of the religious celebration. On the day itself, after the mandatory prayers and ceremony, the sheep are slaughtered and the meat is divided up and shared with the entire extended family, neighbours, and the poor. On each Festival of Sacrifice we marked during our nearly seven years in Bamako, our kitchen counter rapidly filled with roasted legs of sheep and large chunks of mutton offered to us by just about everyone we knew and even some people we didn't, who came bearing meat.

In Mali, on this holy day, about three million sheep are slaughtered and roasted. Perhaps just as many are exported to neighbouring countries such as Senegal and Côte d'Ivoire, some of them led there on foot by herders and in urgent need of fattening up once they plod and straggle into the livestock markets at their destinations.

Grilled or roasted meat is a culinary treat found across Africa, where it's barbecued over charcoal or wood fires on roadsides or in small *rotisseries* set up in markets or at major intersections. These imbue roadside markets and neighbourhoods with the smell of wood smoke combined with the aroma of sizzling meat. But the methods of grilling and the condiments used to flavour the meat are as variable as are the names by which it's known.

In Kenya, it's *nyama choma*, Kiswahili for "grilled meat." In parts of Nigeria and in Cameroon, it's *suya* or *soya* and the vendors who sell it are known as "Ministers of Soya." In The Gambia it's called *afra*. In Senegal it's sold in *dibiteries*, and it's *kankan* in Guinea. And so on. I can't recommend it highly enough to anyone who likes meat. (For those who don't, it may be best to skip this chapter altogether.)

I more or less lived on barbecued goat and mutton picked

up from roadside grills when travelling in Mali on reporting assignments and in northern Côte d'Ivoire when I was reporting on the conflict there in 2002 and 2003. The BBQ barons, the men for whom roasting and grilling meat is their life's calling, all have their own individual mixes of spices with which they sprinkle the meat – dried hot peppers, finely ground peanuts, wild herbs and onions, and usually some monosodium glutamate (MSG) or Maggi seasoning, if you so wish. Some do the grilling over brick fireplaces and wood fires, sometimes using wood from only certain kinds of trees that imbue the meat with a distinctive flavour. Others prepare the meat over charcoal stoves, often fashioned from half a barrel sliced in two lengthwise and then welded onto metal legs. On these they may place grills or smooth and shiny sheets of recycled metal into which holes have been punched and across which they slide the sizzling meat. It is a process that pleases the eye, the nose, and the tongue. Just writing about this makes my stomach grumble in yearning.

Usually the barbecued meats are from domesticated live-stock or poultry – beef, goat, sheep, or chicken. But not always. As elsewhere on the planet, some ethnic groups in Africa eat dogs and cats. I learned this by chance one afternoon in Tamale, during a visit from a couple of Ghanaian women involved with the school that a group of us was setting up. From our back veranda, they spied our two tabby cats sleeping peacefully under a bamboo bench and were inspired to offer me a recipe for them. There was talk of a certain kind of grill, a particular way of cutting up the cat and a list of spices. I failed to register the details because I'd shut my ears and was concentrating on concocting a lock-jawed smile.

When one day our caretaker and handyman caught and killed a rat so large that not even our cats would dare tackle it, I asked him how we should dispose of the corpse. I suggested we burn it, recalling that rats carry many diseases and that the bacteria responsible for bubonic plague is spread by rat fleas. But

Rukaya, our babysitter, was appalled at this suggestion. She said she would take the rat home, hang it for two or three days, and then cook it. "The meat is so sweet!" she exclaimed.

And then there is bushmeat, game from wild animals. It's a subject to which I come reluctantly. Bushmeat has been a major source of food for people ever since there have been people on this planet. In spite of the rise of sedentary agriculture and domesticated livestock, game has continued to be an important part of diets the world over, and that includes tropical Africa. Although individual cultural or religious beliefs and taboos may exist among different ethnic groups that prohibit eating the flesh of certain animals, there are precious few species of wild creatures that can't be found in a cooking pot or roasting over a grill somewhere in the world.

In Cameroon, during the two years we lived there and several subsequent visits, I sampled – mostly unwittingly – game that I would happily have gone to my grave life without ever tasting. This included a round of tender white flesh that was served at a banquet hosted by our wealthy landlord in Foumban. I tucked into it with gusto, thinking it seafood (which, come to think about it, is also meat harvested from the wild unless it's the fruit of aquaculture). It had a gentle flavour, something borrowed from two of my favourites, lobster and haddock, with just a hint of poultry thrown in. It wasn't until I asked what it was and they told me it was python that I felt queasy. Dead or alive, I do not relish physical contact with snakes and I didn't care for the idea of the meat from a very large snake in my stomach. Which makes no logical sense at all, but there it is.

I once found myself staring down at a bowl cradling a baby crocodile basted in a grey sauce in a restaurant in Cameroon's biggest city, the port of Douala. On that occasion I quietly pushed it aside, although years later in Kenya, at a crocodile farm I discovered that a kebab made with chunks of white crocodile meat is rather good, reminiscent of shellfish but not quite so flavourful.

Then there was the fateful evening when we were invited to a gathering in a restaurant in the south of Cameroon where we were served monkey (the people around me called it "chimpanzee"). The large bowl of sauce was plonked in the middle of the table. There was a baby-sized hand sticking out of it. It made me want to weep, retch, and run. I ate nothing, pleading nausea that I was not faking.

For personal reasons, I have a powerful aversion to eating primates. I studied monkeys, wrote a thesis on the social behaviour of spider monkeys in Guatemala – and came to have a strong affinity for the tree-swinging playful primate acrobats that moved about in large extended families, enjoying late-morning romps with each other after early morning fruit-feeding frenzies. I watched juveniles lining up like children in a playground to slide down the smooth limb of a giant tree right into the lap of a waiting male monkey. Like a favourite uncle or grandpa, he hugged and tickled each of the young ones as they landed on him. I took data for hours on doting spider monkey mothers moving about with their infants on their backs, watched them seek out comfy resting places where branches meet trunks of those enormous tropical trees and then pull their infants off their backs to spend what could be called "quality time" grooming their little bodies, removing whatever insects or debris they dug out of their infants' fur.

So I am coming at this issue of bushmeat with very strong biases, especially when it involves monkeys or apes. I avert my eyes every time I pass a dead monkey on a roadside, freshly killed, dangling from a stick on a roadside for sale, or flayed and smoked and awaiting purchase in a market.

Of course, not everyone in Africa likes bushmeat; as elsewhere in the world, people are very selective about which animals they will and won't eat. Across the continent, there are taboos against many kinds of bushmeat. Some clans or even entire ethnic groups may view a particular animal or reptile as their totem, sacred, which means it would be a sacrilege to kill or consume it.

One Sierra Leonean friend, a Muslim, explained to me that Muslims shouldn't eat monkey meat – and he doesn't – because "it's like eating people," which echoes my own thoughts on the matter. Then he went on to talk about the advent of Islam in the country, centuries ago. As the story goes, people were instructed not to go to their farms on Fridays to work in the fields because Friday is the holy day on which they should go to the mosque for prayers. Those who insisted on farming on Fridays, he says, were turned into monkeys. So to eat a monkey is to eat an ancestor.

Some weeks after he told me this, I visited the Tacuguma Chimpanzee Sanctuary in the remnant forests on the spectacular mountains of the Western Peninsula near Freetown. It's a large enclosure where chimps are safe from hunters and cooking pots. There the guide told me that before the civil war ravaged the country between 1991 and 2002, Sierra Leoneans did not eat chimpanzee meat. But influence from peacekeeping forces from other African countries, he said, and of course rampant hunger that drove desperately hungry people to try new sources of food, cracked the ancient taboo. Today, he says, some of the chimps that have been given sanctuary at Tacuguma are orphans of adult chimps killed for bushmeat.

Friend, filmmaker, writer, and former colleague Arwen Kidd wrote an essay about bushmeat and what it was like trying to come to terms with some culinary choices while she was working on a journalism project in Liberia.[136] "Driving down the main streets of Monrovia," she wrote, "I have encountered brightly painted signs boasting pictures of endangered animals, stating 'Don't eat these' – advice necessary in a country home to such quickly disappearing species as the pygmy hippo (an animal whose near extinction I recently heard bemoaned by one of my reporters, who remembers from his childhood their taste, 'so sweet-oh!')." Arwen also reflected on the many times her African friends and colleagues had expressed bemusement about "white people's" delicate sensibilities when it came to food.

This, in turn, got me reflecting on my own culinary sensibilities, habits, and food decisions, especially about different kinds of meat. Why would I not eat some creatures, but continue to eat beef, for example? Scientists have been telling us for years about the very high toll that meat production takes on the environment and the climate, that if we are serious about tackling climate change, we should reduce or even cut out our meat consumption.[137] And beef, which I loved, was the worst – requiring twenty-eight times more land to produce than chicken or pork, and producing five times the greenhouse gas emissions.[138] Yet I still ate beef (at least as of this writing), and I still ate far, far more meat every year than the average person in Africa. I was hardly well placed to make judgements about ethical or environmentally friendly eating.

For all my wallowing around in the mucky realm of relativism, bushmeat remains a highly controversial issue. Many wild animals are such popular fare and their habitat so diminished by logging, agricultural development, and deforestation that they are now becoming rare. Some are on the endangered species list. In 1999, experts from organizations and agencies around the world met in the United States to talk about the "commercial bushmeat crisis in tropical African countries" and its impact on threatened and endangered species, particularly great apes.[139] They represented a worldwide network of conservationists, zoo biologists, animal welfare advocates, and medical researchers and they then established the Bushmeat Crisis Task Force.

The consensus of the Task Force was that the commercial bushmeat trade in Africa was unsustainable, and if it continued unchecked there would be dire consequences for both animal populations – great apes, forest elephants, and some species of monkeys – and for human populations as well. It's estimated that bushmeat provides up to 80 percent of the protein and fat in rural diets in Africa.[140]

For ten years, the Task Force worked to find ways to end illegal and unregulated hunting of endangered animals and the commercial bushmeat trade. It drew attention to the responsibility logging companies, mining firms, and other extractive industries bore for the growth of the unregulated commercial bushmeat trade, calling on them to provide alternative sources of food for their workers. It examined an array of solutions, including giving local people rights and incentives to manage and hunt their own resources, more public education, and better anti-poaching laws and enforcement. The Task Force ended its "formal collaboration" in 2009, which is a polite term for saying it ran out of funding, but it continues to provide information highlighting the bushmeat crisis and the risks to endangered species. Their salvation may depend in part on whether local people can succeed in raising these wild animals in captivity or ranching them like any other domestic livestock, with all the environmental implications that would have.

Researchers from the Center for International Forestry Research (CIFOR), where I worked in 2014 and 2015, have undertaken extensive studies on bushmeat, its importance for nutrition and food security in Africa, how it may relate to diseases such as Ebola, and how best it might be regulated. They've found that stunting in children in the Congo Basin is almost nil where people have access to bushmeat. People in the Congo Basin consume about five million tonnes of bushmeat each year. To replace that with beef in the region would require the conversion of 20 to 25 million hectares of forest to pasture, an area about the size of Great Britain. There are no simple answers or solutions when it comes to bushmeat.[141] I keep trying to remind myself of the complexities of the issue the day two of my food guides in Sierra Leone, Rachel and Esther, decide to tell me their fondness for bushmeat. They start with details of the roasted monkey they bought and shared earlier that day at a roadside market while travelling in the east of the country. I try very hard to keep things in perspective. I remind myself – yet again – what the industrial food system has been doing to us, what cruel crimes against livestock, the environment, and climate are committed every day by CAFOs (concentrated animal feeding operations) in the name of cheap beef, chicken, or pork. Mentally, I tick through the list of wild animals, the bushmeat I've eaten in Canada – black bear, moose, deer, and snowshoe hare.

Rachel and Esther seem not to notice that I really don't want more details about their monkey lunch, that it's *too much information*.

Rachel: "I was having the hand [of the monkey]."

Esther: "I like the head and the tail. They are the best parts."

Rachel: "Yes, the tail is the best part. But the head and the hands, the fingers, are also good. And the buttocks! I like the buttocks too."

Rachel: "Some people like eating dogs and some like cats. I don't."

Esther: "I like viper, the kind with two horns. They can leap right over a village."

Me: "A snake? That can leap? Over a village?"

Esther: "Oh yes, it's the little snake that has horns. They can fly right over a village."

I decide I don't really need to know any more about this mysterious edible viper, so ask nothing more.

Both agree the best kind of bushmeat is the rodent called "cutting-grass." I'm pleased to hear this. If there's one source of bushmeat that is not endangered in Africa, it's the Greater Cane Rat (*Thryonomys swinderianus*), popular all the way from Sierra Leone to the Democratic Republic of Congo. It can weigh up to ten kilograms in the wild and grow as long as sixty centimetres. Changing habitat and deforestation appear not to be harming the population of these animals; some believe it's actually increasing. Known in Sierra Leone as "cutting-grass" and in Ghana as "grass-cutter," it certainly has the choppers for the job that has given it the name. Its big sharp teeth are crammed into its small jawbone and can slice easily through any grass or cane and, much to the annoyance of farmers, also through a lot of crops.

Fortunately, cane rats can be reared in captivity, which transforms them into regular old livestock, eliminating some of the stigma about eating them, at least among those who believe human beings should be eating animals.[142] I agree with Rachel and Esther that I should really give cutting-grass meat a try. After all, it's a rat in name only; its closest taxonomic cousins are actually porcupines and guinea pigs.[143]

They tell me one of the best places to find cutting-grass meat in Sierra Leone is at Mano Junction, an intersection of three bush roads linking major regional towns. One comes from Koidu, via Tongo Fields – a major diamond mine owned and operated by a complex tangle of foundations and subsidiaries held by BSG Resources, which belongs to the controversial Israeli billionaire, Beny Steinmetz.[144] The BSG Group had reportedly agreed to improve the road between its Koidu and Tongo Fields mines. The only discernible work that has been done on the rutted, rocky mud track leading through forest and small farming villages is a few loads of gravel dropped on one particularly steep hill. During the rainy season, the rest of the road is often impassable to all wheeled vehicles except the *okadas,* or motorcycle taxis, driven by young men, many of whom developed their riding skills and fearless recklessness during the war in which they fought on one side or another. The *okadas* seem able to get through no matter what time of year, sometimes with two or three passengers plus giant bags of market produce piled high and lashed onto the backs of their motorcycles.

It is a road spectacularly suited to the word in the Krio language for "bump," which is *galohp.* We are doing some bone-rattling *galohping* from Kono towards Mano Junction in the four-wheel-drive Land Cruiser. We're being jostled up and down and back and forth, as if on the back of a bronco that's been stoked with several tabs of Ecstasy.

By the time we reach Mano Junction, any appetite I had has been *galohped* right out of me. But as we pull to a stop at the intersection, the vendors come running. They swarm the vehicle, all shouting at once as they vie for our attention and business, thrusting platters laden with local delicacies through the open windows. I'm being assaulted by avocados and bananas and bags of peanuts. Others proffer trays heavy with kebabs of yellowish fleshy things fried, I'm told, in red palm oil. Some kebabs are made with slices of fried sweet potato. And some are made with the meat of cutting-grass. The rodents' heads can be purchased separately, but these are more expensive, says Ivan Kajue, the driver, because they are a very special culinary treat.

I buy four of each kind of kebab, enough to share with the others in the vehicle. The cost is negligible (by my standards), about 25 U.S. cents for each sweet potato kebab and about 50 for a kebab of cutting-grass. Our intrepid driver Ivan convinces me to buy a head too, for later. "It's very sweet!" he informs me. I assure him he'll have to eat the head; I won't touch it. Then I realize this is precisely what he had in mind. Hesitantly, I nibble on the first chunk of meat on the stick. It's tender, the grainy texture of cow's tongue, a mild flavour. I pull off the next chunk, chew and swallow. It's good, not gamey at all, reminiscent of pork.

But I still have no intention of even looking at the head that is tucked away in a black plastic bag. This, I admit, is irrational and unreasonable. There are many foods that I eat without qualm – oysters, clams, sardines, shrimps, even some sausages – that don't warrant detailed analysis or close examination before being eaten. But I can pop these into my mouth whole, without searching for the right place to bite off a bit and coming face to face with a pair of eyes.

When we reach Kenema, I gladly hand over the cutting-grass head to Ivan and he gladly receives it.

19

Fishy fears and ocean delights

If you want to eat a monkey, don't look in its eyes.

– Guinean proverb
The Wisdom of Africa
Pete Lewenstein, editor

Learning to cope with eyes in the food on my plate was something I should have managed during the years we lived in the Malian capital, Bamako. During that time, I spent many evenings at an impromptu eatery that Janet and Maurice, a Cameroonian couple, set up every day just after sunset on a wide dusty road in the city. The menu was simple, extremely so. On offer were plantains and grilled mackerel, fish that were trucked north daily from neighbouring Côte d'Ivoire. Janet smothered them in a miracle of flavours, a marinade she made with a myriad of peppers, local condiments, and onion. She served them on a bed of crispy fried plantains, one of my favourite foods, known as *aloko* in Mali and *plantains mûrs frits* among the Cameroonians. Maurice dealt with the beverages, soft drinks and beer. No frills, not even a fork to eat with. Instead, Janet brought around a pitcher of water, a bar of soap, and a towel, and poured as each of us washed our hands before tucking into our meals.

The first time one of these fish was plopped in front of me, I stared down at it for some minutes while it stared right back. My companions, of several African nationalities, had already dug in. They asked me what was wrong, what I was waiting for and then advised me that if it was cutlery, I was wasting my time. There wasn't any; fish tasted far better eaten with the hand. I had been hoping for a knife with which to hack off the offending head, but I didn't tell them this. Instead, hesitantly, I began to pick away at the body of the fish, inexpertly pulling back the skin and separating the delicate and succulent white flesh from the bones.

I used my fingers to mash up the small pieces and check for bones before putting them into my mouth. Once I had picked away at the largest chunks of flesh, I sat back and pushed the plate away, pronouncing the fish very tasty. While their fish had been picked clean, nothing left but bare bones, mine looked like something a spoiled child had picked over. As if reading my mind, my Cameroonian colleague and friend Seydou chided me, "Not even a child would eat a fish like that. What a waste! You've hardly touched it. What's wrong with you? *Qu'est-ce que tu as?*" With that he pulled my plate towards him and polished off the rest of the fish himself. Watching him, I understood why we use the term "polish off" to describe a dinner well and truly finished; when he was done with the mackerel, its bones almost shone.

Regrettably, in many ways I am still like a finicky child when it comes to eating fish. I've not managed to develop an affinity for any serving of fish that involves eyes, whiskers, or bones lurking in fillets. On many occasions over the years, generous African hosts have served me dishes made with various kinds of mudfish that burrow into the muck in swamps, rivers, and lakes. Some can survive months in the mud after the rain-fed pond in which they live dries up during the annual drought.

Although there are many species of such fish, they tend to have blunt heads and cat-like whiskers that make me recoil. African friends seem reasonably tolerant of my dislike of the mudfish that they tell me is delectable; that is, they don't push me to eat it. I expect they just chalk it up to "strangers" (foreigners) being like "children," as the Ghanaian proverb says we are.

Although I grew up in Nova Scotia, an ocean-bound province full of fisher folk and fresh fish, where local songsters proclaimed you couldn't claim to be a real local if you didn't like fish, that didn't mean we *all* liked *all* the fish – bones, fins, head, and eyeballs. One chilly February evening in an upscale European restaurant in an upscale suburb of Banjul that caters to tourists in the Gambian capital, I was seated with several fellow Nova Scotians studying the menu of mostly Swiss and German dishes. It offered fresh local seafood, and one of my companions decided she'd try the butterfish, which the waiter highly recommended. When the waiter placed the plate in front of her, she let out a shriek that turned heads (mostly European and a few Gambian) at neighbouring tables. She shouted at the waiter to take it away, saying she couldn't eat a fish head. I was mortified, but only because in her reaction I saw myself struggling to overcome my own disquiet at the sight of a whole fish on my plate. And I felt for her; the butterfish had a particularly unnerving head with large front teeth that looked almost human.

The Europeans around us muttered and tsked-tsked at this show of uncultured behaviour. The African diners present simply looked aghast at such an outburst of incomprehensible outrage over the presence of a large, delicious fish on one's plate.

From the mud ponds along the banks of the Niger River in northern Mali, to the swamps in eastern Sierra Leone, to the fishing hamlets along the Volta River in northern Ghana, to the beaches at Yoff in Senegal's capital Dakar, to the magnificent coral reefs off Kenya's coast on the Indian Ocean, anywhere there is water in which fish can breed, Africa's fishers are there harvesting them. Smoked, dried, fresh, fried, or salted, from rivers, lakes, oceans, and swamps, big and small, fish and molluscs are a mainstay in many African cuisines. Shrimp and crayfish are often ground up to "enliven soups, stews and sauces" and along with various combinations of fish oil, ginger, garlic, and other spices, they are a key ingredient in Ghana's pungent peppery condiment called *shito*.[145]

Cameroon's name derives from the Portuguese "Rio dos Camarões" or River of Shrimps. And once upon a time, shrimps swarmed the waters around the coastal town of Kribi, set on a little stretch of paradise with white sandy beaches backing almost directly onto tropical rainforest. Just south of Kribi, the Lobé waterfalls cascade over volcanic rocks straight into the ocean surf. In the late 1990s, I spent a few nights there in a tiny hotel listening to the crashing waves and the nocturnal orchestra of the jungle fauna, marvelling at the beauty and the bounty of the place. In the morning, fishermen came ashore in small boats loaded to the gunwales with fresh shrimp and fish.

The roadside eateries in the town of Kribi featured the bounty from the sea, offering grilled sole, barracuda, snapper, grouper, and shrimp served up with all manner of delectable side dishes, including what must be some of the world's biggest and most delicious avocados.

Amen, and alas. This was before those in charge of the Exxon-Mobil pipeline, which would carry oil from Chad south through Cameroon, decided it would be laid right through a tropical rainforest to an offshore loading terminal erected on the Eden-like shore just south of Kribi. From there, the oil would be transferred to tankers that would carry it off to energy-guzzling lands far away. The pipeline and terminal belonging to Exxon-Mobil, then the world's wealthiest corporation, were financed in part by the World Bank. Their construction involved blasting away a reef known to be a rich fishing ground just offshore. Since then, there have been several oil spills and today those who once depended on fish for their livelihoods are out of luck. The fish are now all but gone.[146] Christine Badgley gives a very personal eye-witness account of this on her blog Pipeline Dreams.

Fishing, processing, and marketing fish are the lifeblood for untold hundreds of thousands, if not millions of people living in coastal areas on the West African coast. For the most part, the fishing they do is artisanal from small, family-owned boats and with simple nets and sometimes with hooks and lines from dugout canoes. They can't begin to compete with the foreign factory trawlers from Europe and Asia that park themselves in their territorial waters.

Sit on any beach near Freetown in Sierra Leone and you can watch, as dusk fades into night, the lights of the trawlers as they slip closer to land, well inside the inshore exclusion zone. Sierra Leone – like Guinea, Guinea-Bissau, and Liberia – does not have the resources or the political rigour and integrity needed to police its territorial waters to protect against illegal and overfishing by the foreign trawlers. Some of them are unregistered, some dishonest about what and how much they are catching, and some simply transfer their catches offshore for shipping to Asia and Europe without the knowledge of the government. Sierra Leone suffers from the world's highest rate of the plague officially known as Illegal, Unreported and Unregulated fishing or IUU.[147]

The effect on local fishers and on local supplies of fish is devastating. Nets set overnight just a few hundred metres off-shore or along beaches during the day may bring in a sorry catch, a mere handful of fish, even if the haul of rubbish may be a bumper one. I've watched as a dozen men hauled, chanted, and strained for more than two hours to pull in a net on Freetown's Lumley Beach, only to bring ashore a net with six barracuda bare-ly bigger than fingerlings, a lot of plastic bottles and old shoes, and a toilet seat. To make matters worse, those who venture out at night in their small motorboats to cast their nets just offshore run the risks of being mowed down by pirate trawlers or destroying their motors when propellers get wound up in plastic in the garbage slicks that abound in coastal waters.[148]

Freshwater fish populations are also in trouble. In recent decades, freshwater bodies across Africa – from Mali to Chad, from Kenya to Malawi – have been drying and silting up, ravaged by climate change, pollution, and mismanagement. There has been some effort to develop small-scale fish farming in rural communities to produce tilapia and other kinds of fish, but these are too few and far between to provide a real substitute for the loss of natural fish stocks. The use of small-mesh fishing nets in the Volta and Niger Rivers, among many others, has also hurt fish populations as young fish are caught up along with mature ones and wind up in cooking pots before they can go forth and multiply.

Several large tourism resorts and industrial projects are planned for the Western Peninsula of Sierra Leone, and sand mining is taking a terrible toll on the beaches and coastline itself. Illegal fishing continues and offshore oil exploration is ongoing, so the fish stocks and the health of the coastal waters are at immense and imminent risk.

But the fish are not all gone yet and there are great antidotes to this steady diet of bad fishing news. One of the most powerful I can think of must surely be an excursion with Mohamed, from the village of Tokeh, just down the coast a few kilometres from Freetown.

Tokeh Beach is a sliver of tropical paradise. The startlingly white sand crescent, backed by deep green forest, was once home to the "Africana," a Club Med resort to which tourists were ferried by helicopter from Lungi International Airport that serves the capital, several kilometres and a very wide river away. But the long war years finished the resort. After it closed, its nightclub, swimming pool, tennis courts, and gardens fell into ruins.

In the post-war years, Tokeh Beach became a community of fishermen and of people who catered to foreigners in a very low-key and low-priced way with small thatched structures and cold drinks. Immediately after the war, many of them were United Nations peacekeepers who some local people impertinently christened "beach keepers." In subsequent years, they were joined by the growing ranks of expatriate development workers, employees of the UN-backed Special Court for Sierra Leone, diplomats, business people, foreign military personnel from the International Military Assistance Training Team or IMATT, and mining and private security roughnecks who were flocking to Sierra Leone. Some fishermen turned tour guides-cum-chefs offer one-day excursions from Tokeh to the Banana Islands with a meal tossed in as part of the deal. One day we negotiate a day's outing with Mohamed, one of these entrepreneurs.

We set out in the morning, after Mohamed has loaded a sack of rice, a bag of charcoal, and some bags with condiments for the meal and cutlery, all piled in a heap between narrow slats in the middle of his wooden fishing boat. It is quite slow going; the Yamaha 95 motor struggles and splutters as it pushes the boat across the glassy sea towards the Banana Islands, more than twenty-five kilometres distant.

Our progress is made even slower because Mohamed keeps stopping the boat to shop. First, we intercept a young man in a tiny dugout canoe who is using a fishing line and a hook, no rod. His face and bare torso are covered in fine sand. In exchange for a few dollars, Mohamed relieves him of his morning catch, two magnificent barracuda, each almost a metre long. A short while later we cross paths with a slightly larger fishing boat on its way back to shore after a night on the water. It has a fine haul of crabs and Mohamed buys four.

Now satisfied, he guns the motor and we continue on our way at full throttle. The Banana Islands comprise three small islands, none of which is called Banana. There is Dublin Island, connected at low tide to Ricketts Island, and then a third tiny one called Mes-Meheux. We land on Dublin and head off on foot through a village and across the island to a beach on the other side. Mohamed enlists the help of a couple of local young men to carry the makings of our lunch, and the grill and charcoal needed to cook it.

Mohamed sets to work immediately, cleaning the barracuda and removing the scales. I join him as he chops it into short chunks, chuffed by the progress I decide I've made over the years in suppressing qualms about normal fish anatomy, and getting practical and realistic about food and its origins. I'm now less likely to be plagued by a fish head or guts than by echoes of my daughter voicing her distress that I am even eating the fish, so high up on the food chain and imperilled by overfishing, polluting, acidification, and deterioration of the world's oceans. The beach on Dublin itself is a reminder of that, dotted as it is with rubbish that has washed ashore with the tide – plastic bottles, a pink flip-flop, some waterlogged running shoes, and other flotsam.

Mohamed puts together the rudimentary barbecue, half an old barrel that is a chamber for charcoal, mounted on metal legs and topped by a grill. He lights the charcoal and prepares in a single pot a sauce with tomato paste, hot peppers, onion, some mixed green herbs, and a Maggi cube. Maybe it is the clear salt air, maybe it is just something about the idea of eating fresh fish while basking in the tropical sun that acts as a catalyst for my digestive juices and ignites my lust for food. My stomach starts growling like a predator on the prowl and I am physically aching for the food long before Mohamed has finished grilling the crabs and the chunks of barracuda (marinated in some of the tomato sauce), cooked the rice, and dished it all up in plastic bowls. To distract myself I wade out and take a short swim in the warm water. That only whets my appetite even more.

My memories of the hours we spent on Dublin Island and indeed nearly all my photographs are not, as one might reasonably expect, of the beautiful secluded beach on a tropical island, watching the azure ocean waters and the sapphire sky melting into each other on the wild blue horizon. Instead, my Banana Islands recollections and photos are all about the food. If I were in the business of awarding stars for eating establishments, as Michelin is, I would give Mohamed and that heavenly meal of fresh seafood on the Banana Islands a whole sky full of them.

A fisher in his dugout canoe, using a hook and line to catch barracuda, with the Banana Islands in the background.

A fisher paddling his www.tokehbeach.com boat at Tokeh Beach in Sierra Leone.

20

Grandma's cooking?

I have yet to hear of a traditional diet — from any culture, anywhere in the world — that is not substantially healthier than the "standard American diet." The more we honor cultural differences in eating, the healthier we will be.

– Michael Pollan
The New York Times Magazine
October 2, 2011[149]

I had mentioned to Mohamed that we'd be just as happy if he left the Maggi cube out of the tomato sauce, but he seemed just as happy not to entertain my suggestion. The fact is that today, manufactured flavour-enhancers are ubiquitous in Africa. Television commercials promoting flavour cubes feature smiling and expensively dressed African women lovingly crumbling them into rich African stews bubbling away in stainless steel pots in gleaming modern kitchens. The reward comes when the well-heeled husband – in his suit and tie – arrives home from his office job and offers her a dazzling smile for her efforts. Like reruns of a worn-out American dream.

Entire buildings in cities across the continent are painted in the yellow and red hues of the Maggi brand, turning them into giant advertising blocks for Nestlé seasonings. Throughout West Africa, roadsides and market areas are punctuated with small wooden food stands sponsored by Maggi and emblazoned with the red and yellow name and logo. Billboards abound, and a massive Maggi campaign begun in 2010 featured an oversized image of a lovely young woman and the words, "Rachel. Student. Cook. Star." Then across the bottom of the supersized billboard: "Real Star. Real Maggi. Real Woman."

The Malian cookbook issued by the government to promote the country's cuisine and local foods and crops has hardly a recipe that doesn't include Maggi cubes.[150] Today ever-growing numbers of corporations are pumping out artificial flavour-enhancing cubes and powders to satisfy an apparently ever-growing demand.[151]

Manufactured flavour enhancers have crept in and inserted themselves firmly and permanently into Africa's cuisines, and so it's time I paid more attention to them. That's why I find myself again traipsing through a market on another learning exercise. This time I'm with Mai Diakité, a Malian friend, and we're in the Medina Market in Bamako. A sprawling web of paths, alleyways, and vendor stalls, the Medina market is nestled at the foot of the majestic red cliffs that flank the city's northern edge and squeeze the rampant urban sprawl east and west along the valley of the Niger River. It's primarily an afternoon market, where local growers and traders bring produce harvested fresh each day from gardens and farms outside of town. But much that is sold here is also imported.

We begin in the market's vegetable section. Mai takes my arm and leads me, offering a running commentary about what vegetables are available in the stalls and on the tarpaulins laid out on the ground. There are "immigrant" vegetables introduced over many decades and integrated into local cuisines – tomatoes, carrots, green peppers, cucumbers, celery, zucchini, lettuce, Irish

Mai Diakité at the Medina Market in Bamako. The sacks are bulging with a wealth of local produce, a feast for the senses.

potatoes, radishes, and cabbage. (Cameroonian chef Alexandre Bella Ola calls a dish featuring many non-indigenous vegetables *"Les légumes immigrés"* in his fine 2010 cookbook *La Cuisine de Moussa: 80 Recettes Africaines Irrésistibles*.) And there is more typical tropical produce, the indigenous fare – hot peppers, plantains, cassava tubers, sweet potatoes, red onions and shallots, okra, cowpeas, sorrel leaves or *oseille blanc* used for leafy sauces. There are all shapes and sizes of squash for eating and also as gourds – calabashes – that are grown for use as spoons, bowls, water containers, and musical instruments.

Mai carries on animated discussions with the women vendors, repeatedly exclaiming *"a da ka gelen kosébé!"* This translates literally from Bamanankan as "That's very expensive." But with the inflected dismay that Mai gives the phrase, I figure what it really means is, "Man, that's bloody outrageous!"

In urban Mali, food has already become a luxury and this is one year before drought, political crisis, and conflict would seriously exacerbate an already very difficult situation in 2012. Even before these multiple crises, most Malians were living on less than two dollars a day and, on average, households were having to spend more than 60 percent of the family budget on food.

To put that in perspective, in the U.S., the average family spends only 7 percent of its budget on food. In Canada, the percentage of the household budget spent on food is not even 14 percent.[152]

Not surprising then that the spiralling food prices in 2007 and 2008 led to food riots in many poor countries around the world. Higher food costs didn't mean inconvenience; they meant cutting back the number of meals per day or serving sizes to bare substistence levels, or below.

So while the markets of Bamako are full of food, Mai explains, most people can't afford to buy anything but the very basics to feed their families, if even these. As a result, it takes a lot of financial acrobatics to stretch precious pennies and squeeze menus to stave off hunger, even if this may mean settling for inferior flavours and ingredients. In lieu of meat, fish, or chicken, nutritious local condiments, and vegetables to give a sauce substance and taste, someone cooking for the family may just substitute artificial flavour-enhancing cubes and powders to deceive the tongue into believing something of substance is tickling its fancy. In the Medina market, there is an entire section devoted to condiments, both traditional natural ones and modern manufactured ones.

The small stalls here are strung with red and yellow pennant streamers with a simple, straightforward message: "Maggi, Maggi, Maggi, Maggi, Maggi." No surprise, then, that the stalls are crammed with stacks of bags of Maggi cubes. The market stalls are backed by narrow shelves weighted down with more Maggi products, including bottles of liquid seasoning or *arôme*. On very close inspection, I see the liquid Maggi contains: "WATER, WHEAT GLUTEN, MONOSODIUM GLUTAMATE, SUGAR, POWDERED CELLULOSE, ACETIC ACID, XYLOSE, ENZYME (AMINOPEPTIDASE, SUGAR, POTASSIUM CHLORIDE, POTASSIUM SORBATE), SODIUM HYDROXIDE, DISODIUM INOSINATE, CALCIUM CARBONATE, FLAVOUR AND ARTIFICIAL FLAVOUR, PROTEASE, DIMENTHYLPOLYSILOXANE FORMULATION, LACTIC ACID, ACID STARTER CULTURE."

The label states that this cocktail of tongue-twisting chemicals "improves the taste of soups, sauces, salads and vegetable dishes. A few drops are sufficient."

Nestlé is not alone in its bid to corner the African market on flavour-enhancing products. As Mai points out to me, another player – Adja – has entered the flavour-enhancing fray. Adja offers a selection of substitutes for real foods sized for all budgets. Those who can afford to can purchase them in bulk in large tubs. Those who have just enough money to acquire the ingredients for a single meal can buy them in the teeniest of packets holding just a spoonful of the stuff. Adja products are made by a Senegalese company, Patisen, which specializes in a growing range of processed comestibles – chocolate and peanut spreads, margarine, and "bouillon" powders and cubes. Patisen, following in the footsteps of other corporate food giants, has honed its sales pitch to a simple slogan and would have the consuming public believe that its products and flavour enhancers are like "Grandma's cooking."[153]

I pick up one of the tiny envelope packets of Adja "tomato seasoning powder." The package features a beautiful African woman holding and smiling rapturously at a large platter of vegetables stewed in rice, probably Senegal's traditional dish *Benachin,* known elsewhere in Africa as *riz gras* or Jollof rice. She is wearing an elaborate peach-coloured headscarf folded and tied so elegantly that it resembles a giant orchid perched on her head. On the back of the package, in four languages and miniscule print, the ingredients of the tomato seasoning powder are listed as: IODIZED SALT,

MONOSODIUM GLUTAMATE, CORN STARCH, WHEAT FLOUR, SUGAR, AROMAS, ALIMENTARY COLOURING. On the front it proclaims "The Best Taste."

I ask the vendor how much it costs, and then pull out a coin for 200 West African francs (about 40 U.S. cents) and stick the packet in my purse. As I write, it still sits there right in front of me on the windowsill. I regard it as a totem of the alchemy of modern food processing: Adja "tomato seasoning powder" contains not even a whiff of tomato.

The food scientists and chemists who beaver away in sterile labs, a world away from the living plants and creatures that have nourished our species for thousands of years, may know what chemical compounds hide behind the generic and vague terms "aromas" and "artificial flavour," which are listed as ingredients in so many modern foods. But we the lay public on the outside, average consumers on all continents, may be left scratching our heads about the ingredients.

Author Eric Schlosser penned a vivid account in *Fast Food Nation: The Dark Side of the All-American Meal*, of what he saw when he visited the New Jersey factory of the world's largest flavour company, International Flavors & Fragrances (IFF): "Wonderful smells drifted through the hallways, men and women in neat white lab coats cheerfully went about their work, and hundreds of little glass bottles sat on laboratory tables and shelves … The long chemical names on the little white labels were as mystifying to me as medieval Latin. These odd-sounding things would be mixed and poured and turned into new substances, like magic potions."

From what I'm seeing in Medina Market, this brave new future of manufactured flavours is now bearing down on Africa and its traditional cuisines. But they've already been largely conquered by monosodium glutamate, or MSG, which is a key component of many manufactured flavour enhancers in African diets. MSG is the sodium salt of glutamic acid, a naturally occurring amino acid. Japanese chemist Dr. Kikunae Ikeda patented it in 1908 and called it Ajinomoto, literally "essence of taste," which then became the name of the company that sold the new flavour enhancer to the world. Just a year after the patent, Japan's Interior Ministry declared MSG "harmless in terms of health and safety."[154] Despite numerous reports to the contrary, which suggest possible side effects and evidence that MSG consumption can cause kidney damage in rats,[155] MSG (also known as E621) has managed to retain its clean bill of health.

In 1995, a study for the U.S. Food and Drug Administration determined that MSG was safe when "eaten at customary levels."[156] This, in turn, meant it did not have to be regulated as a food additive and was considered instead a "flavour-enhancing ingredient." Health agencies around the world used the U.S. study to decide there was no need to regulate the amount of MSG that can be added to foods, although they seemed to have some concerns about safe doses. Health Canada, for example, stipulates: "only the smallest amount needed to enhance the flavour should be added to food."[157] It doesn't say why that is or what it means by the "smallest" amount.

Ajinomoto's conquest of the West African market happened in the late 1980s and early 1990s.[158] We watched it make its advance on northern Ghana with campaigns that spread the MSG gospel through the region with the zeal of an army of missionaries. Small vans with enormous loudspeakers strapped to their roofs made their way from village to village, playing non-stop Ajinomoto advertisements at full blast and distributing free MSG to curious villagers. A couple of decades later, the white MSG crystals, sold in plastic bags and easily mistaken for coarse salt, can be found everywhere on the continent. In Sierra Leone the pure MSG is known as "white Maggi."

If you are one of those who react poorly to large doses of MSG (as I am), prone to the palpitations, headaches, and other symptoms associated with "MSG syndrome complex,"[159] its liberal

use in African dishes can be problematic. It is increasingly difficult to find MSG-free food, given that most sauces are laced not
just with pure MSG, but also with some form of flavour cube
that is also heavy on the stuff. I've had MSG-induced headaches
from Douala to Dakar. It's very difficult for the eating public in
Africa to follow the edicts of health agencies and limit their intake
of MSG to "only the smallest amounts."

Mai tells me that at the same time as Maggi and other flavour enhancers are conquering Malian tastes and cuisine, the
quantities of indigenous, nutritious condiments and ingredients
that most people use are dropping. This is partly because of decreasing availability and rising costs of healthy local foods that
give dishes substance and flavour, and also because of advertising
and notions that processed or imported foods confer a kind of
elite status on those who consume them.

Now, before I go on any further, I can already hear some
voices, even a contrarian one in my own head, arguing that I'm
being a food Luddite, that I just want to stop economic growth
and progress, and why shouldn't Africans enjoy the same fast and
convenient processed foods that have been filling North American
supermarkets and stomachs for decades? And if all this spares a
woman the backbreaking work of pounding seeds and vegetables
to a pulp in a wooden mortar to produce traditional condiments
and ingredients, why not?

But then in my mind I recall the words of scientists, nutritionists, and defenders of healthy food and smallholder farms
raised in warning against the corporate takeover of Africa's foods
and the inevitable negative ramifications of the "nutrition transition."[160] This involves a rapid shift from traditional diets to ones
that have emerged in industrial societies, which include more fats,
especially imported edible oils, more sweeteners, more animal-
source foods. People making this nutrition transition start to suffer from obesity and diet-related non-communicable diseases such
as diabetes and cardiovascular ailments.[161]

And I also recall the voices of African friends reminiscing fondly about – *pining* for – their grandmothers' and mothers' cooking, singing the praises of their own indigenous condiments, seasonings, and spices, even as they are disappearing or falling out of favour. And I hear them worrying aloud about the influx of what they recognize as unhealthy processed and imported products in their markets and diets.

One of these voices is Mai's, as she catalogues for me the imported comestibles for sale in the stalls of Medina Market. She asks vendors if they have any cooking oil made in Mali, any shea butter or peanut oil. They say she will have to find that elsewhere. They sell only greasy-looking plastic bottles of imported palm oil or derivatives thereof.

One of the cooking oils on the shelves of the stalls is Dinor, highly processed and industrially produced palm oil from neighbouring Côte d'Ivoire. If you trace its roots you find it's produced by a company called Sania, the offspring of a corporation called Sifca, which is part of a corporate family stretching across West Africa. The corporate parents, however, are found further afield – in Asia and Europe. Among them, the mighty Michelin Group, better known for tires and its iconic tubby Michelin Man (who looks to have eaten a few too many foods deep-fried in Dinor oil), Wilmar (Asia's biggest agribusiness group, with more than 400 subsidiaries), and Olam (another heavyweight atop Singapore's corporate food chain).[162]

Also on the vendors' shelves in the Medina market in the capital of a country that exports raw green beans to France are canned green beans from ... France. But all that is local is not yet lost in Medina. In front of the imported cans and bottles and Adja and Maggi products are giant sacks filled to the brim with local condiments, upright bags stuffed with an abundance of local produce like a silent symphony of sumptuous colours, textures, and smells.

There is *soumbala* from *dawa dawa* trees. There are bags full of dried tamarind. There is garlic, lots of it – some local but a good deal, Mai says, now coming in from China. There are mountains of deep red hibiscus petals or *dah,* mounds of dried and fermented onions formed into small round bombs of flavour for any sauce, dried red peppers, raw peanuts, a dizzying number of kinds of beans and lentils. There are hot peppers of all shapes and sizes.

There are the black seed pods from a shrubby tree (*Xylopia aethiopica*), which double as a spice to flavour sauces and also as medicine. The pods go by many names – grains of Selim, African pepper, Moor pepper, Ethiopia pepper, Senegal pepper, Guinea pepper, Kani pepper, Kili pepper, and in Sierra Leone, it's just called "spice." The names alone attest to its widespread popularity and importance to people scattered from one side of Africa to the other. Chronicling its multitude of uses, it's small wonder that it has collected so many colourful names for itself. As a spice it adds a musky, peppery taste with a hint of nutmeg. The fruit (seed pods), leaves, stem, and root bark are used to treat an astounding number of ailments, including bronchitis, dysentery, and bacterial infections. When the bark has been soaked in palm wine, it is used to treat asthma, rheumatism, and stomach aches. The wood of the tree is termite-resistant, and greatly valued in house and boat construction. In the Middle Ages the pepper itself was an important export to Europe.

Yet in more than a quarter-century of living and eating in Africa, I'd never heard of this remarkable condiment or plant. Of course, this is largely my fault because I failed to go looking and asking for information on local food. But it does make me wish I had a million dollars to develop an advertising campaign that would put some of Africa's own flavour-enhancing treasures in lights on billboards and on television screens across the continent and beyond, the way Nestlé and Ajinomoto do with their substitutes. Anything that would promote their cultivation and consumption for generations to come.

Today, I often toss a couple of the African pepper seed pods into my stews and soups to enhance the flavour – *sans Maggi*. Cooking can be a political act.

21

Dutch onion disease

Unless you're a corporate food executive, the food system isn't working for you. Around the world, farmers and farmworkers are dying, with the connivance of elected officials, at the whim of the market.

– Raj Patel
Stuffed and Starved:
Markets, Power and the Hidden Battle for
the World's Food System

When I first landed in Africa, more than half my lifetime ago, it was in Niger, the landlocked country to the north of Nigeria. Much of the country is covered by the Sahara Desert and the United Nations persistently ranks it at or very near the bottom of its Human Development Index. It's a major source of uranium for the French and Chinese, and a source of gold, especially for Canadian companies. The country made world headlines in 2002 when George W. Bush claimed that Saddam Hussein had been trying to procure uranium from "Africa" (by which he meant Niger) for an alleged Iraqi nuclear arsenal in the making. Apart from those few minutes of fame, Niger has rarely made world headlines, unless it's because of droughts, crop failures and famines, and, more recently, floods. Climate change is turning these catastrophes into almost annual events.

Niamey, capital of a very hot, dry, and impoverished nation in Africa's Sahel, wasn't a soft landing for a pampered city girl from North America. I felt as if I'd just landed on the moon, about which I probably knew more than I did about Niger.

After a few days in Niamey, we set out – Karl (my future husband) and I – on the two-day drive across the country to Zinder. He was working in Niger on a food security project, as an advisor with the national produce office, OPVN, or *Office des Produits Vivriers du Niger*. OPVN operated warehouses throughout the country, buying up harvested grains from farmers each year and selling them off throughout the long annual dry season to stabilize prices and prevent wild speculation on food and thus, widespread famine. In times of food shortages, OPVN could also provide emergency stocks of food to affected populations.

The national food storage and distribution services, together with grain marketing boards and agricultural extension services, had been set up in the 1970s, supported by the World Bank. By the 1980s, however, the World Bank began to see such things as obstacles to development, contrary to the ideology of the neo-liberal "Washington Consensus." It began to push its debtors in Africa to do away with such national grain banks and anything else that might tame the hand of The Market.

Despite its harsh arid climate and the persistent growth of the Sahara Desert, about a quarter of Niger's GDP comes from agriculture. Eighty percent of its population is engaged in small-scale agriculture, farming and pastoralism both requiring a great deal of skill and knowledge in such a difficult landscape and climate. In 2009, 64 percent of export earnings were from uranium, about 20 percent from livestock, and about 6 percent from other agriculture, most notably onions.[163]

But in the 1980s, newly landed in Niger, I wasn't aware of any of this. I was far more concerned about my own perceived discomfort than I was about any complicated economic or political realities in Niger. First, I needed to survive the scorching, two-day drive from Niamey to Zinder. Karl's official vehicle was a miniature Suzuki jeep that looked like a toy suitable for a California beach. Instead of a permanent roof, it had a snap-on plastic tarpaulin that afforded almost no protection from the blast furnace of the desert wind and the blowing sand that were constants on that landscape.

Towns were few and far between on that long, straight ribbon of pavement across Niger. There was also a dearth of the kind of modern amenities that I suddenly missed desperately and longed for: roadside restaurants and hotels with running water, electricity, and cool, clean interiors away from the heat and the dust of the great Nigerien outdoors.

Dusk was descending when we eventually stopped in a small market town called Birnin-Konni, pulling up in front of a genial little hotel. The proprietor proudly showed us all three of the rooms, which were full of spanking new electric appliances – a refrigerator, a television, and very showy and elaborate light fixtures, even air conditioners imported from across the border in Kano, Nigeria. These modern luxuries would have been useful had there been electricity to power them, but the town had none. It was a hot night. We got up, washed with the help of a flashlight, a cup, and a bucket of water, and left before morning had broken.

The sun was just appearing on the craggy horizon as a shard of red when we stopped for breakfast at the first eatery we found on the roadside. It consisted of a rough wooden bench and a low wooden table covered with a plastic tablecloth bearing the logo of Canada Dry. The table served as the dining table, counter, and kitchen cupboard. On it stood a couple of battered cans – coffee and Nestlé sweetened condensed milk, a box of Lipton teabags from Unilever, two very large pink thermoses, a flat of eggs, some fresh baguettes, some red onions, a plastic container of sugar cubes, and a few plastic cups and plates in primary colours. Behind it all sat the cook. His tools were basic, a small charcoal cook-stove and a battered and blackened frying pan. On the menu was omelette. With onions.

The young proprietor began by slicing up a small red onion with a large knife and scooping the slivers into the blackened frying pan over the stove, along with a generous dollop of cooking oil. Then, while the onion sizzled, the omelette maestro broke four eggs into a red plastic cup and with a spoon, whipped them to a frenzied crescendo. His hands and arms swooped and danced as if he were conducting a symphony and not conjuring up a roadside breakfast for a couple of straggly foreigners. With unabashed panache, he poured them into the frying pan, holding the cup high so that the molten egg dropped elegantly in a thin stream into the hot sizzling oil. At the same time, with the other hand, he swirled the pan to spread the egg.

While the aroma of the frying eggs infused the cool dawn air, awakening a hunger I really thought I'd left behind me in Canada, he started on the Nescafé. He sprinkled a few brown crystals into two plastic mugs. Then, I watched in stunned silence as he poured in copious amounts of viscous sweetened condensed milk. I could have asked him to stop pouring, told him I wanted a cup of coffee, not a lethal sugar overdose, but I was curious as to just how much of the syrupy stuff he considered normal. About a third of the cup, as it turned out. He then filled the mugs to the brim with hot water from one of the large thermoses, placed them on small plastic saucers. On these, just in case the sweetened condensed milk wasn't enough to satisfy our sweet teeth, he added half a dozen sugar cubes.

He swiftly scooped up the scrambled eggs, and divided them in two portions on two plastic plates, each adorned with half a fresh baguette. *Et voilà!* Breakfast on the highway in Niger. Fast food, Sahelian style. I marvelled at how much I enjoyed breakfast out there on the edge of the desert, with the air still remarkably fresh and the sun still a red globe rising over a wan rocky horizon.

Then it was time to hit the road again, the *hot* road, as the sun took possession of the sky, and the grey pavement ahead began to squirm and quiver with heat. This was October and the annual rains were ending. Harvesting was nearly done, so what I was seeing were farm fields in the dry season, shorn of annual crops and exposed to the relentless sun and wind. The desert was consuming the country, moving south at an alarming rate, swallowing up arable land, killing off vegetation and burying the country in sand. Remnant forests and woodlands were disappearing. The lonely Tree of Ténéré, the last tree standing in a 400-kilometre radius in northeast Niger, had been knocked down by a stray Land Rover in 1973. Its memory had been captured in a sad black-and-white photograph exhibited at Niger's national museum in the capital.

The only crop I saw thriving, just about the only green thing I saw in the nearly thousand kilometres we covered between Niamey and Zinder, was onions, countless fields of them. I was amazed any plant could survive the insane heat. It would be many years before I would finally learn what is special about that Niger onion and why it can survive – even thrive – in such inhospitable dry heat and store well under the same conditions.

Enlightenment on the onion question comes decades later. The occasion is a meeting of the Coalition for the Protection of African Genetic Heritage, or COPAGEN, in Benin. There I learn the plucky purplish onion that perplexed me with its growing powers for so many years is the *Violet de Galmi*. It was bred by the people of the Ader Region of southeast Niger after its ancestors were brought to the area by caravan from Egypt in the 1600s.[164] In the intervening years, the farmers of Niger developed the cultivar to cope with the difficult climate of the Sahel, sharing out their seeds with other farmers as was their tradition, calling the onion "Galmi" after a village in the area, or "Maggia" after the valley in which it was bred. This cultivar became popular throughout West Africa, greatly appreciated for its tangy flavour, excellent storage, deep violet colour and for the way it thickened sauces in which it was used. In the 1960s, agricultural researchers working with the onion in Niger dubbed it the *Violet de Galmi.*

Several national institutions now maintain their own strains of this precious violet onion for posterity, including those in Mauritania, Senegal, Côte d'Ivoire, and Burkina Faso. In the latter, one gene bank holds thirty-eight onion lines. Onions are a crucial cash crop for family farmers in the region, and nowhere more so than in Niger, where they produce 200,000 tonnes of them a year.[165]

In 2006, the Senegalese company Tropicasem applied to the African Intellectual Property Organization, headquartered in Cameroon, for a patent for the *Violet de Galmi.* Tropicasem is a "sister" of the French company Technisem,[166] and it has affiliates in thirteen other countries.[167] Eleven of them are African, with another in Guadeloupe and one in the United States. Tropicasem says its mission is to breed and market varieties of important tropical crops.

The Tropicasem application for a patent on the *Galmi* onion caused a firestorm of controversy. Activists from COPAGEN denounced it as "theft."[168] Tropicasem argued that its purpose was to *protect* African biodiversity and the invasion of the continent by expensive hybrid and genetically modified seeds from giant agrichemical corporations, that it wanted to prevent the disappearance of this invaluable onion variety and other African crops.[169] It stated its attempt to register the name *Violet de Galmi* was to prevent it from being stolen or appropriated by bigger multinationals and to improve the cultivar for widespread distribution in Africa and the Caribbean. In the end, after Niger's onion producers protested, Tropicasem's patent application was rejected.[170]

Regardless of where one stood on the issue of who owned or could own the purple onion, it highlighted an important issue, that of seed and food sovereignty in Africa. Although it's a broad and complex concept, "food sovereignty" essentially means the right of peoples to define their own food, agriculture, livestock, and fisheries systems, as opposed to having food and farms largely subject to international market forces. The term was coined in 1996 by La Via Campesina, the world's largest association of farmers, which represents the interests of peasant organizations, small- and medium-scale farmers, agricultural workers, rural women, and indigenous communities from Asia, Africa, America, and Europe. It counts as members close to 150 organizations and coalitions of organizations, all advocating food sovereignty through family-farm-based sustainable agriculture.

They are concerned that the biotech and agrichemical juggernauts that now control most of the world's seeds and pesticide sales are digging into seed banks in Africa and around the world to get their hands on genetic material, patent it, and also manipulate it with genetic modification so they can sell it back to the world's farmers with their own copyright on it. Their fears seem well founded.

By 2006, the biggest ten seed corporations controlled 64 percent of the world's seed markets. Just one of those, Monsanto, controlled a staggering one-fifth of the global market, while Monsanto together with Syngenta, Dupont, and Limagrain accounted for about half of all proprietary seeds sold on the planet.[171] Monsanto continued to buy up seed companies around the world, concentrating and solidifying its grip on our food.

By 2016, the world's six largest seed and agrochemical companies were working on mergers that would reduce their numbers, putting the control of the majority of global sales of seeds and chemicals in the hands of just three gargantuan corporations.[172] This corporate control of seeds, and thus our food, robs the rest of us – the eaters and the food growers – of food sovereignty, the control over our food system, what we grow, how we grow it, and what we eat. And Monsanto does not limit itself to seeds; many of its GM "Round-up Ready" seeds are intended to be planted with glyphosate-based Round-up pesticide, which has spawned an epidemic of super-resistant monster weeds that are taking over America's farmland.[173] The World Health Organization research arm has also categorized glyphosate as a Group 2A substance, meaning it's "probably carcinogenic to humans."[174]

But it's not just the genetic rights for the humble African onion that are threatened by forces beyond the reach of West African family farmers. The global marketplace, and all the financial and corporate forces it has to reach into every last nook and cranny on the planet, also affects family farmers who earn income by selling their onions in local and regional markets. These days the African onion, that succulent Sahelian gem, has to struggle for a place even in local African markets. As Dorcas had told me in Freetown, sometimes you can't even find African onions in African markets.

It is almost impossible to walk through a market in West Africa without tripping over piles of fifty-kilogram bags of drab yellow onions from The Netherlands, just like those "Ladybug" ones that Thelma and I bought in Makeni Market. I've seen Dutch onions in markets in The Gambia, Senegal, Guinea, Sierra Leone, Liberia, Mali, and Ghana. Dutch onions have flooded West African markets; exports of onions to the region have tripled in the past ten years.[175] Until very recently, The Netherlands was the world's largest producer of onions. As it lost markets in Russia and the rest of Europe, it ceded this position to India. With an annual production of 1.3 billion kilograms, however, The Netherlands still has excess onions in need of markets, and these were found in West Africa.

From 2006 until 2011, Dutch onion exports to Senegal rose 70 percent. From there and from the other main dumping centre in West Africa, Côte d'Ivoire, the bland, mass-produced and travel-weary Dutch onions are laboriously re-exported and distributed throughout the entire region. The flooding of the markets with Dutch onions was happening at the same time that the government of Senegal was trying to stimulate local onion production with the construction of storage facilities, establishing fair pricing for producers, and even placing seasonal restrictions on onion imports to try to protect their own farmers, build rural economies, and fight poverty.

Think of it as Dutch Onion Disease. Except it's a disease that goes well beyond onions.

22

Let them eat imports

Farmers are … leaving their fields in droves because their crops can't compete with cheap products from Europe, the United States and Asia. Stacks of onions from The Netherlands are sold in markets in the capital, Dakar. The tomato paste comes from Italy, the powdered milk from France and the chicken parts from all across the EU.

– Michaela Schiessl[176]

For the first ten or fifteen years we lived in Africa, I failed to fully appreciate just how good so much of the food was, how much of it was fresh, direct from a farm somewhere nearby. Back in the 1980s and early 1990s, nearly everything we ate came from local markets. Much of it was also pesticide-free, although there was one exception, namely vegetables and produce that had been treated with the pesticide hexachlorocyclohexane, a toxic organo-chloride often called HCH for short.

HCH was introduced initially by the Canadian Interna-tional Development Agency (CIDA) and other aid organizations that funded aerial spraying programs to kill agricultural pests in Sahelian countries. When the production and use of HCH were banned in most Western nations, aid agencies continued to acquire it from other sources and to fund its use in the Sahel. Because it was so abundant, market gardeners and vendors began to use it liberally on vegetables. Sometimes it was spread around seedlings and I also saw vendors in markets douse tomatoes with the fine powder.

Apart from that, most local produce we were consuming in those years was organic, by default if not by design. In the case of local poultry, it was also generally humanely produced, fresh and delicious.

During the four years we lived in Tamale, we went almost every Sunday to an open-air locale called the Drop In to dine on fresh guinea fowl breasts, procured from local producers. On our bicycles, it took us about a half-hour to get to the Drop In. The ride took us through Forestry Department plantations of teak trees, along deep sandy paths, and then over the worn pavement on Education Ridge, a cracked and ailing road lined with schools and administration buildings that dated back to the colonial era. Giant shade trees planted way back then had grown up and over the road to create a leafy tunnel where the temperature was at least ten blessed degrees cooler than it was elsewhere in Tamale, helping to whet our appetites for the feast of fowl at the end of the road.

The Drop In was an unpretentious place, consisting of a few thatched roofs over wooden tables and benches. The women who ran the place and prepared the guinea fowl were not as selfish with their recipe as was Colonel Sanders with his secret spices for Kentucky Fried Chicken. It all had to do, the women told me, with the way they tenderized the breasts by boiling them and then anointing them with hot peppers and herbs, before plunging them into hot peanut oil in cauldrons perched on small charcoal stoves. In subsequent years I've tried, over and over, to replicate their magic with guinea fowl and chicken breasts, and never succeeded.

I also have very fond memories of the local chicken on which we dined in Cameroon. In the two years we lived in the town of Foumban on a beautiful, mountain-studded plateau, we practically lived off dishes made with "native" chicken. At private residences in Foumban that doubled as restaurants, we often dined on a chicken and vegetable dish called *Poulet DG* or, roughly translated, Director General Chicken. It was popular with a new and growing breed of *nouveau riche* businessmen in the country, and the name was a wry poke at their predilection for self-important titles. The native chickens were commonly known as *poulet bicyclette,* possibly because their little thighs were so lean and tough that it seemed the birds might have ridden little chicken bicycles in the Tour de France before they landed in the cooking pot. Tough they may have been, but their taste was unbeatable.

In the past couple of decades, though, all that has changed. In West and Central African markets, it has become increasingly difficult to find local, native poultry. The live local chickens have been replaced by imported, industrially produced poultry parts from America and Europe – turkey necks and backs, fatty little pink tails and fetid little chicken feet like the ones I saw (and smelled) in the market of Kailahun and the flabby, unappealing chicken thigh Dorcas used in the yam pottage. This has crippled local poultry producers.[177]

In Ghana, until the early 1990s, the country produced all the chicken and eggs it consumed. Over the next decade, imported poultry parts from Europe and the United States decimated the indigenous poultry sector. By the start of the new millennium, 89 percent of the chicken consumed by Ghanaians was "imported," dumped on the country.[178] By 2010, more than 200,000 tonnes of frozen chicken made its way each year to Ghana from the European Union, Brazil, and the United States.[179]

Cameroon's poultry sector suffered the same fate. Until the

late 1980s, the country was self-sufficient in poultry. Then came the 1990s, the age of trade liberalization and so-called "free" trade agreements, and imported chicken usurped the market in Cameroon. An estimated 120,000 jobs in local and small-scale poultry production were lost. A study on the safety of imported frozen chicken in the country showed that 83 percent of it was not fit for human consumption.[180] Activists took to calling the imported poultry the "chicken of death."

In Senegal, a formerly thriving local poultry industry that provided employment for 10,000 people and generated about US$3.8 billion for local economies was destroyed by the dumping of cheap chicken parts from Europe and the U.S. Some 2,000 small-scale poultry producers were put out of business.[181]

All this can, at least in part, be laid at the feet of the World Bank, which pushed African nations to liberalize their trade. In 2000, the World Bank persuaded the countries of the West African Economic and Monetary Union to slash their import duties for chicken parts to less than half what they had been, from 55 to just 20 percent. Large poultry producers in Europe and North America and large egg producers in India were able to take full advantage of the open doors on African markets. Excess chicken parts, or bits of the bird that didn't appeal to consumers in wealthy lands, could be packed up and shipped off to Africa, turning what might have been a waste product or good only for fertilizer and pet food into very profitable exports for industrial producers. In Senegal, three-quarters of the imported chicken parts came from Belgium and The Netherlands, and sold for half the price of local chicken.

The European Union contends that this is not unfair trade because the poultry sector in Europe is not subsidized. It is, of course; it's just that the subsidies are indirect – call them camouflaged. Between 1990 and 2002, when chicken exports to Africa were escalating, Europe was dramatically increasing subsidies to grain producers. That meant the cost of chicken feed, the bulk of the cost of producing poultry, dropped by about two-thirds. African producers had no chance of competing on a playing field as tilted as the deck of a sinking ship.

What may be called "free trade" may not look quite so free or appealing when it's followed from corporate factory farms to Africa's markets and kitchens. The chicken parts are shipped frozen to Africa, but by the time they go on sale in markets, they have been thawed and may sit for hours – sometimes days – under the hot sun before they are bought. Traditionally, chickens were sold live in markets so there was no need to worry about spoilage. Unfortunately, the market women may not realize that the chicken parts they are selling can become bacterial bombs by the time they are purchased and taken home.

Free trade deals have turned Africa into a profitable disposal ground for industrialized countries in Europe and North America,[182] and increasingly also for Brazil, Southeast Asian nations, India, and China. The story of liberalized trade in Africa is a narrative influenced by and written to favour multinational corporations and industrial agricultural producers. What makes the free trade deals less than free – and far from fair – is that many of the corporations that benefit from them also benefit from agricultural subsidies, which are not available and sometimes even forbidden to African farmers.[183]

Between 1995 and 2012, the U.S. government bestowed more than US$292 *billion* in agricultural subsidies on American producers, the bulk of them on just five commodity crops of corn, soybeans, wheat, cotton, and rice.[184] While the subsidies are generally promoted as measures to preserve the family farm, this is hardly the case. Giant agribusinesses tend to get the bulk of the subsidies and small producers a mere pittance or nothing at all – fruit and vegetable growers are almost completely excluded.[185] Many of those receiving subsidies in the United States are billionaires.[186]

Europe's subsidy scheme, the Common Agricultural Policy,

is worth about 50 billion Euros a year. The subsidies are presented to the public as a way of providing European farmers with a reasonable standard of living, providing consumers with quality food at fair prices, and preserving rural heritage. What isn't included in the sales pitch to the public that pays the bills is that just as in the U.S., the subsidies are generally not for struggling small, *family* farmers. The larger the farm in Europe, the bigger the subsidy. More than two million European farmers receive only 4 percent of the subsidies, while half the subsidies are lavished on just 5 percent of Europe's poultry producers, all very large ones.[187]

So in both the U.S. and the European Union, the rich and powerful skim off the most public money dished out as agricultural subsidies, while the small and cash-starved farmers continue to struggle or fail altogether.[188] The agricultural subsidies allow American and European agribusiness to produce surpluses. Export subsidies then compound the problem by helping producers offload the surpluses in Africa, at less than production cost, where they undermine local produce and farmers. To make this even easier, the European Union has been negotiating Economic Partnership Agreements that permit easy access to local markets throughout Africa.

This has led to what are benignly termed "import surges" of subsidized commodities in developing countries.[189] Import surges account for the preponderance of everything from Dutch onions to European and American chicken parts in Africa's markets.

The dependence on imported foodstuffs becomes a huge problem for urban populations throughout Africa when food prices skyrocket, as they did in 2008. Neo-liberal economists, billionaire philanthropists, and giant agrochemical companies quickly used the skyrocketing food prices as a pretext to justify their call for still more industrial corporate agriculture, blaming the food crisis on global food shortages, a growing taste for and the capacity to afford meat in China and India, and on poor productivity of smallholder farms. In 2012, many of the world's biggest chemical, food, fertilizer, and seed corporations threw their support (and plenty of money) behind President Obama and the G8's New Alliance for Food Security and Nutrition,[190] already looking ahead to the profitable opportunities this private sector investment in industrial agriculture in Africa offered them.

Many others, especially those whose bottom line was the public good and not corporate profits, disagreed. They preferred to listen to the wisdom of the hundreds of experts behind the most in-depth study of global agriculture ever undertaken, the International Assessment of Agricultural Knowledge, Science and Technology for Development (IAASTD).[191] The Assessment, which took years to complete, was unequivocal, concluding that to feed the world, business as usual was not an option and agro-ecological agriculture that respected and worked with ecosystems was the only approach.

Food security, as the IAASTD showed, can only be ensured by food and crop diversity. Fortunately, there's no shortage of plant diversity out there to help our species meet its food needs. About 50,000 vegetable food species are known to exist world-wide, but increasingly industrialized agriculture and a food system more and more under corporate control have been whittling down the numbers of the ones that show up on our plates. Today, humanity is using only about 200 food species on a large scale. The Food and Agriculture Organization of the United Nations (FAO) thinks we could do better, use more, and warns us that it is "ecologically and nutritionally dangerous" to make use of so few edible species. Back in 1997, the FAO concluded that it was "time to rediscover forgotten and neglected food plants and to broaden the food base using significantly more of the available resources."[192]

There is a growing chorus of voices being raised in praise of Africa's farmers and foods. The chorus includes African chefs and food writers who have been producing beautiful recipe books that celebrate the continent's gastronomy. African food-lovers are using the Internet to talk up their favourite African foods, dishes, ingredients, and cuisines. Around the world, countless numbers of people are seeking out restaurants that serve up the tastes of Africa. At the same time, African farmer coalitions together with La Via Campesina and their allies around the world, including the United Nations Special Rapporteur on the Right to Food, continue to defend and promote the family farming systems and agroecological agriculture that can assure Africa's food security and sovereignty. And, I venture to say, also save its wonderful cuisines.

23

Slow fast food

If a family's shared meal around a communal bowl remains a moment of formality with a set of fixed customs, in the city the "cuisine of desire" tempts us at every corner, in the form of kebabs, bean cakes, donuts (froufrou), roasted peanuts or icy bags of ginger juice or bissap or tamarind …

– Malian Ministry of Employment and Professional Training
Recettes des mets Maliens

The road to junk food, rural poverty and agricultural pollution was paved with good intentions.

– Wayne Roberts
The No-Nonsense Guide to World Food

Fast food – in the form of franchised outlets cloned and implanted around the world by global corporations – has yet to completely conquer the African continent. This may well change very soon as some of the world's largest food, drink, and agri-chemical corporations and other foreign investors set their sights there. But so far, much of Africa has been left off the globe-straddling location maps of the big players in the big business of fast food. McDonald's has outlets in close to 125 countries, but only two – South Africa and Morocco – are on the African continent. In 2013, north of South Africa and south of the Maghreb, you could still cross the continent without spying a single Wendy's, Burger King, Taco Bell, Dunkin' Donuts, Tim Hortons, or any of the chains that have made it possible to eat and drink the same things in almost the same décor around the globe. Today, however, familiar chains such as Pizza Hut and Subway are starting to pop up in large cities across Africa.

There are some African upstarts working to follow in the footsteps of the big chains. Nigeria has its Mr. Bigg's "Village Kitchen." In 2003, it branched out and opened outlets in Ghana as well, where it invites customers to come for "meals in your mother tongue." If Mr. Bigg's statistics are anything to go on, it is filling a growing appetite for fast food in the region. It boasts having 100,000 visitors and selling 25,000 pieces of chicken every day. And in its first quarter-century of life, it sold 148 million doughnuts and 635 million meat pies.[193] Mr. Bigg's is a subsidiary of UAC of Nigeria PLC, with roots stretching back to colonial days, and which, until 1994, was a subsidiary of the British giant, Unilever.[194]

I had occasion to sample Mr. Bigg's fare on a working trip to Ghana in 2011. It came at the end of a long, hot day wandering through flood-prone shantytowns in the Ghanaian capital, seeing firsthand the calamitous effects of climate change on the coastal communities on the outskirts of Accra. I was thirsty and hungry, and for reasons I failed to question at the time, my Ghanaian colleagues decided to take me to Mr. Bigg's for a late lunch from a menu that offered a host of Ghanaian specialties. I ordered a plate of "red-red," black-eyed peas done up in red palm oil.

Our orders placed, we went upstairs to sit down and wait.

The décor looked to have been borrowed directly from Ronald McDonald's playbook – large windows and lots of bright red, yellow, and orange plastic everywhere. We waited. And we waited. After the heat of the day, it was unpleasantly cold inside, as if the air conditioner were set to replicate an Arctic chill.

Less patient than my colleagues, I went downstairs to check that the food was indeed coming. The pleasant young woman assured me it would ready in seconds. Back I went up the stairs. We were the only customers in the place, never a good sign in any eatery. It was interesting, I thought, that instead of "fast food," Mr. Bigg's calls itself a "quick service" restaurant. If this was quick service, I wondered aloud, what did slow service look like? Meals prepared overnight? My Ghanaian companions smiled politely at my impolite impatience.

When my plate of "red-red" finally did come, it was congealed, cold, and inedible.

The next day I told my colleagues I'd prefer to eat just about anywhere but Mr. Bigg's. This time, they took me to a local canteen where women catered in an outdoor setting to nationals working at a cluster of gated international development and research organizations. Here, the "red-red" was about as good as it gets. The black-eyed peas in their oil and peppery sauce were piping hot, as were the accompanying fried plantains, and to top it all off, the waitress appeared with a fresh salsa of tomatoes, onions, and hot peppers. Traditionally, this salsa was prepared in a three-legged ridged clay plate known as an *asanka,* with a wooden masher that just fits in the palm of your hand. According to African food specialist Fran Osseo-Asare and Ghanaian food scientists with whom she consulted on the advantages of this old-fashioned kitchen gadget, the mashing of the vegetables in the *asanka* enhances and preserves the flavours and the textures in ways that pulverizing in a blender does not.[195]

And the food was indeed heavenly. Because it had been made from scratch in the morning, ready to eat at noon, this was authentic slow food with genuinely quick service.

Despite the absence of the fast food outlets, there are many, many places to find quick meals and snacks throughout Africa. Major thoroughfares, intersections, markets, and just about any place where large crowds of people gather are all locations for ready-to-eat street foods and snacks, many of them prepared well in advance in kitchens at home.

In his marvellous cookbook *La Cuisine Moussa*, Cameroonian chef and restaurateur Alexandre Bella Ola divides African cuisines into three broad categories. There is the cuisine of the *gargotes*, restaurants in private homes in which small individual rooms offer private dining experiences. These are particularly popular in Cameroon. During the two years we spent in the highland town of Foumban in the 1980s, we often ate in overstuffed sofas and chairs adorned with lacy doilies, surrounded by the bright pink and green walls that were so popular in the *gargotes* owned by princesses belonging to the royal family headed by the king of the Bamoun people.

Then there is Africa's "family cuisine," which offers the "taste of tradition" with dishes found at any large family gathering, such as a baptism, wedding, or funeral. And there is *la cuisine de la rue* or street cuisine that offers what Chef Bella Ola calls the "taste of celebration." The fact that he identifies the food available on roadsides as a separate cuisine speaks volumes about the incredible variety and quality of Africa's street fare.

The list of tastes to celebrate on roadsides is extremely long. Freshly roasted peanuts. Peanuts boiled in their shells in sugar water. Caramelized peanuts roasted with sugar and a little lime juice. In Sierra Leone there is the sweet *kanya* that is often sold by young women who move about with it in plastic containers they carry on their heads. *Kanya* is made from roasted peanuts pounded into a powder in a large mortar, to which rice flour or *gari* can be added along with sugar or honey and worked until it becomes a smooth paste that is placed in a mould or rolled out and cut into appealing squares or trapezoids, like cookies.

In Benin, a variation of this delicate sweet is *nougat,* which is cooked before it is cut into pieces. Or the delightful *andou,* made by grinding (or pounding in a mortar) grilled peanuts and maize, hot pepper, black pepper, and salt, the paste of which is rolled into delectable little balls.

There is almost always fresh fruit – bananas, avocados, oranges, coconuts full of thirst-quenching liquid and delicious, satisfying flesh, and countless other indigenous fruits that would take an army of botanists to document. There are roasted or boiled cobs of maize. Freshly grilled sweet potatoes, cassava tubers, cobs of corn. Barbecued meats. Fried plantains or yam chips.

There are the almost ubiquitous roadside outlets that set up for morning and evening meals, preparing omelettes on the spot and offering Nescafé with sweetened condensed milk and bread, much like that memorable first roadside breakfast I had a few days after landing in Niger. There are bean cakes, boiled eggs, sandwiches made with sardines, margarine, mayonnaise, sometimes with boiled potatoes, and even sandwiches made by pouring sweetened condensed milk onto baguettes.

There is also the peppery cake of mashed black-eyed beans and fish and spice, which is steamed in banana leaves or small recycled tin cans. Versions of this snack of many names – *oleleh* in Sierra Leone, *moimoi* in Nigeria, *koki Bamiléké* in Cameroon, *abla* in Benin – are found throughout West and Central Africa.

There are homemade doughnuts and biscuits too. Among the very best I've tried are the peppery biscuits made from fresh ginger or the almost heart-shaped sugar cookies known as "kill driver" in Sierra Leone, so named because they are said to be so tasty that if drivers dare to sample them while at the wheel, they are almost sure to swoon and drive off the road to their deaths.

As for quick meals grabbed at roadside eateries, I'd happily trade in a coupon for a free lunch in every single golden arch on the planet for just one afternoon meal *chez* Nene in Moyamba Junction in Sierra Leone. Every morning, she and her family cook up fifty kilograms of rice in a massive aluminum cauldron on a three-stone hearth in the thatch-roofed kitchen hut behind her "Good Food" restaurant, the small structure that doubles as family home and eatery. As the perfect culinary companions for the rice, they prepare two separate soups in giant cauldrons, big as small bathtubs. One is Nene's incomparable groundnut soup, rich with red palm oil, chunks of local beef, hot peppers, and the local eggplants, *jakato*. The other is a leafy soup, made usually with (sweet) potato or cassava leaves and fish. When the food is ready, Nene wraps the huge cauldrons in layers and layers of cloth, blankets, and sheets, and then enlists several young men and women to carry them from the kitchen out back to the front of the small roadside restaurant. While the morning clientele, mostly travellers taking a food break, work their way through the contents of those big pots, back in the kitchen Nene and her team prepare a second round of the same for evening clients.

The décor and amenities are best described as, well, minimalist. The dining area is a small porch-like room at the front of a clapboard structure just a couple of metres from the busy highway that links the capital, Freetown, with the rich agricultural (and mining) regions in the east of the country. Some lengths of locally made batik, known as "gara" cloth, dyed in hues of royal blue and grass green, have been strung up as curtains to keep out the worst of the sun and some of the fumes from ailing diesel engines of passing trucks and vans. Deep blue oilcloth has been stapled onto the low-slung tables and benches.

But Nene's is not about fine facilities or comfort; it's all about good food – bowls of delicious and nutty local rice drenched in rich, peppery sauces. I once asked a member of her extended family for the recipe for her groundnut stew. Like the rest of the family, he had migrated to Sierra Leone from his native Guinea, a French-speaking country next door. Translated from the French, this is the recipe he painstakingly wrote out for me:

Nene (Isatu Sow) dishing up her scrumptious groundnut soup in Moyamba Junction, Sierra Leone.

"Preparation of the sauce. Before anything else: Light the fire, she puts the cooking pot [*marmite*] on the fire, after a few minutes, she pours some red oil [palm oil] into the pot, when the oil is hot she adds the meat and after that the condiments such as tomatoes, onions, *jakato*, peppers, shallots, bay leaves, etc. ... At the end, the mama adds groundnut paste and takes a big spoon to stir the sauce very well in the pot for about one hour. Reported by Anatha Diallo 28-11-09, Moyamba Junction at 13 h, 37 minutes and some seconds."

I greatly appreciated his attention to detail and also his assumption that I would know what to add in the way of "etc." But most of all, I loved the slow food that Nene dished up fast at her Good Food restaurant. And given the lack of facilities, the rather relaxed approach to washing dishes in large bowls of dubious water, I do still wonder how it was that we never once experienced the slightest stomach problems after eating there regularly for many years.

24

Peppered with misconceptions

Rich people sometimes eat bad food.

– Kikiyu proverb, Kenya[196]

If you see a man in a gown eating with a man in rags, the food belongs to the latter.

– African proverb[197]

At the beginning of the 1960s, when many African countries were becoming independent nations, the continent was more than able to feed itself. Until 1970, it was even exporting food, more than a million tonnes a year.[198] Today, after more than half a century of foreign development assistance and food aid, as well as decades of economic development doctrines from the World Bank Group and International Monetary Fund, the continent imports a quarter of its food.

This lands us right in the middle of the kitchen staring into the eyes of the big elephant of a question that is sitting there: Why has Africa become synonymous in many people's minds with malnutrition, famine, and hunger and not with wonderful and nutritious foods?

Some of the causes are evident. The continent has suffered enormously from political instability and turbulence; in the half-century before 2004, it saw 186 coups and 26 major wars, which produced 16 million refugees. Farmers need stability and also a voice that is heard and respected by political elites, and in much of sub-Sahara Africa they have had neither. Rapid population growth has put additional strain on resources and social services: the population of the continent more than doubled between 1975 and 2005. Governments have tended to ignore rural areas, which suffer from poor roads, a lack of health and education facilities, and other infrastructure that would make rural living more appealing. There is also the unfair competition that local farmers face from subsidized produce from abroad.

Small scale and family farming deserves respect as the profession that feeds a nation. But it has generally been seen as a desperate, last resort choice in life. Children in Sierra Leone are warned that if they don't work hard and do well at school, they will wind up being a farmer, as if it's the worst occupation there is rather than a respected and fulfilling way to make a living by feeding the world, which it should and could be. Unfortunately, this is the same the world over.

The myths and misconceptions about African farming, foods, and even eating habits certainly come in all shades of bleak and even ridiculous and pathetic. In 2001, the mayor of Toronto, Mel Lastman, managed to decimate the city's chances of getting the 2008 Olympics when, just before he was to travel to Mombasa in Kenya to lobby African delegates, he said, "I'm sort of scared about going there, but the wife is really nervous. I just see myself in a pot of boiling water with all these natives dancing around me."[199]

In 2012, a jet-setting British national and CEO of a gold prospecting company with interests in Liberia was asked by an online management publication what his worst travelling experience was. He responded thus. "On one of my first trips with my business partner, we broke down in the middle of the jungle [in Liberia]. We walked into a village and waited while the villagers decided what to do with us – were they going to put us in a pot and eat us? But they made us welcome and offered a bed on their mouse-infested floor in a mud hut. I always find these experiences entertaining."[200] He then slagged off Liberian food as "horrendous."

Where do such arrogant and condescending notions about Africa and its food habits come from? Many seem to have been shaped by historical or media reports about Africa written primarily by Europeans. And many of those are imbued with an inflated sense of superiority or written by individuals suffering from terminal *Hubris eurocentricis* (okay, I made that up, but I maintain it is a verifiable condition). What can be said of Western attitudes towards Africans when, for decades, it was considered acceptable to produce penny candy bits of licorice gummy things shaped like human infants, call them "nigger babies," and give them to impressionable little children to eat? Speaking of cannibalism.

School curricula around the world, with some notable and fairly recent exceptions in Afrocentric programs, have given short shrift or none at all to Africa's complex history, cultures, rich oral traditions, and wisdom captured in proverbs and fables, to its literary, artistic, scholarly, and musical accomplishments, and to its immense contribution to human development. Sadly, this is also the case in some African countries that inherited so many texts and concepts with deep-rooted prejudices from former European colonial powers.

Nor has enough attention been paid to the amount of wealth African slaves created for white plantation owners and economies in the Americas with their forced and free toil in rice, cotton, and sugarcane fields. Since this African agricultural prowess has been so neglected, it's not really surprising that school curricula have also failed quite spectacularly to give the rich heritage of African crops, foods, and food cultures its due.

In lieu of much meaningful education about Africa, much of the "knowledge" floating around out there about the continent has been brought to us by Disney and Hollywood, by charities seeking funds, and even tired old colonial biases and misconceptions handed down through generations. As a consequence, much of the purported knowledge is wrong, skewed, distorted, and self-serving, meant to prop up delusions about Western superiority in just about everything. Much of it falls into the category of myth, half-truth, sometimes even spurious fiction.

Some believe there is a language called "African," whereas there are perhaps *three thousand* languages spoken on the continent. This language fallacy is so common that frustrated Africans have a Facebook page devoted to it: "Do you speak African? Well do you speak European? – IDIOT."[201]

Africa is the most diverse continent on the planet. It boasts all manner of contrasting ecosystems, from snow-capped mountains (at least until climate change began their meltdown) to inhumanly hot salt flats more than half a kilometre below sea level and surrounded by a lake of sodium carbonate brine. In fact, these two spectacularly different landscapes are found in just one small part of East Africa. Parts of the continent are covered by rainforests; much of it is desert. Some of Africa is mountainous. Some is flat. Some is merely hilly.

Nevertheless, some people are under the impression the whole continent is uniformly and constantly hot and dry. Or else always terribly hot and wet. Some believe it is covered almost entirely by savannahs on which lions and elephants roam unchecked. Some believe that nearly everyone is starving and living in a refugee camp. Others believe you can't walk down a road in Africa without meeting a rebel soldier brandishing a sub-machine gun or a machete, braying for blood. A well-meaning and pleasant young woman cutting my hair in a Canadian hair salon once asked me if I wasn't afraid of "headhunters down there in Africa." Who knows, it could well be that some believe Africa is ruled by a Lion King.

None of this is really surprising, given the factoids about Africa many children in Europe and North America have been served in their early years. Odd notions about the continent are drilled into our heads by films or cartoons and a host of aid agencies intent on drumming up support for their work overseas with fund-raising campaigns featuring stereotypes and sometimes horrific imagery that lasso the compassion and good intentions of adults and children far away. Out of this emerges the implausible but often unquestioned myth that no one in Africa could possibly survive without Western help and food aid, as if life in the cradle of humankind did not tick along for millennia, and indeed give rise to the species to which we all belong.

This notion has in turn spawned a corollary myth that famine strikes because people don't know how to farm and are sitting there twiddling their thumbs until a Western youngster, missionary, economist, or volunteer aid worker comes to "teach" them how to coax crops out of the soil.

Many in the wealthy world aren't aware of how much their country's foreign policies, corporations, consuming habits, industries, financial institutions, and even pension plans may be causing or exacerbating problems in Africa. Until they do, they will be ill-equipped to offer much useful help and may find themselves unwittingly part of what Nigerian-American writer and thinker Teju Cole has drily dubbed the "White Savior Industrial Complex."[202] "The white savior," tweeted Cole, "supports brutal policies in the morning, founds charities in the afternoon, and receives awards in the evening."

The global food crisis of 2007 and 2008 was not of Africa's making. Nor was it caused by global food scarcity. Rather, food prices were driven sky-high because of the new mania for converting food into fuel for vehicles, by financiers fanning the flames of famine by speculating like mad on food commodity prices, by the ravages of climate change and erratic rainfall, by changing diets in rapidly developing China and India, and by high fuel prices.[203]

In dozens of countries around the world, hungry and angry people took to the streets to protest the new hardship of the rising food prices. Among them, many violent demonstrations occurred across Africa, in Burkina Faso, Cameroon, Côte d'Ivoire, Egypt, Mauritania, Mozambique, Senegal, and Somalia.

In the midst of the multiple crises breaking out over the planet – fuel, financial, food, and climate – all of a sudden many of those who had been ignoring agriculture for decades, strangling budgets for agricultural extension agencies and for participatory research, rediscovered the importance of agricultural investment.

But what kind of agricultural investment? The World Bank, World Trade Organization, and the U.S. Department of Agriculture prescribed solutions that were more of the same that had led to the food crisis – still more deregulated global trade in agricultural commodities, ill-targeted food aid, more investment in industrial agriculture leading to climate change, more technological and genetic fixes. Joining the bandwagon was also the prominent economist Paul Collier proposing that "modern" industrial agriculture, with all the environmental and health consequences that entails, is the solution for feeding the planet.[204]

Rather than put an end to this speculation on food, investment banks and hedge funds (and pension funds) continued to increase their investment in food commodities, which went from US\$65 million in 2007 to US\$126 billion by 2012.[205] This helped push food prices to thirty-year highs and caused dramatic fluctuations in the prices of food.

Yet there is still no sign that international finance and development institutions think it's time to challenge the corporate control of our food and farms or the unfettered financial markets.[206] Those who suggest that smallholder agro-ecological farms could feed Africa, were they given half a chance against the global financial system that was killing them, are frequently dismissed as "romantics."[207]

What is romantic and unrealistic about healthy, diverse farms and landscapes, foods, and people?

The percentage of the global population that is now officially underfed is indeed higher in Africa than anywhere else in the world, at close to a third. But the majority of the world's hungry are not in Africa. In 2010, about 925 million people on the planet did not have enough to eat, a slight decline from the previous year but still higher than before the financial and food crises of 2008.[208] While 98 percent of them were in developing countries, two-thirds of the hungry people live in just seven countries, only two of which are in Africa. One is the Democratic Republic of the Congo, a country that for many years suffered from conflict, much of it related to its rich natural resources. The other is Ethiopia, where the authoritarian regime that is congratulated and supported by Western donors for its economic progress has been throwing countless farmers off their own land and killing those who protest.[209]

Over 40 percent of the people in the world who don't have enough to eat now live in China and India, two nations often feted as emerging economic superpowers, home to a burgeoning number of billionaires and gaping, bewildering economic and social disparities.

On this planet plagued by famine, there is also a good deal of excessive eating, particularly the over-consumption of unhealthy foods. Globally, more people are now lugging around too much fat on their frames than there are people carrying around too little. One and a half billion people are obese or overweight, and 65 percent of the people on earth live in countries where excess weight and obesity kill more people than does being underweight.[210]

And the obesity epidemic, in turn, is caused by a food system that seeks not to nourish the world with healthy foods but to maximize its profits feeding people whatever it is cheapest to produce and easiest to sell.[211]

Africa hardly needs an obesity epidemic on top of all the other health issues it faces, but that is precisely what is happening in urban areas as diets shift from traditional to more processed foods.[212] Between one-fifth and one-half of urban Africans are estimated to be overweight or obese. A study of nutritional status of women in urban areas of seven African countries, some known more for hunger and famine than for excessive caloric intake and weight, such as Burkina Faso and Niger, revealed an alarming trend. Between 1993 and 2003, the prevalence of overweight/obesity in urban areas increased by nearly 35 percent, and the rate of increase was much higher among the poorest, where it rose by 50 percent, than among the richest, where it rose by just 7 percent. Women who had either attended only primary grades or had no formal schooling at all were the ones most likely to become overweight or obese.

Despite rampant poverty in cities, the urban poor have more access to cheap processed foods with high contents of fat and sugar than do their rural cousins, whose diets are more traditional, consisting mostly of vegetables and fruits, tubers, cereals, and grains. Traditional diets do not an obesity epidemic create, nor are you likely to find a family farmer in Africa who is obese. But with modernization and urbanization, nutritionally superior traditional and indigenous foods are rapidly being replaced by modern processed foods.[213]

We've known for almost a century that an industrial diet of fast and processed foods makes people sick and fat.[214] And now Africa is suffering at both ends of the dietary scale – both undernourishment and hunger from lack of food, and obesity brought on by over-consumption of processed foods.

Many people in North America and Europe grew up with this dinnertime cliché: "Finish your dinner. There are children starving in Africa." This is a curious non sequitur. The meaning of the first sentence is clear but the second sentence about kids starving in Africa is more perplexing. Its probable purpose was to remind well-fed and complacent children in affluent homes living in affluent lands in the second half of the twentieth century that they should be immensely grateful for their good fortune, for not having to go to bed with hunger pains gnawing at their bellies, for even having a bed to sleep in.

But has anyone, anywhere found that this comment really works? A friend of mine recalls very clearly, fifty years later, how she responded when her parents used this line on her. She would tell them they were free to package up the leftovers on her plate and mail them to Africa. And I found that being pressured to eat food I didn't want or found disgusting – slimy canned green beans were my nemesis – merely made the food even more unpalatable and caused my digestive tract to seize up. It certainly precluded my sympathy for anyone but myself.

But that's the least of what's wrong with this tired old horse. "There are children starving in Africa" may be the very first and most powerful message children in Europe and North America ever receive about a continent that may barely figure in their education. So the phrase sticks to the mind the way oatmeal porridge sticks to the ribs, creating a lasting impression, the absolute nonsense that *everyone* in Africa is starving and the corollary that clearly they don't know how to farm or feed themselves, don't have any gastronomy or food cultures and etiquette worth noticing.

One of the continent's strongest and most admirable traditions is its culture of sharing. Not just money and material possessions, but seed, labour, and most of all, food and meals. Sharing and communal eating are still the norm in much of Africa. Sierra Leonean food writer Rachel C.J. Massaquoi recalls her mother telling her not to cover her face when she was eating so she could "enjoy the privilege of inviting people passing to share" her meal with her.[215]

I've never experienced anywhere the same generosity with food, even when it's not abundant, that I have in Africa. I can't count the number of times I've been walking through a village, or a market, and come across a group of people sharing a meal from a communal bowl, who, on spotting a passing stranger, extend the bowl in my direction and say, "You're invited."

Late one afternoon in eastern Sierra Leone, I was following my husband, an avid jogger, up a steep path to a mountain peak in a forest reserve on the outskirts of the town of Kenema. I lagged behind and got horribly lost. I wound up going down the wrong side of the mountain, making my way along paths that led me through compounds where whole families were seated around large bowls, eating their dinners. When they caught sight of me, and I must have seemed an odd apparition in their compounds in my running shorts and T-shirt, without exception they smiled, extended greetings, and invited me to stop and join them for some food.

An African proverb says it all: "The man who eats alone, dies alone."

Celebrities who take on Africa as a "cause" sometimes help perpetuate myths about Africa. Sometimes they may diminish the dignity of its people, misrepresenting them or presenting them as objects of pity.

In 1984, the BBC alerted the world to a famine in Ethiopia. The famine, widely attributed to drought, was "in fact a political crisis characterized more appropriately by war than by drought."[216] This fact, however, was not part of the campaign to do something about the suffering and solving the root problems. Instead, to pluck at heartstrings to raise funds to help tackle the famine in Ethiopia in 1984, Bob Geldof and Midge Ure wrote the song, "Do They Know It's Christmas?". Sir Bob (he later earned a knighthood for this work) then put together Band Aid, a group of top British and Irish artists to sing it. It became a Christmas hit and sold 3.5 million copies in the U.K. alone.

Its lyrics include phrases such as "nothing ever grows" in Africa, and "no rain nor rivers flow." "Do They Know It's Christmas?" was always a peculiar title for a song intended to raise money to help ease the plight of people in Ethiopia. The majority of its population, some 32 million people, are Orthodox Christians. Christianity is nothing new to the country; it dates back to the first century C.E. So *of course* Ethiopian Christians know when it's Christmas; on their calendar it falls on the seventh of January. Non-Christian Ethiopians would also certainly know what day is Christmas because it's a public holiday.

Another line in the song bemoans the fact that "there won't be snow in Africa this Christmastime." Now really, Sir Bob. What's snow got to do with it? White Christmases and the other recently concocted trappings of the season don't figure at all in the traditional Ethiopian Christmas. Theirs is called *Genna* and is preceded by a period of fasting. On *Genna* itself, Christian Ethiopians traditionally dress in white wraps with magnificent colours woven along the borders, and head off to church. Ethiopian Christmas is not a time for giving gifts; rather, it's a time for faith, games, and feasting. Ethiopia has an incredible history; it was the cradle of great ancient civilizations, home to remarkable cultures, and it has its own distinctive and fabulous cuisines, with its spongy sourdough bread, *injera*, made from the highly nutritious grain called *tef*, and an amazing variety of stews and soups and unique spices. Ethiopia gave the world coffee, finger millet, the important root crop of *enset* or "false banana," *lablab* beans, and castor beans.

But after all the fund-raising was done and the tear-jerking songs had been sung for Ethiopia, how many people were left with the impression that there was nothing, absolutely nothing in the country but starving, wide-eyed women and skeletal babies?

In her powerful book, *Damned Nations: Greed, Guns, Armies and Aid*, Samantha Nutt recounts a bad joke that sums up that fallout from the one-dimensional image of Ethiopia promoted by Geldof & Company: "You're going to an Ethiopian restaurant? What do they serve, an empty plate?"

25

Jam delicious dishes and adorable fast food

When he had asked for all that white man's food, the beautiful long rice in the packet with the Afro-American Uncle Ben smiling on it, the tinned cake which had traveled thousands of miles from rich man's countries, and the New Zealand butter, he had known it was stupid to be feeling so good just because he was buying these things he could not in the end afford, yet he could not help the smile that came to his lips and spread this feeling of well-being over all his body.

– Ayi Kwei Armah
The Beautyful Ones Are Not Yet Born

It's the afternoon of Easter Monday, and in Freetown that means party time. My husband and I have donned sunhats and sunglasses and we're headed on foot towards Lumley Beach. I do so with some trepidation. My fear of large crowds has been growing steadily along with my advancing age, and on this day each year tens – if not hundreds – of thousands of Sierra Leoneans make their way to the beautiful crescent of sandy beach in the west of the capital.

The stream of people is already epic, becoming a torrent of toddlers, children, teenagers, women, and men dressed up and moving towards the beach for a frolicking good beach party. These are not rich people. Many qualify as extremely poor, live in squalid and flood-prone shantytowns on the east side of town, and can only dream of eating three square meals a day. A good number of them have walked several kilometres, braving the raging April sun and the wet blanket of humid heat that covers the city, because they cannot afford even the few coins that a ride in a packed *poda poda* van would cost. The wealthy will come later, in showy and expensive cars, for the high life and nightlife on the beach, when the masses are already making their way back home. But right now, the rip current of humanity is flowing towards the beach.

It's wild. Insane. Wonderful. Frenzied. Fun. The young people have scoured the markets to adorn themselves in the latest second-hand fashions currently drowning the continent. Young men model name-brand underwear, riding high above tight jeans worn below the buttocks, secured in that awkward place with rhinestone-studded or Stars-and-Stripes belts, white plastic sunglasses perched on their heads or slick streamlined shades covering their eyes. Young women literally sparkle. There are sequined headbands and even crowns, satiny pink evening dresses, the shortest of shorts. Nothing is too flashy, shiny, slinky, blingy, or risqué for this day of partying and fun.

My husband and I fall into step like interlopers in a parade, borrowing and soaking up the excitement. We pass a row of tiny roadside eateries. Their names are hand-painted, some a little unevenly, on their closed doors. "Adorable Fast Food Restaurant," "Eat All Restaurant," "Penny Penny." Another is called "Jam Delicious Dishes," which is the delightful Krio way of saying "come together for really good food." During the week, you can have a quick meal in these hole-in-the-wall places for just a dollar or so, with a thin, Maggi-flavoured groundnut sauce or *plasas* on top of some white (imported) rice and sometimes some fried (imported) chicken. Today they're all closed for the holiday.

We move past the intimidating walls of the former Mammy Yoko hotel complex that for years was the headquarters for the United Nations peace mission to Sierra Leone. It has been transformed into a Radisson Blu Hotel and now provides the city with luxurious accommodations for visiting elites and business people.

Billboards line both sides of the pot-holed road. They herald the rapid change in the country's – the continent's – eating and drinking habits. One billboard, featuring a Heineken beer bottle, suggestively shaped and erect, blasts out the promise of "POSSIBLY TONIGHT." Another, topped with the words "SIMPLY THE BEST," gives equal billing to a handsome man in a tailored suit, clutching car keys and a mobile phone and the giant bottle of Best whisky he's standing next to.

One invites us to GET ENERGIZED WITH STING ENERGY DRINK and underneath the image of the can floats the disembodied word VITAMIN. Another features an energy drink called BURN, a high-sugar and caffeine drink from Sweden that is distributed internationally by Coca-Cola. Nearby is another large billboard pushing Maggi cubes, adjacent to a still bigger one advertising ATOMIC ENERGY DRINK (SHARE YOUR ENERGY). In the steady stream of pedestrians and vehicular traffic – motorcycle *okada* taxis and the four-wheeled variety, *poda poda* vans – there is a truck emblazoned with ads for POWER HORN ENERGY DRINK, featuring a stylized bull's head in a ring of fire.

Another billboard features enormous images of tins of Vega "evaporated filled milk" that is IMPROVED FOR GREAT AFRICAN TASTE." This milk, which I often buy for my coffee, is "filled" with more than just milk. Its ingredients are SKIMMED MILK, VEGETABLE FAT, STABILISERS (E-407, E-339), EMULSIFIER (E-522), VITAMIN A AND D. Labels on the tins say it's manufactured in Peru for Vega Foods, a division of Vega Foods Corp. Private Ltd. of Singapore. "Life is tasty" ™ and "Better Foods for Better

Life," chirps Vega on its website, along with this intriguing information: "In Africa alone, more than a dozen people are enjoying Vega Foods every single second. By the time you finish reading this paragraph, close to two hundred people would have enjoyed the taste of Vega Foods."[217] Vega says it realized in 2005 that Africa, "with its 900 million people and immense opportunity was the final frontier" for food businesses.[218]

The advertising onslaught continues as we walk. Another promotes Jago chocolate milk powder FOR THE CHAMPIONS OF TOMORROW, followed by yet another encouraging consumers to buy and use Gino tomato paste. Both are produced by the Watanmal Group, a transnational with a wide range of product groups: a culinary division, animal proteins, beverages and confectionery, spices and seasonings, branded commodities, and a breakfast division that produces sweetened condensed milk and "fresh sterilized UHT milk," as well as the Jago powdered chocolate drink that the billboard would have its beholders believe will make Olympians out of happy and smiling little children who drink it. The Watanmal Group – "Enhancing Life" – has offices in India, the U.S.A., Singapore, and Hong Kong and its markets are mostly in Africa.[219] It's difficult to tell where or from what any of its products are made.

Finally, we reach the Lumley Beach roundabout, where we could head to the right towards one large and flashy casino, or follow the throngs fanning out along the beachfront, in the direction of a newer, even flashier Chinese-owned casino. The bedlam has reached an ear-splitting crescendo, with giant speakers set up all over the place and belting out a cacophony of West African highlife and American hip-hop tunes duking it out at deafening volumes.

Instead of continuing, we cross the street to a bar and restaurant overlooking the beach and find a place to sit at a small table in the blessed shade of an umbrella. In the six years I've been coming to Lumley Beach, I've never seen it so full of people.

Earlier today, just after dawn, when my husband and I jogged its length, our only company was a handful of young men playing soccer, a few fishermen hauling in a net, and a dozen or so other walkers and runners. Now, as far as the eye can see, it is seething with humanity – humming, vibrating with it.

Half of the people here seem to have come to party and play; the other half appear to have made their way to the beach intent on earning a little money peddling foodstuffs, drinks, and just about everything else under the dazzling sun. But everyone is here to revel in the moment, to enjoy being part of the multitude on this special day on their beautiful beach in the country they affectionately call "Swit [Sweet] Salone."

I am longing for a *swit* fresh coconut and that's what I say to the waitress when she comes to take our order. The choice of beverages seems to be limited to only industrially canned and bottled drinks involving a lot of sugar, caffeine, or alcohol. There is not a single one on tap that is made with local ingredients such as ginger, cola nuts, tamarind, or other fruits and crops that abound in the country. There's not a coconut in sight, even though the coconut palms grow like mad along the coast, producing a thirst-quenching drink and delectable tender flesh in their own insulated packaging designed by the wondrous invisible hands of nature. I find myself lecturing the poor young waitress to this effect, extolling the virtues of the tree and its fruit while she stands patiently with a polite smile pasted on her face.

The coconut palm (*Cocos nucifera*) has to be one of nature's most generous gifts to the tropics and some have dubbed it the "tree of life," even "the world's most useful plant."[220] In West Africa it is usually harvested by young men and boys who nimbly shinny up the trees to collect the large green immature coconuts, known sometimes as jelly-nuts or just *jelie* here in Sierra Leone. It's usually possible to find them in the centre of Freetown, where vendors – always men for some reason – pile them into wheelbarrows and move about from one street corner to another.

Flag one down, request a coconut, wait while they shake and knock a few to find one with lots of liquid, then watch as they cradle it with one hand while using a machete in the other to carve away a little of the green outer skin and decapitate it. Then, oh bliss, take hold of it in two hands, tip it back, and drink.

The slightly tangy milky liquid is a perfect pick-me-up in the sweltering heat of a tropical day. It is rich in vitamin C, riboflavin and calcium, dietary fibre, magnesium, potassium, and manganese. And once you've finished imbibing all those nutrients and quenching your thirst, you just hand it back to the vendor who uses his machete to open it up and scoop out the soft white flesh that you can then eat. A genuine energy drink that comes in its own drinking vessel. The going price for a *jelie* in Freetown at the time? 1,500 Leones, less than 30 U.S. cents.

But just as the many bars and restaurants along Lumley Beach don't serve local country rice, neither do they offer fresh coconuts. The waitress pledges to keep an eye out for any vendors passing with *jelies* for sale. In the meantime I have a choice. I can order a sugary soft drink that comes in a bottle. Or I can order one that comes in a can. I choose the bottle.

From my vantage point overlooking the beach, I watch food sellers working their way through the crowd. Girls peddle pieces of fried (imported) chicken. Young men move about with huge bowls on their heads, stuffed with biscuits from Sri Lanka and China ... going for the price of a whole day's meal for a whole family, 10,000 Leones or about US$2.50 at the time.

An ambulant vendor approaches us with a cardboard box on his head that overflows with colourful packages and bags. Tucked under his arm are several cylindrical packages of Pringles. He lowers the box, offering us a better view of the contents. Partly because I feel sorry not to give him a little business and partly out of curiosity, for 2,000 Leones, or about 50 U.S. cents, I agree to buy a bag of what may possibly be potato chips. I use my teeth to tear open the package and place a chip in my mouth.

At first I think I've mistakenly been chewing the bit of plastic I tore off the bag when I opened it. Nope. The small crispy thing I've bitten into is identical to the rest of the ones still inside the bag. Intrigued to see if there are any potatoes or corn or soy or something generally considered edible in the "chips," I turn the bag over and read the ingredients. There is only one; the contents of the alleged chips are "snack pellets." Made in China.

Consumer protection and regulations on product labelling in most African countries aren't up to coping with the inundation of processed food and drink to which they're being subjected. Nor is the public being warned to be cautious with processed foods and drinks in fancy packaging. Rather, they're being wooed to consume them by powerful marketing campaigns that have been so successful in roping in consumers around the world and convincing them that a modern diet of processed chemicals, sugar, and fats is somehow superior to one of local, diverse, delicious, and more natural foods.

Next to approach us are three teenage girls with platters on their heads. Two of them lower the large metal plates and unwrap layers of cotton cloth to expose some freshly roasted peanuts. We place an order for 2,000 Leones and they each tear off a small piece of paper from a collection of paper scraps on their trays, and use a tin that once held (imported) tomato paste to scoop out 1,000 Leones worth of peanuts, still warm from recent roasting over grills in their homes. The peanuts are small and delicious, tastier and more addictive than any of the over-salted and adulterated kinds available on the North American market. The scraps of paper they are wrapped in evoke mysteries. How did a Dutch-language newspaper wind up in Sierra Leone and where did these girls get it? And how did a page of a United Nations expense account form come to be in the public domain, being used by young vendors to wrap up peanuts?

The third young woman is not selling peanuts, however. Next to the mounds of peanuts on our table, she places her heavy platter, covered with small plastic bags full of a brown substance and sealed with miniscule knots. I ask her what's in the bags, how it's made. Six years I've been coming to Sierra Leone, eating and drinking everything I can find, combing the markets, roadsides, and eateries for interesting edibles, and still it seems there is so much to learn. She tells me it's *"thombi"* mixed with sugar, Maggi, pepper (hot), and a little water.

"It's very sweet," she says.

I ask her what it comes from, this *thombi.* She earnestly explains that it comes from a plant with a flower and a fruit. I thank her for this, and buy a couple of packages of *thombi* for mere pennies. It's tongue-tingling good, sweet and sour and peppery all at once and I immediately know what plant produces it from the flavour. I'm almost sure it's tamarind, something I will confirm later when I have the chance to consult a 1967 book about the trees of Sierra Leone, which says that *Al-Thombi* is the word in the Temne language for the tree *Tamarindus indicus.*[221]

Apart from the peanuts and the *thombi,* and a few vendors selling fried fish, I see nothing else in the way of local food or drink on display and for sale here today. On the beach, young men maneuver baby carriages and even wheelchairs through the melee. In them are cool boxes full of soft drinks, beer, and energy drinks. One enterprising fellow wheels another ingenious contraption up and down the beach. It's a large wooden box, the front half of which is glassed in and filled with cones for ice cream. The rear half is an icebox, and it looks as if it's been made by cutting in half a wagon and a walker for the elderly and then welding together the two disembodied parts. The icebox is painted red, white, and blue and emblazoned with the words "Ice cream bomber" and "God Bless My Costomers" [sic]. The ice cream itself is made from an imported powder mix.

Just as the food and drink are mostly Made In Another Country, so are the consumer items and trinkets and clothes that peddlers are trying to sell today. There are young men walking

An ingenious ice cream vendor peddles his wares on Lumley Beach, Sierra Leone, on Easter Monday. (Photo by Karlheinz Eyrich)

about with bouquets of plastic blow-up beach balls and airplanes. Women move about trying to sell lengths of coloured cloth that look, on first glance, like the beautiful cotton prints for which Africa has been known so long. But they're not. The cloth comes from China and it's a thin synthetic material rough to the touch. The necklaces, bracelets, and shawls that women vendors carry up and down the beach, mostly plastic beads moulded into Africa motifs, come from Asia too. As do the endless stacks of DVDs full of pirated movies, some of them filmed inside theatres, some of them graphically pornographic with lewd photos on their covers and in case we missed the point, graphic titles such as *Too Big to Fit.*

Apart from a few hand tools, cooking pots made from recycled aluminum cans, some local vegetables and grains, these days very little of what is sold in the markets of Freetown and many African cities is Made In (or Grown Anywhere Near) Africa. In the Lebanese supermarkets, almost nothing is local and so nothing is fresh. The "Heavy Duty" Blue Plate margarine bears a label tracing its origins to New Orleans. The Woodburry coconut milk comes from The Netherlands where no coconuts grow. The industrial-sized cans of Woodburry tropical fruit cocktail come not from Africa, where the fruits grow in abundance, but from China. Nestlé products fill whole shelves. Energy drinks, soft drinks, Heineken and Carlsberg beers fill the fridges.

The majority of the young people on this beach today are either unemployed or underemployed, trying to make a living at odd jobs, most of which involve trying to sell all this imported stuff and food. How can a nation employ its people when nearly everything it consumes is imported, creating jobs elsewhere, and its natural resources – its diamonds, gold, bauxite, iron ore – are exploited and exported raw by foreign companies? When these foreign "investors" are permitted to repatriate up to 100 percent of their profits, and when many of them and their tangled web of subsidiaries are registered in tax havens? And when the nation is now enabling the grabbing of its prized farmland and water resources by foreign investors looking to make a buck, or a billion of them, by speculating on food, agrofuels, and "land banks"?

The answer is: It can't. No nation can thrive and gainfully employ its youth and maintain a healthy society and population when it is a dumping ground for manufacturers and corporations elsewhere. When its natural resources are flowing out of the country to enrich investors in high places and distant cities, leaving only the environmental destruction and social upheaval behind. Nor can its farmers and farms thrive and keep the country fed with local foods produced sustainably when subsidized and unsustainably produced imports undermine them. Nor can its people nourish themselves and their health when their own healthy foods are being replaced by processed industrial junk.

Where some see the wealth of family farms and local foods that should be supported to promote food sovereignty, the neo-liberal economists see only lost opportunities to create a dependence on genetically modified seeds, toxic agrochemicals and fertilizers, a handful of commodity crops for a global marketplace, and inferior processed food products that will wipe out Africa's cuisines before they have even become known and appreciated internationally.

The continent's rich and varied culinary and crop heritage is rarely acknowledged, let alone praised, by Africa's leadership. Today, younger generations are rejecting traditional foods and opting instead for exotic ones as a way to show that they are "modern" consumers.[222] I recall listening to two young women in Cameroon, both flight attendants with the national airline, laughing derisively about how their less worldly and hopelessly "unsophisticated" peers who had never experienced Paris (as they had countless times) didn't even know how to eat a baguette "correctly," and to this day I wonder why I neglected to ask her how one does *correctly* eat a baguette. They derided their countrywomen for eating Cameroonian couscous, a staple dish made from maize, with their hands rather than with a "civilized" fork like *un blanc,* a white person.

Young people are often on the move in search of paying work, and attitudes about foods change rapidly during times of great social and political upheaval brought on by globalization and new communications. Advertising helps, of course, in shaping attitudes. There is an enormous amount of advertising and messaging promoting imported or "modern" processed food and drinks bombarding the continent every day on televisions, billboards, and also in pirated videos that are screened in small video halls in even remote villages in Africa. This erodes the vast library of collective but unwritten indigenous knowledge passed down through countless generations, about local foods, seeds and crops, their cultivation and preparation, and how they are eaten.

Traditionally in many parts of West Africa, before anyone touched a celebratory meal or a beverage, a libation was poured on the ground in honour of deities and ancestors that bequeathed life and knowledge to current generations. Today, this acknowledgement of the past and what is owed to those who went before and supreme beings in the spiritual world is disappearing. In the case of Ghana, it is *being* disappeared by overzealous religious fundamentalists.[223]

As food knowledge, food cultures, and indigenous crops are neglected into oblivion, Africa risks descending into even deeper dependency on the global industrial giants that dominate the food chain, and the biotech and agrochemical behemoths that dominate agriculture. And it will be condemned to follow the path towards industrial agriculture and industrial diets, heavy on unhealthy additives and a few commodity crops and not the least resilient to difficult and changing climates.

I must have sighed out loud. My husband glances at me, recognizes the mood that is descending on me as my thoughts pound against my skull like a caged headache, and he gently urges me to snap out of it, to relax. This is not the time to be dwelling on all these ponderous and worrisome trends. Today is a day for festivities, merrymaking, and around me it looks as if just about everyone is caught up in the joy of the moment. People with far more reason than I have to worry and fret are dancing, laughing, running, swimming, frolicking in the waves, kicking balls about, wrestling in the sand, flirting, or just hanging out and sharing the experience of each other and this holiday Easter Monday on the beach.

For today, at least, they are putting aside all their daily worries and trials. I lean back, and decide to follow their example, bask in the vicarious enjoyment to be had by watching others enjoy themselves. Learning how to enjoy the moment is a gift, one of just many that Africa has offered me along with the knowledge and flavours of a whole new world of wonderful crops, dishes, and cuisines. Long may they last and may the gods save them from the Lords of Capital waging war on Africa's farms – and foods.

It is a sign of the times that the only bottle I have to raise to honour this toast is one containing a sugary soft drink that originated in America, even if it stole its name from the African cola or kola nut and possibly still contains some. I tilt the bottle and pour a little onto the sand at my feet. I hope the ancestors don't mind that this is the liquid I use to pour this libation, to offer my thanks for all the wonderful crops and foods that countless generations have developed and bequeathed the world.

I watch the splash of brown liquid fizzle then disappear into the white sand, as I offer silent but infinite gratitude for the joys of African crops, cuisines, cooking – and for the continent's unsung farmers and cooks.

Endnotes

1. Susanne Friedberg. 2005. "French beans for the masses: a modern historical geography of food in Burkina Faso." In James I. Watson and Melissa I Caldwell, (Eds). *The cultural politics of food and eating: a reader.* Malden, MA: Blackwell Publishing. p. 24.

2. Statement by Civil Society Africa. May 15, 2013. "Modernising African agriculture: Who benefits?" Available at http://www.acbio.org. za/activist/index.php?m=u&f=dsp&petitionID=3 [Accessed June 4, 2013]

3. Slow Food Movement. http://salonedelgustoterramadre.slowfood.com/ dettaglioStampa.plp?tipo=UltimaOra&id= 82fd59bb312843f94293472f4aa9d78fen [Accessed August 2, 2012]

4. Fumiaki Imamura, Renata Micha, Shahab Khatibzadeh, Saman Fahimi, Peilin Shi, John Powles, Dariush Mozaffarian, on behalf of the Global Burden of Diseases Nutrition and Chronic Diseases Expert Group (NutriCoDE). "Dietary quality among men and women in 187 countries in 1990 and 2010: a systematic assessment." *The Lancet* March 3, 2015. www.thelancet.com/lancetgh

5. National Research Council of the National Academies. Washington, DC. The National Academies Press. 1996. *Lost crops of Africa: Volume I: Grains.* p. 5. http://www.nap.edu/catalog/2305.html [Accessed September 21, 2011]; 2006. *Lost crops of Africa: Volume II: Vegetables.* http://www. nap.edu/catalog/11763.html [Accessed September 21, 2011]; 2008. *Lost crops of Africa: Volume III: Fruits.* http://www.nap.edu/catalog/11879. html [Accessed September 21, 2011]

6. Fran Osseo-Asare. 2005. *Food culture in sub-Saharan Africa* (part of the series: Food culture around the world). Westport, Connecticut: Greenwood Press. pp. 13-14.

7. V.F. Doherty, O.O. Olaniran, U.C. Kanife. July 2010. "Antimicrobial activities of Afromomum Melegueta (Alligator pepper)." *International Journal of Biology*, Vol 2(2). Canadian Centre of Science and Education. http://ccsenet.org/journal/index.php/ijb/article/view/4860/5211 [Accessed November 23, 2011]

8. Ayoade A. Adesokan, Musbau A. Akanji, and Gabriel S. Adewara. December 2010. "Evaluation of Hypoglycaemic efficacy of aqueous seed extract of *Aframomum melegueta* in Alloxan-induced diabetic rats." *Sierra Leone Journal of Biomedical Research.* 2(2), 91-94.

9. Cheryl Lyn Dybas and Ilya Raskin. 2007. "Out of Africa: a tale of gorillas, heart disease ... and a swamp plant." *BioScience* 57(5), 392-397. Available at: http://www.bioone.org/doi/full/10.1641/B570503 [Accessed November 16, 2013]

10. A. Agueguia, D.A. Fontem, J.C. Mboua, M. Mouen, J. Ngo Som, M. Segnou, M. Tchuanyo, and S. Zok. 2000. "Les ignames: la richesse des paysans." *Les richesses du sol: Les plantes à racines et tubercules en Afrique: une contribution au développement des technologies de récolte et d'après-récolte.* Ed. A. Bell, O. Muck, and B. Schuler. Germany: GTZ, FAO. http://www.fao.org/wairdocs/x5695f/x5695f04.htm [Accessed June 8, 2013]

11. Fran Osseo-Asare. pp. 18-19.

12. "Les ignames: la richesse des paysans." FAO. http://www.fao.org/inpho_archive/content/documents/vlibrary/move_rep/x5695f/x5695f04.htm [Accessed June 7, 2013]

13. A. Dansi, A. Adjatin, H. Adoukonou-Sagbadja, and K. Akpagana. March 2009. "Production and traditional seed conservation of leafy vegetables in Benin rural areas." *Bulletin de la Recherche Agronomique du Bénin*, Numéro 59.

14. Rachel C.J. Massaqoui. 2011. *Foods of Sierra Leone and other West African countries: A cookbook and food-rerlated stories.* Bloomington, Indiana: AuthorHouse. p. 76.

15. Krio is a lingua franca spoken widely in Sierra Leone, which is related to pidgin English spoken elsewhere in anglophone West Africa. It developed into a complex and intricate language in Freetown in the late 1700s and early 1800s when there was an influx of former slaves into the city and a need for a common language, as it is estimated that as many as 200 African languages were spoken in Freetown at that time. [Peace Corps. *Krio Language Manual*, revised edition, 1985. Freetown: Peace Corps-Sierra Leone]

16. *Amaranthus: production guideline.* 2010. Pretoria, South Africa: South Africa Department of Agriculture, Forestry and Fisheries.

17. National Research Council. 1984. *Amaranth: modern prospects for an ancient crop.* Washington, DC: National Academies Press.

18. *Lost crops of Africa: Volume II: Vegetables.* 2006. p. 6.

19. A. Dansi, A. Adjatin, H. Adoukonou-Sagbadja, and K. Akpagana. March 2009. "Production and traditional seed conservation of leafy vegetables in Benin rural areas." *Bulletin de la Recherche Agronomique du Bénin*, Numéro 59. p. 60.

20. A. Dansi, et al. 2009. p. 60.

21. Personal communication, July 2013, Anna-Sarah Eyrich.

22. Judith A. Carney and Richard Nicholas Rosomoff. 2009. *In the shadow of slavery: Africa's botanical legacy in the Atlantic world.* Berkeley and Los Angeles, California: University of California Press. p. xv.

23. V. Fernandes. 1951. "Description de la Côte Occidentale d'Afrique (Sénégal au Cap Monte, Archipels)." T. Monod, T. da Mota, R. Mauny, (eds). *Centro de Estudos da Guinée Portuguesa, Bissau, Guinea-Bissau.* Vol. 11, p. 59, cited in O. Linares. 2002. p. 16361.

24. Jessica B. Harris. 2011. *High on the hog: a culinary journey from Africa to America.* New York, NY: Bloomsbury. p. 13.

25. U.R. Wagenigen. December 11, 2008. *"Green list" of 7000 useful African plants a step closer.* http://www.wur.nl/U.K./newsagenda/archive/news/2008/Plants081211.htm [Accessed December 16, 2011]

26. Carney and Rosomoff. 2009. *In the shadow of slavery: Africa's botanical legacy in the Atlantic world.* Berkeley and Los Angeles, California: University of California Press. p. 7.

27. Carney and Rosomoff. p. 23.

28. Carney and Rosomoff. p. 35.

29. Carney and Rosomoff. p. 31.

30. Charles C. Mann. 2012. *1493: Uncovering the New World Columbus created.* New York: Vintage Books. p. 7.

31. Charles C. Mann. 2012. p. 321.

32. Pat Mooney. December 2012. *Oxfam: Who will feed us all?* https://blogs.oxfam.org/en/blogs/12-12-20-day-9-who-will-feed-us-all

33. Carney and Rosomoff. 2009. pp. 124-125.

34. Susanne Freidberg. 2005. "French beans for the masses: a modern historical geography of food in Burkina Faso." In James I. Watson and Melissa I. Caldwell, (eds). *The cultural politics of food and eating: a reader.* Malden, MA: Blackwell Publishing. p. 23.

35. Carney and Rosomoff. p. 15

36. ETC Group. November 2009. "Who will feed us? Questions for the food and climate crisis." *ETC Group Communiqué*, Issue 102.

37. ETC Group. 2009.

38. Miguel A. Altieri. 2009. "Agroecology, small farms and food sovereignty." *Monthly Review* 61(3) July-August, 2009. http://monthlyreview.org/2009/07/01/agroecology-small-farms-and-food-sovereignty [Accessed August 7, 2013]

39. Salone des Gusto Terre Madre, Slow Food. http://salonedelgustoterramadre. slowfood.com/dettaglioStampa.plp?tipo=UltimaOra&id=c81c1ec058cee7348be87d7620dc365aen [Accessed June 9, 2013]

40. CENAFOD/AGEFORE. *Recueil d'espèces végétales ligeneuses dans la region de Bamako.* 1997. Bamako, Mali: Editions Jamana.

41. National Research Council of the National Academies. 1996, 2006, and 2008. *Lost crops of Africa: Volume 1: Grains; Lost crops of Africa: Volume II: Vegetables; Lost crops of Africa: Volume III: Fruits.*

42. For more detail on the baobab, its remarkable history and the legends surrounding it, and the incredible variability of the tree in Africa, see Thomas Parkenham. 2004. *The remarkable baobab.* London, U.K.: Weidenfeld & Nicolson.

43. M. Sidibé, J.F. Scheuring, D. Tembely, M.M. Sidibé, P. Hofman, and M. Frigg. 1996. "Baobab – homegrown vitamin C for Africa." *Agroforestry Today* 8(2): 13-15.

44. M. Sidibé, et al. 1996. 13-15.

45. *Lost crops of Africa: Volume II: Vegetables.* 2006. p. 7.

46. *Lost crops of Africa: Volume I: Grains.* 1996. p. 59.

47. *Lost crops of Africa: Volume II: Vegetables.* 2006. p. 60.

48. The mother of a Malian friend of mine is a specialist in the "*secrets de femme*" and a "marriage counsellor" who makes and sells *wusulan* and a whole fascinating range of herbal products designed for the woman. Her website is: http://lesecretdefemme.canalblog.com/

49. Rod Chavis. October 2, 1998. *Africa in the Western media.* Paper presented at the Sixth Annual African Studies Consortium Workshop. http://www.africa.upenn.edu/Workshop/chavis98.html [Accessed December 6, 2011]

50. Miranda Dodd's spouse, Shindouk Ould Najim, contributes his perspective on the recent history of northern Mali in Laurence Aïda Ammour, Shindouk Ould Najim, and Jen-Luc Peduzzi. 2013. *Je reviendrai à Tombouctou: un chef Touareg témoigne.* Brussels: Ixelles Publishing SA.

51. Miranda Dodd. *Explore Timbuktu.* http://www.exploretimbuktu.com/culture/culture/food.html [Accessed January 24, 2012]

52. Esther Garvi. August 12, 2008. *Hanza and aid prejudice in Niger.* http://www.esthergarvi.org/2008/08/12/hanza-and-aid-prejudice-in-niger/ [Accessed November 6, 2013]

53. Sarah van Gelder. November 15, 2013. "Vandana Shiva on resisting GMOs: 'saving seeds is a political act.'" *Yes Magazine.* http://www.yesmagazine.org/issues/how-to-eat-like-our-lives-depend-on-it/vandana-shiva-freedom-starts-with-a-seed [Accessed November 24, 2013]

54. Sean Callahan. July 16, 2008. *Delivering international food aid and providing foreign agricultural development assistance.* http://crs.org/newsroom/testimony/entry.cfm?id=1499 [Accessed November 6, 2013]

55. Esther Garvi. August 12, 2008.

56. Edouard G. Bonkoungou, Mamadou Djimdé, Elias T. Ayuk, Issiaka Zoungrana, and Zacharie Tchoundjeu. 1998. *Taking stock of agroforestry in the Sahel – harvesting results for the future, end of phase report: 1989-1996.* Nairobi, Kenya: International Centre for Research in Agroforestry. p. 41.

57. CENAFOD/AGEFORE. *Recueil d'espèces végétales ligeneuses dans la region de Bamako.* 1997. Bamako, Mali: Editions Jamana.

58. World Agroforestry Centre. *Faidherbia albida: Keystone of evergreen agriculture in Africa.* http://www.worldagroforestry.org/sites/default/files/F.a_keystone_of_Ev_Ag.pdf [Accessed December 17, 2013]

59. See, for example: Joan Baxter. 2010. *Dust from our eyes – an unblinkered look at Africa.* Hamilton, Ontario: Wolsak & Wynn. pp. 80-106.

60. Green Commodities Facility. "Shea Butter Scoping Paper." August 2010. United Nations Development Program (UNDP) Internal Working Paper.

61. J-M. Boffa, G. Yaméogo, P. Nikiéma, and J-B Taonda. 1996. "What future for the shea tree?" *Agroforestry Today* 8(4), pp. 5-7.

62. Green Commodities Facility. "Shea Butter Scoping Paper." United Nations Development Program (UNDP) Internal Working Paper. August 2010.

63. J-M. Boffa, G. Yaméogo, P. Nikiéma, and D.M. Knudson. n.d. *Shea nut (Vitellaria paradoxa) production in agroforestry parklands of Burkina Faso.* World Agroforestry Centre. http://www.worldagroforestry.org/units/library/books/book%2015/non-wood%20forest%20products%209/htmlold/shea_nut.htm?n=21 [Accessed May 24, 2013]

64. J-M. Boffa, G. Yaméogo, P. Nikiéma, and J-B. Taonda. 1996. *Agroforestry Today* 8(4) October-December, 5-7.

65. Global Shea Alliance. http://www.globalshea.com/about/15/Mission-Vision [Accessed December 10, 2015]

66. ETC Group. November 2009. Issue 102.

67. B. Vira, C. Wildburger, and S. Mansourian (Eds.), 2015. *Forests, trees and landscapes for food security and nutrition. A global assessment report.* Vienna: International Union of Forest Research Organizations (IUFRO) World Series Volume 33.

68. World Agroforestry Centre. *Agroforestry tree aatabase. A tree species reference and selection guide: Dacryodes edulis.* http://www. worldagroforestrycentre.org/sea/products/afdbases/af/asp/SpeciesInfo. asp?SpID=641#Uses [Accessed June 6, 2013]

69. *New Agriculturalist.* July 2007. "Branching out – safou goes global." http://www.new-ag.info/en/developments/devItem.php?a=172 [Accessed May 29, 2013]

70. International Union for Conservation of Nature and Natural Resources IUCN red list: http://www.iucnredlist.org/search [Accessed May 30, 2013]

71. Olayinka O. Adegbehingbe, Saburi A. Adesanya, Thomas O. Idowu, Oluwakemi C. Okimi, Oyesiku A. Oyelami, and Ezekiel O. Iwalewa. 2008. "Clinical effects of Garcinia kola in knee osteoarthritis." *Journal of Orthopaedic Surgery and Research* 2008, 3:34.

72. N. Ralebona, C.R. Sewani-Rusike, and B.N. Nkeh-Chungag. April 15, 2012. "Effects of ethanolic extract of Garcinia kola on sexual behaviour and sperm parameters in male Wistar rats." *African Journal of Pharmacy and Pharmacology* 6(14), 1077-1082. Available online at http://www.academicjournals.org/AJPP [Accessed May 30, 2013]

73. National Research Council. 2008. *Lost crops of Africa. Volume III: Fruits*, Washington, D.C.: The National Academies Press. p. 206. http:// www.nap.edu/catalog/11879.html [Accessed June 6, 2013]

74. Roger Leakey. 2012. *Living with the trees of life: Towards the transformation of tropical agriculture.* Oxfordshire, U.K. and Cambridge, USA: CABI.

75. World Agroforestry Centre. *Agroforestry tree database. Ricinodendron heudelotii* http://www.worldagroforestrycentre.org/sea/products/ AFDbases/AF/asp/SpeciesInfo.asp?SpID=1449 [Accessed September 27, 2012]

76. *Irvingia gabonensis.* World Agroforestry Centre. http://www. worldagroforestry.org/treedb2/AFTPDFS/Irvingia_gabonensis.pdf [Accessed May 30, 2013]

77. Judith L. Ngondi, Julius E. Oben, and Samuel R. Minka. 2005. "The effect of Irvingia gabonensis seeds on body weight and blood lipids of obese subjects in Cameroon." *Lipids Health Dis.* 4:12.

78. http://africanmangomart.com/ [Accessed May 30, 2013]

79. R.J. Whitehead. November 5, 2013. "The debate: palm oil and troubled waters." *Food Navigator-Asia*. http://www.foodnavigator-asia.com/Policy/The-debate-Palm-oil-and-troubled-waters [Accessed November 6, 2013]

80. Fran Osseo-Asare. p. 135.

81. O.O. Oguntibeju, A.J. Esterhuyse and E.J. Truter. 2009. "Red palm oil: nutritional, physiological and therapeutic roles in improving human wellbeing and quality of life." *Br J Biomed Sci* 66(4), 216-22. http://www.ncbi.nlm.nih.gov/pubmed/20095133 [Accessed December 11, 2015]

82. Tan Choe Choe. May 30, 2010. "We brought the weevils in from Africa." *New Straits Times*. Available at: http://www.highbeam.com/doc/1P1-180462279.html [Accessed October 11, 2013]

83. See for examples: Friends of the Earth International. November 3, 2009. "'Certified' palm oil not a solution." http://www.foei.org/en/media/archive/2009/certified-palm-oil-not-a-solution [Accessed August 2, 2013]; Sutherland, Laurel. "What is the price of palm oil?" Rainforest Action Network. http://understory.ran.org/2013/07/03/what-is-the-price-of-palm-oil/ [Accessed August 2, 2013]

84. Joan Baxter. July 2013. *Who is benefitting? The social and economic impact of three large-scale land investments in Sierra Leone: a cost-benefit analysis.* Available at: www.christianaid.org.uk/images/who-is-benefitting-Sierra-Leone-report.pdf

85. HarvestPlus. *Breeding crops for better nutrition.* http://www.harvestplus.org/content/about-harvestplus [Accessed May 1, 2012]

86. Michiel S. Korthal. April 20, 2010. "Don't medicalise micronutrient deficiency." *SciDev Net*. http://www.scidev.net/en/editor-letters/don-t-medicalise-micronutrient-deficiency.html [Accessed May 1, 2012]

87. Joan Baxter. July 2013.

88. N. Gilbert. October 2012. "One-third of our greenhouse gas emissions come from agriculture." *Nature*. http://www.nature.com/news/ one-third-of-our-greenhouse-gas-emissions-come-from-agriculture-1.11708

89. Oakland Institute. 2016. *The unholy alliance: five Western donors shape a pro-corporate agenda for African agriculture.* Oakland, CA: Oakland Institute. http://www.oaklandinstitute.org/sites/oaklandinstitute. org/files/unholy_alliance_web.pdf [Accessed July 19, 2016]

90. United Nations Conference on Trade and Development. September 18, 2013. *Trade and Environment Review 2013: Wake up before it's too late – make agriculture truly sustainable now in a changing climate.*

91. Roger Leakey. January 14, 2013. "Three steps to bridging the yield gap." Global Food Security, http://www.foodsecurity.ac.uk/blog/index. php/2013/01/three-steps-to-bridging-the-yield-gap/ [Accessed October 11, 2013]

92. Catherine Ward. October 11, 2013. *Working for a fairer, more sustainable food system: an interview with Shiney Varghese.* http://www. worldwatch.org/node/13825 [Accessed October 12, 2013]

93. Caroline Henshaw. March 8, 2011. "Farmers must be weaned off using oil, says U.N. expert." *Wall Street Journal.* http://online.wsj.com/ article/SB10001424052748704758904576188220051993828.html

94. GRAIN. April 2010. "The U.S.'s Millennium Challenge Corporation (MCC): Turning African farmland over to big business." *Seedling.* pp. 2-11. http://www.grain.org/article/entries/4062-turning-african-farmland-over-to-big-business [Accessed July 18, 2013]

95. Oakland Institute. 2011. *Understanding land investment deals in Africa. Country report: Sierra Leone.* Oakland, CA: Oakland Institute. http://www.oaklandinstitute.org/understanding-land-investment-deals-africa-sierra-leone [Accessed July 18, 2013]

96. Mphoweh Jude Nzembayie, Mesmin Tchindjang, and Alfred Homère Ngandam Mfondoum. *The degradation of raffia palms and its socio-economic and ecological consequences: the case study of Bamunka, Ndop, North West Province Cameroon.* cameroon-tour.com/geography/ Jude_article.pdf [Accessed October 22, 2011]

97. Worldwatch Institute. *State of the World 2011, Innovations that nourish the planet: Africa's indigenous crops.* [www.worldwatch.org]

98. Ibid.

99. *Lost crops of Africa: Volume II: Vegetables.* 2006. pp. 6, 8.

100. *Plant resources of tropical Africa. Prota* 7(1): Timbers/Bois d'œuvre 1: Record display. http://database.prota.org/PROTAhtml/Beilschmiedia%20mannii_En.htm [Accessed March 28, 2012]

101. Olga F. Linares. December 10, 2002. "African rice (*Oryza glaberrima*): History and future potential." *Proceedings of the National Academy of Sciences (PNAS) of the United States of America.* 99(25), pp. 16360-16365. www.pnas.org_cgi_doi_10.1073_pnas.252604599

102. National Research Council. 1996. *Lost crops of Africa: Volume I: Grains* (Washington, DC: National Academies Press), Vol. 1, p. 21. http://www.nap.edu/openbook.php?record_id=2305&page=17

103. Joseph A. Opala, *The Gullah: rice, slavery and the Sierra Leone-American connection.* http://www.yale.edu/glc/gullah/02.htm

104. Ian Smillie, Lansana Gberie, and Ralph Hazleton. January 2000. *The heart of the matter: Sierra Leone, diamonds and human security.* Ottawa: Partnership Africa Canada.

105. G. Kennedy, B. Burlingame, and V.N. Nguyen. 2002. "Nutritional contribution of rice and impact of biotechnology and biodiversity in rice-consuming countries." *Proceedings of the 20th Session of the International Rice Commission.* Bangkok, Thailand. July 23-26, 2002: FAO Corporate Directory. http://www.fao.org/docrep/006/y4751e/y4751e05.htm [Accessed June 1, 2013]

106. Rachel C.J. Massaqoui. p. 76.

107. Rachel C.J. Massaqoui. pp. 77-79.

108. *Lost crops of Africa: Volume II: Vegetables.* p. 137-138.

109. Ibid.

110. Coastal & Environmental Services (CES). March 2009. Sugar cane to ethanol project, Sierra Leone, Draft ESHIA. p. 60.

111. Sierra Leone Network on the Right to Food and Bread For All. September 2012. Concerns of civil society organisations and affected land users on Addax Bioenergy. p. 11.

112. "The great African land grab," a radio documentary on the Addax Bioenergy project, is available at: http://www.cbc.ca/player/play/1481108512 [Accessed February 16, 2017]

113. Michael Pollan. 2008. *In defense of food: an eater's manifesto.* New York, NY: The Penguin Group. pp. 1-14.

114. R. Herz. 2012. *That's disgusting: unraveling the mysteries of repulsion.* New York, USA: W.W. Norton & Co.

115. See for example: Prof. Massimo Marcone. 2010. *Acquired tastes: on the trail of the world's most sought-after delicacies.* Toronto, Ontario: Key Porter Books.

116. Charlie Cooper. March 1, 2013. "Monkeys in my pants? No, just 94 kg of caterpillars in my luggage." *The Independent.* http://www. independent.co.uk/news/uk/home-news/monkeys-in-my-pants-no-just-94kg-of-caterpillars-in-my-luggage-8517350.html [Accessed May 21, 2013]

117. A. van Huis. 2005. "Insects eaten in Africa (Coleoptera, Hymenoptera, Diptera, Heteroptera, Homoptera)." In M.G. Paoletti, (Ed.) *Ecological implications of minilivestock: Potential of insects, rodents, frogs and snails,* pp. 231-244. Enfield, New Hampshire, USA: Science Publishers.

118. A. van Huis. 2005. pp. 231-244

119. Susanne Freidberg. 2005. "French beans for the masses: a modern historical geography of food in Burkina Faso." In James I. Watson and Melissa I. Caldwell. (Eds.) *The cultural politics of food and eating: a reader.* Malden, MA: Blackwell Publishing. p. 31.

120. A. van Huis. 2003. "Insects as food in sub-Saharan Africa." *Insect Science and its Application,* 23(3): pp. 163-185.

121. T. Muyay. 1981. *Les insectes comme aliments de l'homme:* Series II, Vol. 69. Democratic Republic of the Congo: Ceeba Publications.

122. *The Guardian* datablog. 2013. https://www.theguardian.com/news/datablog/2013/jan/10/how-much-water-food-production-waste#data [Accessed July 13, 2016]

123. Arnold van Huis, Joost Van Itterbeeck, Harmke Kulnder, Esther Mertens, Afton Halloran, Giula Muir, and Paul Vantomme. 2013. "Edible insects: future prospects for food and feed security," *FAO Forestry Paper.* Rome: FAO. http://www.fao.org/forestry/edibleinsects/en/ [Accessed May 20, 2013]

124. Ibid.

125. Ibid.

126. Committee on the Status of Pollinators in North America, National Research Council. 2007. *Status of pollinators in North America.* Washington, DC: National Academy of Sciences.

127. Sharon Guynup and Nicolas Ruggia. July 15, 2004. "For most people, eating bugs is only natural." *Natural Geographic.* http://news.nationalgeographic.com/news/2004/07/0715_040715_tvinsectfood.html [Accessed May 21, 2013]

128. Arnold van Huis et al. 2013.

129. Arnold van Huis et al. 2013. p. 36.

130. Arnold van Huis et al. 2013. p. 23.

131. Arnold van Huis et al. 2013. p. 35.

132. C.A. Silow. 1983. "Notes on Ngangela and Nkoya ethnozoology. Ants and termites." *Etnologiska Studier,* 36. p. 177.

133. Arnold van Huis et al. 2013. p. 40.

134. G.R. DeFoliart. 1999. Insects as food: Why the western attitude is important. *Annual Review of Entomology,* 44, 21-50.

135. Current worldwide annual meat consumption per capita (2009). http://chartsbin.com/view/12730 [Accessed May 22, 2013]

136. Arwen Kidd. 2010. *No longer in the land of Betty Crocker* (unpublished essay).

137. David A. Davidson. 2012. Representative concentration pathways and mitigation scenarios for nitrous oxide. *Environ. Res. Lett.* 7: 024005

138. Gidon Eshel, Alon Sherpon, Tamar Makov, and Ron Milo. 2016. "Land, irrigation water, greenhouse gas, and reactive nitrogen burdens of meat, eggs and dairy production in the United States." *Proceedings of the National Academy of Sciences* 111(33), 11996-12001. http://www.pnas.org/content/111/33/11996 [Accessed December 15, 2016]

139. http://www.bushmeat.org/about_bctf/consensus_statement [Accessed October 27, 2011]

140. James Morgan. September 16, 2008. "Calls for bushmeat ban rejected." *BBC News.* http://news.bbc.co.uk/2/hi/science/nature/7617103. stm [Accessed October 27, 2011]

141. D. Cooney. September 2, 2014. "Ebola and bushmeat in Africa: Q&A with leading researcher." *CIFOR Forests:* http://blog. cifor.org/23924/ebola-and-bushmeat-in-africa-qa-with-leading-researcher?fnl=en [Accessed December 15, 2015]

142. Orla Ryan. April 3, 2006. "Bushmeat's boom benefits Ghana's farmers." *BBC News.* http://news.bbc.co.uk/2/hi/business/4864714.stm [Accessed October 27, 2011]

143. National Research Council. 1991. *Microlivestock: Little-known small animals with a promising economic future.* Washington, DC: The National Academies Press. pp. 233-239.

144. Ian Cobain and Afua Hirsch. July 30, 2013. "The tycoon, the dictator's wife and the $2.5 billion Guinea mining deal." *The Guardian.* http://www.theguardian.com/world/2013/jul/30/africa-guinea-mining-bsgr-steinmetz [Accessed August 4, 2013]

145. Fran Osseo-Asare. p. 25.

146. Pipeline Dreams by Christine Badgley. *Missing fish.* http://www. pipelinedreams.org/2009/11/missing-fish/ [Accessed August 29, 2012]

147. 6th World Fisheries Congress Edinburgh 2012. May 9, 2012. *Press Release: World Fisheries Congress investigates the impact of illegal fishing on the industry.* www.6thwfc2012.com/wp-content/uploads/.../IUU-Panels-FINAL.pdf [Accessed August 30, 2012]

148. Environmental Justice Foundation. *Pirate fishing: the scourge of West Africa.* http://www.ejfoundation.org/page275.html [Accessed August 30, 2012]

149. Micheal Pollan. October 6, 2011. "Michael Pollan answers readers' questions." *New York Times Magazine.* http://www.nytimes. com/interactive/2011/10/02/magazine/29mag-food-issue.html#/pollan?ref=todayspaper [Accessed October 26, 2011]

150. Agence Nationale pour L'Emploi (ANPE). 2010. *Recettes des mets Maliens.* Bamako, Mali: Ministère de l'Emploi et de la Formation Professionelle.

151. Among them is Promasidor with its "Onga" line of seasonings or "Mama's Helping Hand." http://www.promasidor.com/new_brand_onga. php [Accessed January 10, 2014]. In Nigeria, the struggle for dominance in the seasoning market has led to a veritable "turf war" among giant corporations such as Maggi and Unilever. See: http://allafrica.com/ stories/201209230142.html [Accessed January 10, 2014]

152. Government of Canada, Statistics Canada. http://www.statcan. gc.ca/daily-quotidien/150122/dq150122b-eng.htm [Accessed July 14, 2016]

153. Patisen. http://www.patisen.com/view/fra/produit.php?produit_ sid=32&produit=MAMI%20tomate%20bol [Accessed November 13, 2011]

154. Ajinomoto Group. http://www.ajinomoto.com/en/aboutus/history/ chronology/ [Accessed December 1, 2013]

155. A.O. Eweka. 2007. "Histological studies of the effects of monosodium glutamate on the kidney of adult Wistar rats." *The Internet Journal of Health*. 6(2). http://www.ispub.com/journal/the-internet-journal-of-health/volume-6-number-2/histological-studies-of-the-effects-of-monosodium-glutamate-on-the-kidney-of-adult-wistar-rats.html [Accessed November 14, 2011]

156. *Analysis of adverse reactions to Monosodium Glutamate (M.S.G.)*. July 1995. Prepared for Center for Food Safety and Applied Nutrition, Food and Drug Administration, Department of Health and Human Services, Washington, D.C.

157. Health Canada, Food and Nutrition: Monosodium glutamate (MSG): Questions and Answers. http://www.hc-sc.gc.ca/fn-an/securit/ addit/msg_qa-qr-eng.php [Accessed February 15, 2012]

158. Ruqayyah Yusuf Aliyu. September 15, 2009. "Ajinomoto marks 100-year anniversary." *Daily Trust*. http://allafrica.com/stories/ 200909150203.html [Accessed November 14, 2011]

159. Mayo Clinic. *Food and Health Eating*. http://www.mayoclinic.com/ health/monosodium-glutamate/AN01251 [Accessed August 1, 2013]

160. See for example, the many scientific articles authored by Barry Popkin, who developed the nutrition transition theory. Specifically, Barry Popkin and Shu Wen Ng. 2006. "The nutrition transition in high and low-income countries: what are the policy lessons?" Invited paper

prepared for presentation at the International Association of Agricultural Economists Conference, Gold Coast, Australia, August 12-18, 2006. http://ageconsearch.umn.edu/bitstream/25493/1/ip06po01.pdf [Accessed July 10, 2013]

161. Ibid.

162. Sifca. http://www.groupesifca.com/index.php?option=com_content&view=article&id=2&Itemid=17&lang=en [Accessed November 14, 2011]

163. U.S. State Department: Niger. http://www.state.gov/r/pa/ei/bgn/5474.htm [Accessed November 4, 2011]

164. www.inter-reseaux.org/IMG/pdf_78initiative.pdf [Accessed November 4, 2011]

165. Haim D. Rabinowitch and Lesley Currah, (Eds.) 2002. *Allium crop science: recent advances.* Wallingford, Oxon, U.K.: CAB International. p. 394.

166. http://technisem.com/index.php?m=13&lang=fr&rub=2&opt=2 [Accessed November 3, 2011]

167. http://www.tropicasem.sn/ [Accessed November 4, 2011]

168. *Coalition pour la Protection du Patrimoine Genetique Africain Niger.* April 21, 2009. http://www.semencespaysannes.org/coalition_protectio_patrimoine_genetique_afri_115-actu_73.php [Accessed September 9, 2012]

169. www.inter-reseaux.org/.../doc_tropicasem_revise.doc [Accessed November 4, 2011]

170. Assane Dagna Moumouni. 2012. *La démarche liée à l'origine du Violet de Galmi, Niger.* Rome: Food and Agricultural Organization of the United Nations.

171. ETC Group. April 30, 2007. http://www.etcgroup.org/en/node/615 [Accessed November 4, 2011]

172. ETC Group. March 23, 2016. *Merge-Santo: New Threat to Food Sovereignty.* http://www.etcgroup.org/content/merge-santo-new-threat-food-sovereignty [Accessed July 15, 2016]

173. Matt McGrath. September 18, 2012. "Agent Orange chemical in GM war on resistant weeds." *BBC World News*. http://www.bbc.co.uk/news/science-environment-19585341 [Accessed July 21, 2013]

174. Kathryn Z. Guyton et al. May 2015. "Carcinogenicity of tetrachlorvinphos, parathion, malathion, diazinon, and glyphosate." *The Lancet Oncology* 16(5), 490-491. http://www.thelancet.com/journals/lanonc/article/PIIS1470-2045(15)70134-8/abstract [Accessed July 15, 2016]

175. "Dutch onion exports down overall but increasing to major West African markets." August 9, 2011. *Technical Centre for Agricultural and Rural Cooperation* (CTA) (ACP-EU Cotonou Agreement): Agritrade. http://agritrade.cta.int/Agriculture/Commodities/Horticulture/Dutch-onion-exports-down-overall-but-increasing-to-major-West-African-markets#page=/%28from%29//%28until%29/03-11-2011/%28sortby%29/date/%28search%29/cross/%28nodeid%29/6417/%28topics%29/7817 [Accessed November 3, 2011]

176. Michaela Schiessl. May 14, 2007. "Africa's unfair battle: the West's poverty subsidies. Part 2: Cheap Crops from Europe and America." *Der Spiegel*. http://www.spiegel.de/international/world/africa-s-unfair-battle-the-west-s-poverty-subsidies-a-482209-2.html [Accessed November 11, 2013]

177. Ramtrade Worldwide. "Global meat & poultry exports. Africa." http://www.ramtrade.com/markets-africa.php [Accessed March 14, 2012]

178. Sofia Monsalve, M. Issah, B. Ilge, A. Paasch, K. Lanje, and Patrick Mulvany. 2007. *Right to food of tomato and poultry farmers: report of an investigative mission to Ghana*. Heidelberg: FoodFirst Information Action Network (FIAN).

179. Michael Sarpong Bruce. August 22, 2011. Ghana's poultry farmers battling for survival as country imports $200m frozen chicken. *Ghana Business News*. http://www.ghanabusinessnews.com/2011/08/22/ghanas-poultry-farmers-battling-for-survival-as-country-imports-200m-frozen-chicken/ [Accessed January 10, 2014]

180. "No more chicken please! How a strong grassroots movement in Cameroon is successfully resisting damaging chicken imports from Europe, which are ruining small farmers all over West Africa." Bonn, Germany: Church Development Service. www.aprodev.eu/files/Trade/071203_chicken_e_final.pdf [Accessed April 15, 2012]

181. Michaela Schiessl. May 14, 2007.

182. Wolfgang E. Schoneck. "Africa: the garbage dump of Europe." http://www.africamission-mafr.org/chicken.htm [Accessed April 15, 2012]

183. See: Kevin Watkins and Jung-ui Sul. 2002. "Cultivating poverty: the impact of U.S. cotton subsidies on Africa." *OXFAM Briefing Paper 30.* Washington, DC: OXFAM International. www.oxfam.org.uk/ resources/policy/trade/.../bp30_cotton.pdf [Accessed December 5, 2011]; Richard Mshomba. September 2002. How Northern subsidies hurt Africa. *Africa Recovery, United Nations.* 16(2-3), 29. http://www.un.org/ ecosocdev/geninfo/afrec/vol16no2/162agric.htm [Accessed December 5, 2011]

184. Environmental Working Group: Farm Subsidy Primer. http://farm. ewg.org/subsidyprimer.php [Accessed July 3, 2013]

185. Ibid.

186. Alex Rindler. November 7, 2013. "Forbes fat cats collect taxpayer-funded farm subsidies." *Environmental Working Group.* http://www. ewg.org/research/forbes-fat-cats-collect-taxpayer-funded-farm-subsidies [Accessed November 10, 2013]

187. Eric Holt-Giménez and Raj Patel with Annie Shattuck. 2009. *Food rebellions: crisis and the hunger for justice.* Cape Town, Dakar, Nairobi and Oxford: Pambazuka Press; Oakland, CA: Food First Books; Boston, MA: Grassroots International. p. 66.

188. Eric Holt-Giménez and Raj Patel with Annie Shattuck. p. 64.

189. Food and Agriculture Organization of the United Nations (FAO), Commodities and Trade Division. October 2006. *FAO Briefs on import surges, commodities, No. 1: Import surges in developing countries: the case of poultry.* FAO: Rome.

190. USAID. "More than $3 billion in private sector investment for the New Alliance for Food Security and Nutrition." http://transition.usaid. gov/g8/PrivateSectorFactSheet.pdf [Accessed June 2, 2013]

191. International Assessment of Agricultural Knowledge, Science and Technology, for Development (IAASTD). Available at www.unep.org/ dewa/Assessment/Ecosystems/IAASTD/tabid/105853/Defa [Accessed March 28, 2012]

192. FAO. 1997. *Agriculture, food and nutrition for Africa: a resource book for teachers of agriculture.* Rome: Food and Agriculture Organization of the United Nations. http://www.fao.org/docrep/W0078E/W0078E00.htm [Accessed August 10, 2012]

193. Mr. Bigg's. http://www.mrbiggsonline.com/main.htm [Accessed March 30, 2012]

194. UAC of Nigeria PLC. http://www.uacnplc.com/company/history.htm [Accessed March 30, 2012]

195. Fran Osseo-Asare. http://www.betumi.com/2009/02/food-science-of-african-tastes.html [Accessed April 30, 2012]

196. Jeanne Egbosiuba Ukwendu. Guest author, *African proverbs on food.* African Culture site. BellaOnline: The Voice of Women. http://www.bellaonline.com/articles/art66166.asp [Accessed September 1, 2012]

197. Ibid.

198. Martin Plaut. 2006. "Africa's hunger – a systemic crisis." *BBC News.* http://news.bbc.co.uk/2/hi/africa/4662232.stm [Accessed March 28, 2012]

199. "Mel Lastman kicked off a decade's worth of faux pas." December 19, 2009. *The Toronto Star.* http://www.thestar.com/news/gta/2009/12/19/mel_lastman_kicked_off_a_decades_worth_of_faux_pas.html [Accessed May 20, 2013]

200. Globetrotter: Daniel Betts. http://www.managementtoday.co.uk/news/1133192/ [Accessed November 13, 2013]

201. http://www.facebook.com/pages/Do-you-speak-African-Well-do-you-speak-European-IDIOT/296508039457 [Accessed March 9, 2011]

202. Teju Cole. March 21, 2012. "The White Savior Industrial Complex." *The Atlantic.* http://www.theatlantic.com/international/archive/2012/03/the-white-savior-industrial-complex/254843/ [Accessed 29 March 2012]

203. Marco Lagi, Yavni Bar-Yam, Karla Z. Bertrand, and Yaneer Bar-Yam. September 21, 2011. "The food crises: a quantitative model of food prices including speculators and ethanol conversion." Cornell University Library. arXiv:1109.4859v1 (necsi.edu/research/social/foodprices.html) [Accessed September 17, 2012]

204. Paul Collier. 2008. *The politics of hunger: how illusion and greed fan the food crisis.* Foreign Affairs. November/December 2008. Council on Foreign Relations. http://www.foreignaffairs.com/articles/64607/paul-collier/the-politics-of-hunger [Accessed April 15, 2012]

205. Grace Livingstone. April 1, 2012. "The real hunger games: How banks gamble on food prices – and the poor lose out." *The Independent.* http://www.independent.co.uk/news/world/politics/the-real-hunger-games-how-banks-gamble-on-food-prices--and-the-poor-lose-out-7606263.html# [Accessed April 1, 2012]

206. Grace Livingstone. p. 2.

207. Paul Collier. 2008.

208. Food and Agriculture Organization of the United Nations, September 2010. *Global hunger declining, but still unacceptably high.* Available at http://www.wfp.org/hunger/stats [Accessed November 22, 2011]

209. Human Rights Watch. June 16, 2016. "'Such a brutal crackdown': Killings and arrests in response to Ethiopia's Oromo protests." https://www.hrw.org/report/2016/06/16/such-brutal-crackdown/killings-and-arrests-response-ethiopias-oromo-protests [Accessed July 15, 2016]

210. World Health Organization. Media Centre: *Obesity and Overweight Fact Sheet.* http://www.who.int/mediacentre/factsheets/fs311/en/ [Accessed November 21, 2011]

211. Olivier de Schutter. March 12, 2012. *Obesogenic food systems must be reformed.* Available at http://www.grain.org/bulletin_board/entries/4480-obesogenic-food-systems-must-be-reformed [Accessed August 30, 2012]

212. Abdhalah K. Ziraba, Jean C. Fotso, and Rhoune Ochako. 2009. "Overweight and obesity in urban Africa: A problem of the rich or the poor?" *BMC Public Health* 2009, 9, 465. http://www.biomedcentral.com/1471-2458/9/465 [Accessed December 7, 2011]

213. Ismael Thiam, Kinday Samba, and Priscilla Lwanga. 2006. "Diet-related chronic disease in the West Africa region. United Nations System Standing Committee on Nutrition. Diet-related chronic disease and the double burden of malnutrition in West Africa." *SCN News* 33, 6-10.

214. Michael Pollan. 2008.

215. Rachel C.J. Massaquoi. p. 65.

216. Inter Africa Group: "Famine in Ethiopia." March 18, 1995. "Addis Ababa statement on famine in Ethiopia: learning from the past to prepare for the future." University of Pennsylvania, African Studies Center. http://www.africa.upenn.edu/Hornet/Ben_InterAF.html [Accessed November 17, 2011]

217. http://www.vegafoods.com/corp/?q=corporate/about-us [Accessed April 10, 2012]

218. http://www.vegafoods.com/corp/corporate/about-us/history [Accessed April 10, 2012]

219. http://www.watanmal.com/ [Accessed August 27, 2012]

220. Edward Chan and Craig R. Elevitch. April 2006. *Specific profiles for Pacific island agroforestry: Cocos nucifera (coconut).* Species profiles for Pacific Island Agroforestry. http://www.agroforestry.net/tti/Cocos-coconut.pdf [Accessed May 23, 2013]

221. P.S. Savill and J.E.D. Fox. 1967. *Trees of Sierra Leone.* Private print.

222. Charlie M. Shackleton, Margaret W. Pasquini, and Axel W. Drescher. 2009. *African indigenous vegetables in urban agriculture.* London, U.K.: Earthscan.

223. Ebo Quanoulsah. n.d. "Libation is our soul." *Ghanaian Chronicle.* http://thechronicle.com.gh/?p=19308 [Accessed August 7, 2013]